Before Theological Study

Before Theological Study

A Thoughtful, Engaged, and Generous Approach

Edited by
HARRY O. MAIER,
ASHLEY JOHN MOYSE,
and RICHARD R. TOPPING

Introduction by Joas Adiprasetya
Afterword by Janet Martin Soskice

WIPF & STOCK · Eugene, Oregon

BEFORE THEOLOGICAL STUDY
A Thoughtful, Engaged, and Generous Approach

Wipf & Stock
An Imprint of Wipf and Stock Publishers
199 W. 8th Ave., Suite 3
Eugene, OR 97401

www.wipfandstock.com

PAPERBACK ISBN: 978-1-6667-0655-0
HARDCOVER ISBN: 978-1-6667-0656-7
EBOOK ISBN: 978-1-6667-0657-4

AUGUST 23, 2021

To the past, present, and future students
of Vancouver School of Theology

Contents

~

List of Figures

Acknowledgements

WE WANT TO THANK all the professors and sessional instructors at Vancouver School of Theology who contributed to this volume and to the generous spirit that pervaded the discussion of each essay at our faculty gatherings. It is a pleasure to work with colleagues on such projects and to engage with others on matters other than administration. Bearing witness to deep commitment to excellent theological education on the part of your friends is inspiring. This volume is dedicated to our students, past, present, and future, from whom we teachers learn so much.

Preface

Theological Studies:
A Thoughtful, Engaged, and Generous Approach

THIS COLLECTION BEGAN AS a series of orientation lectures for new students at Vancouver School of Theology. Over the course of three days in the fall, students hear and interact with each of our faculty members in the subject area of their expertise. The half-hour lectures, called Theological 10 Percent, give students the basics and background for an approach to multiple subject areas with lots of overlap and contrast and diversity. We called it Theological 10 Percent because we were naïve and ambitious enough to imagine we could give 10 percent of a subject in a half hour! The feedback from students has been excellent. Right from the start they get a sense of the gravity, fun, diversity, and expectation that surrounds theological formation and education.

The variety of the presentations, both in style and content, give our students a great feel for the diversity of our faculty and the sheer joy we all have for teaching and learning in the service of the church and the world. Like our faculty themselves, these presentations show that we have enough in common to work together and enough difference to make working together interesting. The style and content have range—some talk about learning dispositions for theological studies as a whole, others about the scope of a specific subject matter, still others introduce important background that invites divestment of unhelpful generalities and attention to the context where theology lives to orient the common life of the church. Acquisition of knowledge, skill sets, and character, even holiness, are supposed throughout these essays. All the essays included here are born of experience in the classroom and the congregation. We have drawn on the astute comments of those wonderful students who raise their hand during a foggy lecture and remark, "So what you are trying to say is . . . " and then express the matter succinctly and with greater elegance than they heard it, to the nodding admiration of the class!

At Vancouver School of Theology special attention is given to interreligious studies and Indigenous studies as ingredient to the education we provide. Across the whole range of our curriculum and programing, these are essential to the DNA of the school. We do not think a candidate can be formed for Christian leadership at a time like this without a profound sense of the enduring significance of religious pluralism and the legacy of residential schools and the work of truth and reconciliation with Indigenous peoples.

An enchiridion is a small manual or handbook. The *Enchiridion of Epictetus* (c. 125 ca), a Stoic philosopher, is perhaps the most well-known example. In this manual, one of his followers, Arrian, collected the essentials of his teaching and how they might be applied in life. Saint Augustine picked up the form and produced an *Enchiridion on Faith, Hope, and Love* in about 420. In this handbook, he provides in summary form a model of instruction in the essentials of faith. Augustine seems to have intended his manual for Christian instruction or catechesis in response to a request from a person, otherwise unknown, named Laurentius. We offer this enchiridion in honor of our students, whose names we know and who are known and loved by us.

We are grateful to Professor Janet Soskice, Professor of Philosophical Theology Emerita Fellow, Jesus College, Cambridge, for picking up the thread of our collection in her afterword. She identifies the way in which the whole volume works to make the connection between the particularity of Christian confession and engagement with the broader world. To go deep with God is to go wide with the world. An introduction by Joas Adipresatya, professor of Constructive Theology and Theology of Religion and Dean of Public Relations of Jakarta Theological Seminary, introduces the essays by orienting the study of theology in the church and for the world to the goal of nurturing thoughtful pastor-scholars, engaged mystic-prophets, and generous host-friends. The following chapter by Richard Topping, President of Vancouver School of Theology and Professor of Studies in the Reformed Tradition, continues several of the themes Adiprasetya introduces a study of theology grounded in the particularities of Christian confession with an open-handed stance toward the world. This sets the stage for an orientation to the study of Christian mission by Robert S. Paul, former Dean of St. Andrews Hall and Professor of Mission Theology. Paul outlines a history of Christian missions with attention to the study of mission as a crucial aspect of theological education that invites us to consider the nature of the church, Christian vocation and discipleship, the manner of witness and proclamation as a culturally bound task of faithful translation, respect and advocacy for our neighbors, and a way of knowing God. The study of missions attends to the church's dark history and from it seeks to learn what it means in the context of globalism to be generous host-friends.

The third chapter turns to the study of worship and liturgy. Melissa Skelton is retired Archbishop in the Diocese of New Westminster and Metropolitan of the Ecclesiastical Province of British Columbia and Yukon, and now Assisting Bishop of the Diocese of Olympia in the Episcopalian Church and the Episcopal Visitor to the Society of Catholic Priests. She relates Trinitarian theology to liturgical study and the formation of leaders grounded by practices of spiritual devotion and discipleship. It is through worship that we know God, ourselves, and one another and how to live in the world: *lex orandi, lex credendi, lex agendi*—the way of prayer, belief, and action—are inextricably tied together.

Discussion of worship and liturgy prepares the way for the next two chapters, which focus on denominational and spiritual formation in theological education. Grant Rodgers retired Director of Anglican Formation, describes ways in which denominational formation is shaped by the needs of diverse constituencies that include congregational settings, national church desires, accrediting agencies, and the lived contexts which shape preparation for ministry. Intentional theological formation in community is critical to preparation for leadership in a quickly changing mainline church. Janet Gear, VST's former Professor of Public and Pastoral Leadership and Director of United Church Formation, continues the discussion introduced by Rodgers by consideration of spirituality and spiritual formation as central tasks of theological education. A communally and socially embedded spirituality is the way God calls us to become more fully human and alive.

Chapters 6 to 9 focus on the study of the Tanakh/Old Testament as a historical and literary set of documents, the New Testament, homiletics and biblical hermeneutics, and the relation of biblical exegesis to ethics. Commitment to thoughtful conversation is the red threat that joins them together. In chapter 6, Patricia Dutcher-Walls, until 2020 Dean and Professor of Hebrew Bible, orients students to the study of ancient Israel by furnishing a basic overview of Israel's story as told in the First Testament. Using Paul's Ricoeur's threefold model of the world behind, in, and in front of the text, she considers the Hebrew Bible as a collection of narratives shaped by the material, social, and historical events of the ancient Near East addressed to different audiences. Next, Harry O. Maier, Professor of New Testament and Early Christian Studies, takes up the study of the New Testament as an invitation to a conversation with the authors of the New Testament that starts with close listening through disciplined study and continues through a way of interpretation open to change and conversion. Maier refers to a study of the New Testament that makes the familiar strange and in the next chapter Jason Byassee, Butler Chair in Homiletics and Biblical Hermeneutics, invites readers to the study of preaching (homiletics) and biblical interpretation (hermeneutics) by looking for the weird and then expanding consideration of it by listening to the ways in which the voices of the Bible have been understood in the Christian tradition. In chapter 9, Mari Joerstad, Associate Professor of Hebrew Bible and Academic Dean, takes up the story of Tamar in Genesis 38 to invite readers to consider the ways in which biblical exegesis functions as resource for ethical reflection by facilitating the role of the Bible as conversation partner.

Consideration of the study of ethics continues with an essay by Ashley Moyse, a postdoctoral fellow in Christian ethics at the University of Oxford and sessional lecturer at VST. It orients the study of Christian ethics to the shape of human being made known by Jesus Christ and the question of who is my neighbor. In a way that echoes Richard Topping's understanding of theology as oriented to God's revelation in the desire to address world and self, Moyse considers ethics as engagement with the world through conversation that involves listening, hearing, and exchanging moral speech. This essay captures the tone of this collection as a whole, one of optimism and fearlessness, not because of human potentiality or commitment to humanistic ideals of progress and the realization of utopian ideals, but located in the gift of God's self in creation and God's desire to conform us to God's image. The task of careful listening and allowing the other to remain other furnishes the orientation of the next two essays, dedicated to Indigenous theology and interreligious studies.

In chapter 11, Ray Aldred, Cree Director of the Indigenous Studies Program at VST, considers the contribution of Indigenous studies to the study of theology as a way that moves beyond detached ways of knowing the world toward one rooted in relationship. Similarly, Rabbi Laura Duhan-Kaplan, Director of Interreligious Studies and Professor of Jewish Studies, considers the integral task of interreligious studies as the task of every student of theology. She outlines different models of interreligious studies, together with their relative strengths and weaknesses, and champions a form of learning that attends to the particularities of religious traditions that encourages movement beyond knowledge of beliefs to development or relationships with people of different faiths. By encountering people of other religious traditions and getting to know them, we come to know ourselves and our own beliefs better. Moyse, Aldred, and Duhan-Kaplan invite a way of theological study rooted in encounter with others and immersion in the particularities of the worlds we find ourselves where through our neighbors we come to know ourselves and what it means to live fully as human beings.

All of the essays in this collection are written with a view to theology that faces the world and that orients the teaching of theological disciplines for the sake of the thriving of humans and the whole of creation. The authors of the final two essays bring these commitments to their respective introductions to theological field education and to evangelism and mission in a secular context. Brenda Fawkes is Office of Vocation Minister for the Pacific Mountain Region of the United Church of Canada and was until 2019 VST's Director of Theological Field Education. Her chapter introduces VST's pioneering "Leadership Studio" and its crucial role in forming students to develop theologically reflective practice within the fourfold story worlds of God, Self, Place, and Context. Ross Lockhart, Dean of St Andrew's Hall and Professor of Mission Studies at VST, presents the study of theology directed and sustained by participation in the mission of God in the world. Vancouver is at once one of the most culturally and religiously diverse cities in North America and amongst the top five of its most secular ones. He relates the tasks of evangelism to the secular Canadian and North American order and what joining our voices and lives to the mission of the Trinitarian God calls us to as church. These final two essays lead to the same place all the contributions do—to the door—and ask us to consider theological study as a way of orienting us to a quest for a thoughtful, engaged, and generous theology that gives us courage and strength as we meet the tasks of daily living amidst the concrete realties that shape us as individuals, communities, and societies.

Introduction

On Becoming a Thoughtful Pastor-Scholar, an Engaged Mystic-Prophet, and a Generous Host-Friend

DOING THEOLOGY IS AN adventure of faith taken collectively by Christians as a community called the church. However, while the church receives its identity from the Triune God of the future, who anoints us with superabundant grace, sometimes the church experiences confusion regarding the destiny and the loss of passion in continuing its tiring journey. Theological education is therefore the fuel to keep the journey alive and enjoyable. In my experience as a seminary professor, I have witnessed how fundamental it is for theologians to help the church navigate and endure the long adventure. We need to realize that the journey is more important than the destiny, whatever it is. Even more, the journey is the home![1]

The metaphor of journeying together seems to be more relevant nowadays as we face the disruption caused by the COVID-19 pandemic.[2]

---

1. I borrow the expression from Morton, *Journey Is Home*. However, a close reading of the John 14 will certainly take us to the same idea.

2. Interestingly, such a vibrant imagination was initiated in the 2013 WCC's General Assembly in Busan, South Korea, where the global churches declared to continue

We can no longer imagine the church as a staying community. As "the house of authority," institutionalized churches in many places worldwide have been collapsed to the ground and we must walk together as a wounded community towards uncharted territory (*terra incognita*). This is a new era, as Tod Bolsinger laments, "when you find yourself without a map and recognizing that you have to lead your people into a reality where the world in front of you is nothing like the world behind you. There is no clear plan, no map to follow, no past expertise to give confidence to both the leader and followers."[3] Bolsinger believes that what we desperately need in such a strange time is a kind of leadership that combines three overlapping components: technical competence, relational congruence, and adaptive capacity.[4] In other words, the post-pandemic leaders of the church must be skillful, caring, and flexible.

I believe that this book offers a different, if not much better, alternative than Bolsinger's proposal. We find here the authors of the book saying that theological education should be the birthplace of thoughtful, engaged, and generous leaders of the church. At the very least, the three components that Bolsinger suggests are parallel with the three dimensions of theological education proposed by this book. Yes, we need leadership with technical competence. Still, the leaders who learn any pastoral skill should interact thoughtfully with global issues of our time through a creative *ressourcement* to our rich traditions. Yes, we need leadership with relational congruence, but the leaders should engage with those they relate to in more transformative ways. Finally, generosity must be the core of a leader's capacity to adapt to the changing world because the leaders are called to befriend those affected by the unfortunate changes today.

By offering a thoughtful, engaged, and generous theological education, the authors of this book are both confident and humble. They are confident that theological education, as embodied at the Vancouver School of Theology, where they belong, can provide a fecund land for students to flourish in their uncertain life situations. At the same time, I strongly feel their humility as expressed in the origins of this collection as an introduction to the 10 percent one should know when embarking on theological study. It looks as if they would tell the students that no

---

ecumenical movement by shifting their commitment from "staying together" to "moving together." The commitment was expressed through a theme of "a pilgrimage of justice and peace." See Enns and Durber, eds., *Walking Together*.

3. Bolsinger, *Leadership for a Time of Pandemic*, 7.

4. Bolsinger, *Leadership for a Time of Pandemic*, 11.

matter how long the study goes, they will never be able to provide the perfect theological education for their students. They are trying to say that any formal theological education can never be enough to prepare the church's future leaders. Never! The seminary professors can never say to the students who graduate that they have already reached the finish line. Rather, it must be communicated and emphasized that theology is a lifelong adventure. The students must continue their own journeys, sometimes in solitary, but always in spiritual connection with the faith community called the church.

The three dimensions of theological education—thoughtfulness, engagement, and generosity—make me imagine theological schools as places where everyone is flourishing as a thoughtful pastor-scholar, engaged mystic-prophet, and generous host-friend. The tension of being a pastor-scholar has been a long struggle for both *ecclesia* and *academia*. On the one hand, separating *academia* from the church will make a scholar academically sophisticated yet uprooted from the everyday life of Christians in the community. On the other hand, separating *ecclesia* from theological schools will turn a pastor into a technical leader that lacks theological depth and creativity. In my personal experience, maintaining the tension of being a pastor-theologian has been both painful and rewarding. I have been criticized by church people as being too academic and by my fellow academicians as being too simplistic and shallow. However, being a too-simplistic scholar and a too-academic pastor has put me in a place where I am convinced more than ever that bridging *academia* and *ecclesia* is the best way to keep both publics flourishing.[5] It is precisely at the bridge of the two publics that "the 10 percent" of theological education works, unfolding along with the ever-new development of both *academia* and *ecclesia*.

The second dialectic of theological education is that of being an engaged mystic-prophet.[6] According to David Tracy, *ecclesia* and *academia* are not the only two publics of theology. *Societas* is the third public in which all theologians must be "clearly affected by specific roles in that society."[7] One of the many reasons why theological education has been growing very quickly in the Global South is its power to encourage

5. Wilson and Hiestand, eds., *Becoming a Pastor Theologian*.

6. Such a seemingly odd combination of terms—mystic and prophet—becomes reasonably clear in the entire *corpus* of Dorothee Sölle. See, for instance, Sölle, *Silent Cry*.

7. Tracy, *Analogical Imagination*, 7.

Christians and theological students to engage with their society's bleak reality. For Christians who are struggling with situations where dehumanization is multifaceted, theology is theopraxis. The calling to be a pastor-theologian and a prophet-activist are the same. For example, since my first seminarian year in my primary theological education, I have learned about liberation theology, Dalit theology, and Minjung theology, to name a few. I knew Gustavo Gutiérrez or Sallie MacFague earlier (and better) than John Calvin or Karl Bath. My first field education was a live-in in a local community that engaged with a particular social issue, not in a local congregation. However, such a social engagement can easily dump us into spiritual dryness if we experience it without being continuously attentive to the voice of the One who is calling us with "a sound of sheer silence" (1 Kgs 19:12). In other words, the God who calls me to be a prophet is "the God of silence [who] beckons me to journey to my heart where He awaits."[8] A site of injustice is, therefore, is a site of meeting God, who dwells and stands with those suffering people. It is precisely in the depth of suffering experienced by many people that a theologian as a mystic-prophet was born. Jürgen Moltmann testifies, "My experiences of death at the end of the war, the depression into which the guilt of my people plunged me, and the inner perils of utter resignation behind barbed wire: these were the places where my theology was born. They were my first *locus theologicus*, and at the deepest depths of my soul they have remained so."[9]

While the idea of thoughtful pastor-theologian emphasizes the thinking aspect of theology, although not necessarily so, the image of mystic-prophet combines *orthopraxis* and *orthopietas*, action, and spirituality. In the words of Hans Urs von Balthasar, theology must nourish believers to encounter the "infinite riches of divine truth [in] the finite vessels . . . *in adoration and active obedience*."[10] He continues, "We need individuals who devote their lives to the glory of theology, that fierce fire burning in the dark night of adoration and obedience, whose abysses it illuminates."[11] Therefore, theology can never fully embrace the depth of the longing heart and the lament of the suffering world. "The 10 percent" of theology that we never knew before is always inviting us to go

---

8. This is the first line of a beautiful song by Bukas Palad that, for me, gives the clearest definition of spirituality. See Palad, "God of Silence," YouTube video, 0:17.

9. Moltmann, *Experiences in Theology*, 4.

10. Balthasar, *Explorations in Theology*, 152. Italics added.

11. Balthasar, *Explorations in Theology*, 160.

deeper into our mystical experience and bolder in crying out the peaceable kingdom. But now we shall go further to the third imagination of a theologian, being a generous host-friend.

I genuinely believe that studying theology must be an activity enjoyed within a beloved community. It is not a private endeavor. I have read books about the theology of friendship and hospitality written by those . . . in solitary. The adventure of doing theology is an expression of festive friendship. Not only do we welcome strangers into our vulnerable life, but we are also being embraced as strangers. Unfortunately, we have witnessed how cruel, sometimes, theological education around the world can be. Sadly, competition, rivalry, and enmity have been seen as the unavoidable atmosphere of becoming a successful theologian. Through reading the chapters of this book, I sense the authors' commitment and dedication to theological education through a generous and hospitable community. I observe that the future of theological education will depend on whether we can imagine and generate the relationship among those within the institution—teachers, students, staff, alums, etc.—as friends. Stuart Blythe is correct when he argues that the use of the friend metaphor in theological education can avoid "explicit hierarchical or patriarchal connotations" and conceal "inherent power differentials in supervision."[12] Furthermore, friendship in theological education "signifies the potential for mutual formation and transformation" for those in the educational community.[13] That is why I always commend theological schools that attempt painstakingly to welcome people from diverse cultural and religious backgrounds. They are willing to address misunderstandings that arise from cultural strangeness generously. They celebrate the awkward yet beautiful exchanges between suspicious strangers that turn out to be holy friends. The dynamics will always be surprising and unending, and, therefore, there will always be "the 10 percent" that everyone learns from everyone else.

Read carefully and joyfully each chapter of this book. You will find the three dialectics: a thoughtful pastor-scholar, an engaged mystic-prophet, and a generous host-friend. I wish I could have read this book when I began my theological education a long time ago. But I know that there will be many younger theologians who will benefit from this remarkable collection. For this reason, I am very optimistic about the future of theological education.

---

12. Blythe, "Research Supervisor as Friend," 405.

13. Blythe, "Research Supervisor as Friend," 409.

1

Theological Study

Keeping It Odd

RICHARD R TOPPING

TALK ABOUT GOD IS delightful and difficult. It is difficult in a world in which legitimate explanation does not include recourse to God.[1] That puts Christians (and I think people of all faith traditions) on the defensive. So much of what Christians write these days in the West seems defensive— unduly methodological, halting, preamble, throat-clearing.[2] Apologetic is the mode of most Christian theologies. Apologetic theologies work to show a secular public that belief in God and the gospel is consistent with other kinds of knowledge and the perceived priorities and needs and desires of today. It is not so much that theologians make arguments or confessions about what is true; it is more that they want to demonstrate the meaningfulness of the faith on terms set by dominant systems of thought or current issues. Translation of the content of Christian confession into a more general idiom for broader appeal and availability and above all meaning is usually the apologetic project. The desire seems a sound one, indeed almost a missional one.

1. Taylor, *Secular Age*, 2–3, 550.
2. Stout, *Ethics After Babel*, 184.

The irony is that while this strategy aims to demonstrate relevance to our "cultured despisers," it comes across as needy and, worse still, boring. At times it reduces all religion to the outward expression of inner feeling, a private matter out of public view and influence. It often gives the impression that Christians do not have anything to say or feel or think that a good atheist does not already grasp from affective delight, one of the multiple forms of authentic individualism, or current cultural causes. We imagine apologetic theology as heroic, edgy, and courageous, when in fact it has become a more-or-less sophisticated act of conformity to the ambiance of moment. Christians often end up in a reductive-therapeutic-theistic fog when the solvent of relevance-to-the-moment and "public"[3] norms of intelligibility dissolve Christian confession. Instead of the spicy particularity of the triune God, who comes among us as Jesus to rescue us from ruin and effect the transformation of all things, we can get a saccharine, same-saying substitute. We aim at relevance; we get redundance!

The preceding statement might be worth repeating: We aim at relevance; we get redundance. It isn't that we don't want to engage and make a difference in the world at opportune moments. It is just that we are tempted to a certain cultural respectability that mutes the always-awkward relevance that questions, challenges, and upends the prevailing wisdom of the spirit of the age.

This conformity is a problem for the church. It means that, instead of expanding the imaginative register of our time and place with humane gospel-generated options, we appear to be serving up what everyone already knows better from elsewhere. Remember, we live in a time when six of the seven deadly sins are medical conditions—and pride is a virtue. Philosophical systems, therapeutic expressions, and cultural causes become the template into which Christian confession is pressed and the unique story of Scripture is denuded of its life-giving offer. Flannery O'Connor could have said, "You will know the truth, and the truth will make you odd." Whether she did or not, the words point to how the delightful oddness of Christian theology is doped down when we get too anxious about providing answers to the questions of the time. Theology becomes uninteresting when we think of the Christian faith as answerable to an obligatory God-bereft picture of the world and its problems.

---

3. The idea that there is a "general public" is a problematic assumption. Often public norms of intelligibility are really the norms of the academy or some region of it. Even the phrase "public norms of intelligibility" is not a way of speaking that has currency across multiple cultural publics.

I suspect, instead, that a patient exposition of the content of Christian faith raises the most pertinent questions. The burning issues of the day arise from a gospel reading of the world. Christian relevance is best demonstrated in the prophetic tension that confession of the God of the gospel creates with the times, systems of thought, and causes that are in circulation. *Vive la différence* is a more faithful approach to theological endeavor in the light of the incarnation of the Son of God, Jesus of Nazareth. And strangely, the relevance of Christian confession to the "situation" may be best demonstrated by the distinct sense-making contributions, the framing of where in the world we are, that Christians can make to cultural common life out the distinct shape of Christian confession. The most boring conversations are between people who agree about everything.

In what follows, I want to address some of the intellectual and practical temptations that theology faces and detail some of the practices and convictions that might help hold us accountable to the odd particularity of Christian confession when we engage in theological study. The recommendation of these practices is rooted in the subject matter of theology: God. Just before that, I want to anticipate possible two objections. There are at least two things that holding ourselves accountable to Christian particularity, an unapologetic approach to Christian theology, does *not* mean.

First: this approach does not mean that we absent ourselves from interdisciplinary study and engagement, from ad hoc borrowings and learning from various fields of endeavor, and from joint efforts with a series of conversation partners. Christians have always taught the faith in the language and thought forms of their time. It is not only unavoidable; it is desirable. We want to communicate the meaning of our confession. At their worst, our predecessors got coopted by the thought forms of the time and confused that with Christian confession. At their best, our forebearers in the faith bent those thought forms into the service of the grammar of Christian confession. They used the language and concepts available in their day to make the same theological judgements the Bible does about God, and everything else in relation to God, in a language appropriate to their time and place. That's not translation; it is more redescription and reiteration.[4] It is *andenken*,[5] thinking the thoughts of Scripture after Scripture, a sort of intellectual-spiritual discipleship in which redeemed reason follows the story and provides commentary that always directs attention back to the story Scripture tells and never dispenses with the story for another system or idiom or ethos. As much as our mothers and fathers in the faith wanted to communicate to their contemporaries, it was even more important to be guided by the subject matter of the faith. And so, they bent and contorted language and concepts—"they dug out of the mines of God's providence, which are everywhere scattered abroad"[6]—to serve faithful communication of the content of Christian confession, even if that meant hearers became disoriented by recontextualized use of terms. Fidelity to the system from which language was borrowed got subverted, in the best cases, to the grammar of the Christian story as Scripture tells it. Sometimes to get what the Christian message entails, nothing less than conversion, detoxification, and a senior seminar (catechesis) are required.

Second: holding to Christian particularity, even before audience engagement and internalizing the so-called public norms of intelligibility, does not inhibit Christian participation in public life. Christian theology wants to engage in public life and witness since God loves the world. In the pluralistic society in which we live, we ought to look for partners as we witness to the reign of God and the coming reconciliation of all things through Jesus Christ. And we can do this with all sorts of humane movements of our time. People who do not share Christian convictions also work for the good of the world in ways Christians recognize as consistent with the faith Christians confess. Where we observe common cause or "overlapping consensus"[7] around seminal issues or challenges, we share in the work in Jesus' name with our neighbors. People of other faiths and of good will will have their own motivations and interests born of deep conviction, as do Christians. The motivations may not be the same but the

---

4. See Rigby, *Holding Faith*, xix. Speaking of translation of doctrinal language, Rigby says, "This common approach too often fails to communicate because what is distinctively meaningful about the terms in question can get lost in the process."

5. Paul Ricoeur uses this term to describe "a call to reflection or meditation" in response to encounter with biblical discourse. See Ricoeur, *Critique and Conviction*, 149. On the danger of translation as a form of assimilation and the necessity to "let the untranslatable situation stand," see Asad et al., *Is Critique Secular?*, xvi.

6. Augustine, *On Christian Doctrine*, 75.

7. Taylor, *Secular Age*, 532. Taylor borrows this term from John Rawls.

commitment to the work of human fullness in specific instances will be the same. Swiss Theologian Karl Barth (1886–1968) asserted that because of unconditioned commitment to Jesus Christ, Christians necessarily have provisional commitments to a whole series of movements that help human right and worth in the world.[8] Parables of grace are all over the place in God's good world when we look at the world through the gospel. And so, let's return practices and convictions that foster and fortify Christian imagination for life-giving engagement with God and the world God loves. We can work these in any order since they are connected and overlap. There are at least five 1) keep God central in theological thinking; 2) engage in charitable reading; 3) pray to be permeable—for conversation and transformation; 4) stay specific to Christian confession; and 5) God is excellent at revelation.

KEEP GOD CENTRAL IN THEOLOGICAL THINKING

Karl Barth said, "Theology is not anthropology spoken in a really loud voice."[9] The subject matter of theology is God, and then everything else in relation to God. Barth spotted a problem that is still very much with us. We start off intending to speak of God and then subtly but surely begin to transfer the weight to anthropology—our morals, our experiences, our causes. We even apply for grants to study the physiological and biochemistry of religious experiences and then compare them with other experiences of heightened consciousness so that they become an instance of a class of human experience. We inquire after the social function of religion in a descriptive fashion that focuses only on human actors and historical artefacts. "Did hyssop grow in Palestine?" "Does this reflect a Hittite suzerainty treaty?" These kinds of studies serve some good ends—the ends of moving beyond excavation to exegesis. They could matter to the theological exegesis of Scripture. However, excavation is not theology since attention here is not on God as the subject of the text

8. Barth, *Foundation of the Christian Life*, 267–68. This is the source of Barth's rejection of theologies of experience. He is concerned about the collapse of God into human subjectivity. However—and this is often missed—Barth expresses an interest in theologies of experience if and when they are attempts do theology beginning with the Holy Spirit. He believes this could be the actual theological center from which Schleiermacher works. See Barth, *From Rousseau to Ritschl*, 341.

9. Barth, *Word of God and Word of Man*, 14. This phase can be found throughout Barth's work.

and the active agent in interpretation, but on the social world of a text's production.[10] The subject matter of theology is God. Theologians, while not unconcerned with religious experience and aspects of the ancient world, focus their attention not just on the generated but on the generative. We rivet our attention on the ways and works of the triune God as these are revealed to us through Holy Scripture in the power of the Spirit and witnessed to in the history of the church's testimony. For this very reason, theology sits uncomfortably on the campus of a university. God is a difficult subject matter and so often the closer theology gets to the university, the more colonized by the "immanent frame"[11] it becomes. Instead of Scripture study, we get biblical studies. Instead of theological study, we get religious studies. The defining feature of both moves is that it precludes speech about God; it brackets God out of consideration in the interest of objectivity, which is really agnosticism as default position.

Those who have been educated lately know that "context is everything." We postmoderns understand the situatedness of all work, all our interpretation, all our claims. We do not live above history and culture; no one, except God, has a God's-eye point of view. We interpret Scripture and theological texts with agendas and in the light of problems of a time and place, which is as it should be. The trouble arises when we universalize from our context, get imperious about our interpretative vantage point, and impress it on other people (by "saming" them). This inhibits their opportunity to hear a word from God in their time and place and culture and give expression to the good news as the people they are. Colonial impress has often led to imposition and violence on the part of those who would enforce their interpretation on the world. The later move is especially perverse when Christianity gets mixed up with the imperial aspirations of the regnant order and overrides the dignity and humanity of other people in the guise of paternalism.[12] These important recognitions have become central to much theologizing of the late twentieth and early twenty-first century. They are now collectively a point of departure and unfortunately, at times, they have become a destination.

One of the challenges that accompanies these observations is that we have so foregrounded context, the self-description and cultural place

10. Robert Alter notes that much of the "excavative" work done on biblical texts focuses on "unscrambling an omelette," not tasting it. See Alter, *World of Biblical Literature*, 133.

11. Taylor, *Secular Age*, 550.

12. See Wolterstorff, *Justice in Love*, 223.

of readers and interpreters, that the subject matter of theology, God, gets marginalized. The self-description of the interpreting subject or subjects and their projects overwhelm the interpreted subject matter. We can end up studying lenses (the perspective or world placement of the interpreters) and not what is looked at. I think there at least four doctrinal considerations that insert themselves into this problematic.

First, identity in the history of the Christian church is grounded in baptism. We are through the miracle of the grace of adoption children of God. As the baptized, we are engrafted into Christ and the household of faith and therefore we do theology as children of God, first and foremost. Baptism is what gives theology its character as faith seeking understanding.

Second, while we are creatures and so located in history and time and culture with a variety of secondary identities, our primary context, as the history of Christian confession teaches, is "before God" (*Coram Deo*).[13] Whatever the microclimate of our confession, we live before God, in the presence of the one who loves the world, who sent the Son for the reconciliation of all things, and who gives the Spirit of adoption and mission. That's our context.

Third, the fellowship of the saints extends through time and space in the power of the Spirit. We need to beware of so articulating our identity, our time, our culture, our church that we cut ourselves off from the interpretative fellowship of the saints, both the living and the dead. While other Christian communities through time and across the world now each have or had their own situation in which to confess, their language about God is truth-intending; it gestures toward the God revealed in Jesus Christ, especially in praise and adoration. Catholicity implies that we approach them and include them, not to globalize Western church norms and struggles,[14] but in a spirit of humility and teachableness with a willingness to repent for the error of our ways. None of us gestures in words and witness toward the triune God perfectly or without group interest or error, sometimes serious and pernicious error; but that is precisely why we need to listen and speak with the church catholic.

13. See Stroup, *Before God*. In this book Stroup notes that the sense of life in the presence of God has been eclipsed in modernity and encourages countercultural ways for recovery.

14. See Ward, *History of Global Anglicanism*, 308–15. When we do globalize North American norms and struggles, we are just as colonial as nineteenth-century Christian missions, without the necessity to travel.

Fourth, the church has a mission to witness to the reconciling action of God in Jesus Christ in the power of the Spirit and so has something to say *to* the context. Douglas John Hall, in many ways a parent of contextual theology in Canada, has noted the perils of this good idea. He notes the tendency to treat context as fate, to reduce "the context" to a single issue of cultural currency and to forget that the Christian message gives us things to say that might just challenge the context.[15] It may be that the relevance of the Christian confession to this time and place is its contrary message in the service of life. God enters our context not to confirm it, but to alter it, to reconcile and overturn it. The action of God in Jesus Christ creates a context, a new creation.[16]

ENGAGE IN CHARITABLE READING

When I was an undergraduate philosophy student, I was taught the principle of charity by Prof. Bernard Suits. He told us that before we begin a critique of someone's position, first we take the very best reading of the position we subject to examination. Do not caricature or misrepresent another person's point of view, or we end up shadowboxing with our own bad interpretation rather than offering a legitimate analysis of an argument. Professor Suits told me this principle is observed mostly in its violation.

Whole theological schools of thought have begun in response to a misrepresentation of the longer Christian tradition or aspects of it. For example, I have found critiques of an "interventionist god" to be critiques of theologies of the past that, in fact, do not exist. I have not found a major Christian theologian yet that sets up a theology of creation so that

---

15. Hall, "Future of the Church." Alan Noble makes the point concrete: Christians are not testifying to one more version of human fullness to add to the consumer options. A disruptive witness denies the entire contemporary project of treating faith as a preference" (Noble, *Disruptive Witness*, 81).

16. It is interesting how little this gospel consideration has figured into theologies that simply answer "the context" as it is served up by non- or pre-theological depiction. On the other hand, literary scholar Rita Felski notes the effect of powerful literature. "If we are entirely caught up in a text, we can no longer place it in a context because it is the context, imperiously dictating the terms of its reception. We are held in a condition of absorption . . . transfixed and immobilized by the work and rendered unable to frame, contextualize or judge" (Felski, *Uses of Literature*, 57). Charles Taylor also notes that great spiritual movements "transform the frame in which people thought, felt and lived before . . . Things make sense in a wholly new way" (Taylor, *Secular Age*, 731).

God is estranged from the world God creates and therefore can only engage with creation as Creator by interloping. God doesn't break the natural order of things when God acts in the world. It is God's world; God is always already involved in it—God does not get all "supernatural" from time to time. Islam, Judaism, and Christianity agree: God is creating now; creation and providence are ongoing; the world is now and always upheld "by the word of His [the Son's] power" (Hebrews 1:3, NKJV). All this to say, beware of mischaracterizing a position that is not your own. Take the strong version of what you read; do some historical study to inform your perspective for the sake of justice and charity. Check your interpretations against other interpreters. Talk to others in your class to see if your problem in understanding is, well, you.

If philosophers have a principle of charity, Christian readers ought to have an interpretive disposition of an analogous character. We ought to interpret other people as our theological neighbors, whom we honor as creatures made in God's image, given to us by God for our learning and edification. Their gifts are for us. We ought to linger with our neighbor's writing, as an act of love, to understand what they want to say to us. One way of thinking about interpreting those who have gone before us in the faith is as an act of "communion with the saints." Those who went before us, in different times and places, struggled with making sense of the faith in their circumstances, and, while different from our own, there are always things to be learned, even if they fall into the "errors to avoid" column. When we interpret with imagination, however, often we observe analogues and precedents that are remarkably prescient for our place and time.

Lots of interpreters will emphasize distance; an imaginative interpreter seeking to learn for the sake of salvation and discipleship and praise sees proximity. Hilary of Poitiers (315–368) has things to teach us about the gendered use of language with respect to God. "The Son was conceived in the womb of the Father,"[17] he says. By saying this he contorts what we know of biology so that we speak more truly of God and don't simply project maleness onto God. Marguerite de Navarre (1492–1549), the sister of the king of France, Francis I, can teach us about the importance of theological conversation over "ostentatious debates"—like

17. Hilary of Poitiers, *On the Trinity*, book 12, section 8, 219–20. Kathryn Tanner argues: "The gender-bending use of gendered imagery here—a Father with a womb—might very well present the best hope for avoiding the theological reinforcement of male privilege" (Tanner, *Christ the Key*, 215).

those of Martin Luther and John Calvin—in conversational theological writings.[18] The Barmen Declaration (1934),[19] made against attempts to coordinate the church to National Socialist ideology, was a seminal document. It inspired both the Belhar Confession (1982),[20] made against apartheid in South Africa, and the recent "Reclaiming Jesus" document (2018),[21] which confesses faith in the here-and-now of the struggle of the Christian churches in the US around truth-telling and racism. The Barmen Declaration is itself inspired, in part, by the 1528 Ten Theses argued by Berchold Holler and Franz Kolb at Bern and behind them Zwingli, especially in the use of the phrase "and does not hear the voice of the stranger," from John 10.[22] What shocks a reader of these documents, and of other authors from the past, is not the historical gulf between then and now, but the incredible analogical relevance and immediacy of the past to the present through retrieval. Appropriation of what these friends in the faith teach us requires humility, sustained attention, a teachable frame, and a sanctified imagination open to a word from the communion of saints. We have got to be traditioned to be creative, formed to be transformative, or we repeat the slogans of the age in which we live and call it "edgy."

Another charitable way to construe reading theological texts is by means of the command to "honor your father and mother." This commandment comes in the second tablet of the law, and is in fact part of what it means to love some of our closest neighbors, our parents. Parents are not, of course, always correct in their advice or knowledge. Sometimes parents in the faith fail us and lead us astray—the complicity of the church in residential schools and apartheid are pernicious examples.

---

18. See for example D'Agoulême, *L'Heptameron*. See also Thysell, *Pleasure of Discernment*, 9.

19. See Busch, *Barmen Theses Then and Now* for an excellent treatment of the theses and their ongoing relevance.

20. See Tshaka, *Confessional Theology?* The book argues for the political significant of confession and demonstrates the relationship between Barmen and Belhar.

21. See http://reclaimingjesus.org.

22. See Barth, *Theology of the Reformed Confessions*, 75. Barth's teaching of Reformed confessions in 1923 obviously influenced his imaginative repertoire for the Barmen Declaration of 1934 together with the 1933 Dusseldorf Theses. For the genealogy of these influences on Barmen, see Busch, *Barmen Theses Then and Now*, 21–22. He notes that using past confessions for present confession involves instruction by the past but that "in order to say the same thing that had once been said, it had to be said a new way" (Busch, *Barmen Theses Then and Now*, 22).

However, parents also have been around longer than their children. They have longer life experience and, often, faith experience. Honoring your parents is wise. Listening to those who have struggled with what you now face can save you some unnecessary pain and misspent time, and lead you from thinness to depth. Honoring our mothers and fathers in the faith also presents a challenge. They disturb us; they make it hard for us to relax in *lassez faire* clichés—"you can't fight city hall," "people never change." And then along comes the saints, who wrote and lived in ways that overturned and changed things. They can inspire us to bother writing and acting in Jesus' name in our own situation. Listening to ecumenical confessions and creeds of the past, reading theologians commonly esteemed by the church, can help we people of faith with our struggles to be faithful and effective in our time. It does not mean the authors of these documents or any theological writer is infallible—in either their script or their life; it does mean that they have learned and said things commonly recognized as astute, even definitive, for the life of the Christian community through time. They tried to confess Christ in their time, often in the face of adversity. They can disappoint us with their blindness and prejudice; but they can also encourage, shock, and inspire us by their example. I think a special measure of sympathy and care needs to be exercised here. We should be more skeptical of our explanatory schemes and prejudices and exercise the greatest possible imaginative sympathy to our predecessors, even in disagreement.

A practical note: we are embodied readers, so pay attention to your body when you read. Sometimes reading will make us feel uncomfortable. Our hands will sweat, and our hearts start to race. Be careful not to give up when this happens. Worthy texts have a way of challenging what we have always thought. Learning sometimes involves dislodgement of long-held ideas, and that's threatening. The defensive move is to throw up the safeguard of theory and use sophisticated tools to protect yourself. The more hermeneutics we learn, the greater the temptation. Instead, we should go for a walk and pray. Pray that in our reading we will be permeable to what we need to hear. It could be that an author is just wrong; it could be that we are being taught, even by God. And so, we try and identity what we read that produced this discomfort. At these moments we are discovering our theology. When cherished beliefs come under scrutiny, it is disorienting. We may need to read further to be charitable to the writer. Perhaps he or she has yet to address the other side of the point or go on to a thicker account of the matter. Or perhaps we are being reoriented by means of what we are reading. Great texts have a way of doing that, especially when and where God is or becomes the active agent by whom we are taught. We all start reading as people of a time and place and we think we know what matters and where in the world we are and what our life might mean. And now, now we encounter a new thing, a new reality, and we are recontextualized in the light of it, and we start to read the world, painful as it is, in terms of the God about whom we are reading. It could be conversion, calling, deepening of the love of God. If we experience the grace of that kind of encounter when we are reading about God, give thanks.

> It's astonishing, but Christ is so powerful that he can even manifest himself among the theologians. We cannot force him, but every now and then he permits us to see and hear something.[23]

PRAY TO BE PERMEABLE—FOR CONVERSION AND TRANSFORMATION

The concept of a "teachable frame" comes from John Calvin's commentary on the Psalms.[24] For Calvin, teachableness before the text of Scripture and other esteemed teachers is crucial. When we come to read the Bible and important theological texts, fully armed with inflexible preunderstanding, we miss the opportunity to be instructed and transformed. If reading is simply an opportunity for us to engage in criticism based on high-powered theory that is set, gelled, and hardened (privileged), we will use every important text as an opportunity to hear ourselves think. Calvin's interest in prayer before the reading of Scripture, in a prayer he called the prayer for illumination, is a recognition of our need of God's help to open us up to what is strange and unusual in what we encounter in Scripture. It means that in our encounter with Scripture and in texts that are commentary on the Bible, we participate in dying and rising with Christ.

There are at least three problems encountered by students in seminaries and theological colleges where it comes to a teachable frame. One is that we are distracted with technology, constantly searching for

23. Barth, *Barth in Conversation*, 107.

24. Calvin, *Calvin's Commentaries*, vol. 8, para. 2: "God by a sudden conversion subdued and brought my mind to a teachable frame, which was more hardened in such matters than might have been expected from one at my early period of life."

external stimulation, which makes us incapable of disciplined attention. Alan Noble writes, "Living a distracted lifestyle does more than waste our time, it forms our minds, often in ways that are harmful for deep, sustained thought—the kind of thought so important to religious discourse."[25] Noble, while by no means a Luddite, proposes community and individual practices, acts of discipleship, that grace our capacity for attention to God: silence, saying grace, observing Sabbath, incarnate attention to the liturgy, all for the sake of stoking a disruptive witness in a distracted culture.

Another obstacle to a teachable frame is that professors can give students too much to read and, even when they do not, reading can be minimalist and consumptive. With the flood of compulsory readings coming, a theological student is liable to adopt a rather rudimentary threshold for what counts as reading. Eyes passing over the page is not reading. We as professors can subtly encourage the need for speed, which does not allow students to linger with the words, to contemplate formative matters offered in texts.[26] Texts will not resound and form the reader—contaminate a reader—where speed and extraction for research are the only goals in reading. If every text is simply strip-mined for papers, following a story or an argument for its formative potential is occluded from the outset. Resource mining that glosses texts does not allow us to share in the interpretative fellowship of the saints.

The other temptation in reading the Bible and important theological texts is born of the state of the industry in literary and critical studies. Critical reading in the academy, where most students and professors are formed before they come to theological institutions, has almost exclusively come to mean "suspicious" reading. We have all become aware that texts are located, that authors write from a point of view, and we want to interrogate the moves being worked on us, the "normative" worlds writers assume. Reading, on this approach, is equivalent to smoking out authors and their interested points of view, detective like. It is less suspicious of interested readers, who seem to operate from an immune

25. Noble, *Disruptive Witness*, 20.

26. In a recent *In Trust* article, the disparity between the values of doctoral programs, in which theological professors are shaped, and the needs of theological colleges and seminaries are noted. While professors in theological disciplines are generally taught to value research and teaching in graduate school, the ethos is relatively indifferent to formation of students and actively hostile to administration as part and parcel of the work. See Gin and Williams-Duncan, "Faculty Development," 20.

transcendental standpoint![27] Suspicious reading, as it turns out, is not so much interpretation as diagnosis, most often of power moves on the part of the author. While this mode of reading has produced some interesting and helpful results, an increasing number of literary and educational theorists note how critical-suspicious reading estranges readers from the claims texts make on us. We end up speaking power to truth.[28] It makes us unteachable, aloof to what we are called to consider. "Standing back" and even paranoia is the posture. Diagnosis and exposure are the goals. Affective delight and "heroic pedagogy" are very often the motivation.[29] Lack of surprise—confirmation of strong theory—is almost always the result. Some literary scholars even ask, "Is critical reading really reading at all?"[30]

I think the more devastating comment (we theological types ought to hear) is well articulated by Rita Felski, who asks, "Why—even as we extol multiplicity, difference, hybridity—is the affective range of criticism so limited? Why are we so hyperarticulate about our adversaries and so excruciatingly tongue-tied about our loves?"[31] In our vigilance against texts, we use the "barbed-wire of criticism" to "guard us against the risk of being contaminated and animated by the words we encounter."[32] But that's what Christian readers want as we "pour over the Bible . . . in a state of reverence and joy."[33] Critical-suspicious reading can render us impermeable to Scripture and theological teachers and texts that could instruct and form us.

27. Collini, *What Are Universities For?*, 83.

28. Williams, *Faith in the Public Square*, Kindle loc. 5380–86. Williams writes, "The cost of giving up talking of truth is high: it means admitting that power has the last word . . . . [P]olitical philosophy needs to give an account of suffering for the sake of conscience, and without a notion of truth that is more than simply a list of the various things people prefer to believe, no such account can be given" (Williams, *Faith in the Public Square*, Kindle loc. 5389). Rita Felski believes that questions of greater gravity than power are important to textual interpretation. Rather than simply, "'But what about power?'" she suggests, "'But what about love?'" and "'What is your theory of attachment?'" (Felski, *Limits of Critique*, 17–18). See also Bude, *Mood of the World*, 13–14. Bude describes postmodernity's "fear of truth" and "fear of knowledge."

29. Felski, *Limits of Critique*, 6–7, 186–93.

30. Warner, "Uncritical Reading," 15. Warner notes: "Critical reading is the folk ideology of a learned profession, so close to us that we seldom feel the need to explain it . . . " (Warner, "Uncritical Reading," 15).

31. Felski, *Limits of Critique*, 13.

32. Felski, *Limits of Critique*, 12.

33. Felski, *Limits of Critique*, 55.

For much of the contemplative Christian tradition, reading is analogous to eating. Reading Scripture and important theological texts requires chewing, lingering, and tasting so that the text is digested for nourishment. To use another metaphor, the serious religious reader becomes a "resonant manifold"—a chamber in which the text sounds and resounds so that meaning echoes in our lives.[34] This way of putting it draws our attention to sensuous wholistic engagement with Scripture, theological texts, and traditions.[35] Commenting on the sources from which John Calvin drew his understanding of reading the Bible, Wesley Kort notes his use of the monastic practice of *lectio divina*. This way of reading was designed to allow biblical texts to have their maximum effect on the reader "even to be inscribed on the reader's body."[36] Reading and hearing are acts of communion with God, first with words and concepts and images; *lectio* is inseparable from meditation, from prayer and contemplation. The Bible is, as one of Calvin's favorite authors, Bernard of Clairvaux, put it, "the wine cellar of the Holy Spirit."[37] By reading one receives the text with the palate of the heart. And because of God's agency by means of the Bible, Scripture reading is "inexhaustibly fecund" and "intoxicating" such that the Bible, and formative theological texts, can never be discarded or dominated.[38]

Let me show you an example of how reading Scripture works for Basil the Great (330–379). Here is the beginning and the end of a sermon on Genesis. "In the beginning God created the heavens and the earth" is the text on which he preaches. It is quite disorienting for us to listen to him instruct us on how to comport ourselves for theological study of Scripture and the ends toward which Scripture interpretation moves.

> What ear is worthy to hear such a tale? How earnestly the soul should prepare itself for such high lessons! How pure it should be from carnal affections, how unclouded by worldly disquietudes, how active and ardent in its researches, how eager to

34. Griffiths, *Religious Reading*, 47–48.

35. See for example Wilson, *Research Is Ceremony*. There is much to learn from Indigenous cultures and the practices of other faiths about holistic—sensuous, intuitive, emotional, and interested—engagement in research and reading. "Emotionless, passionless, abstract, intellectual research is a god-damn lie, it does not exist" (Wilson, *Research Is Ceremony*, 56).

36. Kort, *Take; Read*, 19–36.

37. Griffiths, *Religious Reading*, 42.

38. Griffiths, *Religious Reading*, 42.

find in its surroundings an idea of God which may be worthy of Him!

'God created the Heavens and the Earth.' Let us glorify the supreme Artificer for all that was wisely and skillfully made; by the beauty of things let us raise ourselves to Him who is above all beauty; by the grandeur of bodies, sensible and limited in their nature, let us conceive of the infinite Being whose immensity and omnipotence surpass all the efforts of the imagination.[39]

The interpretation of Scripture, engaging with the doctrine of creation in this case, will require nothing less than the conversion of the interpreter. When a person (as a member of the community) takes up what is a holy enterprise, holiness is required. We are not worthy of this kind of familiarity with God's word and work; but can be made so. And Basil is not speaking about the acquisition of interpretative tools and hermeneutical prowess, of "herding divine realities into the approved pens of dialectical arguments and critical studies."[40] We need deliverance from the downward tug of the flesh. We need to shake off the uneasiness and anxiety that the false aspirations of the flesh and the twitchy, multitasking twenty-first-century world engender. This includes the affective delight of showing ourselves smarter than the "interested" author, a critic of the naïve. Without freedom from carnality and disquietude, talk about God goes straight into the service of our personal projects, political aspirations, and hardened ideologies. And then, instead of losing ourselves to the praise of God and God's cause in the world, we will praise ourselves and use God to promote career aspirations.

Basil insists that interpretation is hard work; it will require us to be "active and ardent in our research." This diligence, spiritual and intellectual, is in the service of finding ways of speaking of God that are worthy of God. Sanctified reason scans the world for ideas that do not diminish but extol God. Basil promotes passionate creativity that searches for analogical language worthy to express the eminence of God in ways that are congruent with the scriptural story. He knows the "weakness of our intelligence" to "penetrate the depth of the thought" in the Bible. But he also knows the power of the words of Scripture inspired by the Spirit to produce salvation in those who hear them. The goal of interpreting Scripture is not to display our genius, but to get caught up in the work

---

39. Basil, *Hexaemeron*, §1, 11.

40. McIntosh, *Divine Teaching*, 3.

of salvation by God. Learning Scripture, and theology, is to be taught by God about God.

Where real engagement with Scripture takes place, it moves interpreters to the praise of God. Here the language soars in glorification of God, who makes all things, whose beauty is above all things beautiful, and whose Being is no simple extension of sensible and finite things but is one of a kind (*sui generis*) and surpasses all our attempts to speak of God. And yet, by visible and finite things we raise ourselves up to the invisible and infinite God. We get summoned to "conceive of the infinite Being . . . who surpasses all the efforts of our imagination."
That's the exact space in which theology works: to conceive of the One who eludes our grasp with the very best analogical language we can muster, guided by Scripture, taught by the church's teachers, and empowered by the Spirit. This requires spiritual discipline and awed attention. And it is a task that is not in vain. Christians are not agnostics. We are enabled to speak of the infinite. The confidence to do so is grounded not in our abilities but in God's movement toward us: the incarnation. Stephen Pardue states the meaning of incarnation for speech about God: "The Lord of heaven is in the habit of crossing boundaries, and thereby bringing fecundity where barrenness otherwise reigns."[41] It is not within our grasp to speak truly of God. However, words can bear witness to God, in partial and clumsy but true ways accommodated to human capacity when they get enlarged by divine grace. Theological learning requires a teachable frame, so we are taught by God, through human teachers, and so that with sanctified intelligence we borrow language fit to extol God, which is the proper end of our learning.

STAY SPECIFIC TO CHRISTIAN UNDERSTANDING

The Spanish-American philosopher George Santayana said, "The attempt to speak without speaking any particular language is not more hopeless than the attempt to have a religion that shall be no religion in particular."[42] The point is a crucial one in theological study. We can lose everything that makes Christianity, and other faith traditions, interesting by the quick move to talk about religion in general. People do not speak language in general. They speak English or French or Spanish or Tagalog.

41. Pardue, *Mind of Christ*, 182.
42. Santayana, *Reason in Religion*, 5.

And so it is with religion. People are not religious in general; they belong to distinct traditions that embody and inscribe beliefs, practices, and ways of disposing lives together.

It may be one of the lingering habits of modernity to move quickly to general categories so that particular things become instances of a class. This move can inhibit real surprise, unique practices and beliefs, and odd features for purposes of classification and policing reality. I am not sure there is even such a thing as religion in general, contra Immanuel Kant and *Religion within the Bounds of Reason Alone*. There are religions, even religions that have some common formal features. However, as soon as we press into the language and structure and practice of a faith tradition, we begin to observe subtlety and uniqueness related to the local. We use general language to handle groups of things for the sake of communicative ease. That's impossible to avoid; it is a gift that helps professors name their courses and draw disparate things together so that we have subject matter and a course outline. The difficulty arises when we mistake the general term for the subtle realities we gather under that banner. Let me explain. It is quite possible to have a course on sacred texts or religious communities. It may also be quite possible to observe overlap and intersection between them—commonalities and similarities certainly exist. But to reify general terms like "sacred text" as though the Christian Bible, the Tanakh, the Koran, and the Vedas are instances of class is a fallacy that distorts each of them. Every one of these texts is most at home in the community for which they function authoritatively—like orca in the ocean. Each of these texts is embedded in a world of practice and reading and theological understanding. Remove them from their natural habitat to a clinical world for observation and examination and they are orca in an aquarium—behaving out of keeping with their nature because domesticated.[43] What's more, the things religious texts have in common will not be across the board. The Christian Bible has commonalities with the Tanakh that it does not have with either the Koran or the Vedas. The Koran has things in common with the Tanakh and the Christian Bible that it does not have with the Vedas.

Where doctrinal discussion takes place in Christian theological study, the same difficulty arises. Formal features can replace the storied world of Scripture, which is the primary basis of Christian belief.

---

43. Thanks to my colleague Ross Lockhart for this helpful oceanic metaphor.

If someone asks me to tell them about my spouse, I don't say, "She's a biped."[44] That's a formal feature, an abstraction. To describe my spouse, I'd tell stories about how we met, what she loves, what her family of birth is like. The significant doctrines (teachings) of the Christian faith are related directly to the long story that is the Bible, Holy Scripture, read according to a Trinitarian pattern with a Christ-centered focus, as the creeds of the church teach us. Doctrines are secondary commentary on the story; not designed to replace it with higher order conceptual precision. Indigenous cultures in which storytelling is primary challenge the modernist assumption that abstraction brings us closer to truth. The incarnation also pushes us in this direction. When Christians speak and write about God, Jesus Christ, the Holy Spirit, and salvation they have a particular story, read by particular people, in a particular pattern, in mind. "God" is a cipher term until we identify which God we are speaking about. Christians identify this God through the long narrative of the Bible. This is the God of Abraham and Sarah, the God and Father of our Lord Jesus Christ. It is this God, identified with these people, who creates the world and people and makes and keeps covenant promises with Israel for the sake of the world. This is a God who comes among us as one of us, who lives, dies, and rises again for our salvation as Jesus Christ and sends the Holy Spirit to direct the transformation of all things to God's good ends. That's not God in general, an instance of a general class. The habits of modernity are still alive, and we need to unlearn them to appreciate the rich particularity of Christianity, and other faith traditions. As Ludwig Wittgenstein said, "don't think, but look."[45]

GOD IS EXCELLENT AT REVELATION

> God, after He spoke long ago to the fathers in the prophets in many portions and in many ways, in these last days has spoken to us in His Son, whom He appointed heir of all things, through whom He also made the world. (Hebrews 1:1, NASB)

The assumption that we can speak of God in theological study is a big one and it is an arrogant one if we believe we can manufacture this speech out of the residue of our interiority, community experience, and naked

44. Thanks to my friend Bishop William Willimon for this example of abstraction from the personal to the conceptual.

45. Wittgenstein, *Philosophical Investigations*, no. 66.

observation of the world or current cultural trends. The danger is as Voltaire noted: "God made man in God's image, and man returned the favor." Idolatry is a perpetual danger in "constructive" theology and it is especially acute when theology is forgetful of divine initiative and divine disclosure.

In the history of Christian theology, revelation is what generates our salvation and our thankful, awestruck, bewildered speech about God. We meet God in the places where God has chosen to meet us. And the good news is that God, if the author of Hebrews is right, is loquacious. If we have a problem around God speaking, it will be that God is way too communicative, says too much for us to take in, is overwhelming. Based on biblical testimony, in fact, that's what happens to Isaiah and John of Patmos and to people whom Jesus delivered with a word. They were all gobsmacked, amazed. They asked, "Who is this?" and said, "He speaks with authority." Stammering witness to what disorients and reorients finds a voice. This God wants to be known and loved. This God desires fellowship, opens a conversation[46] with the creatures in the world God made. This God chooses not to be God without us. And so, God talks "baby talk," says Martin Luther. God accommodates to our condition, says John Calvin, so that we can receive words about God, experience fellowship and life as God intended it.[47] Behind both these statement lies the doctrine of the incarnation. God accommodates to the human condition. We understand in Jesus of Nazareth, the Word become flesh, that creaturely reality, flesh, and language is graced to accommodate divine speech. We can know God, not exhaustively, but truly through God's effective downward reach toward us and entry into the human condition. One Trinitarian way of thinking about this we get from Karl Barth.[48] It goes like this: God is revealer, the one who takes the initiative to come to us; God is revealed, the one who comes to us as Jesus Christ to rescue us from all that is less than what God wants to give us; God is revealedness, the very power to receive God's revelation so that it is effective for faith and life is the work of the Spirit and not natural human capacity. God

---

46. Robert Jenson maintains that the possibility of conversation with God is what it means to be made in God's image (Jenson, *Theology in Outline*, 4, 14–16, 68–69. "The blessing of listening to God is not given to Israel for Israel's own sake, but for the sake of opening a *conversation* between the human race and this lively talkative God" (Jensen, *Theology in Outline*, 15; emphasis added).

47. Calvin, *Institutes*, I.13.1.

48. Barth, *Church Dogmatics*, I/1, 295–99.

can effectively deliver the message of reconciliation. "The Holy Spirit is no skeptic."[49]

Having been spoken to, the church speaks. Christians, including theologians, are witnesses with words to what God has done for the world in Jesus Christ. Lately, the church and some of its theologians seem to draw back a bit from speaking about God, as a humble gesture. There is wisdom in this. Apophatic theology ("negative theology," which articulates what we don't know about God since God is beyond any final formulation) is a noble part of the mystic traditions of Christian theology. God's infinity and beauty and grandeur exceed our comprehension, always and everywhere. Awe is the human gesture Scripture records before the revelation of God. And the book of Ecclesiastes councils, "Be not rash with your mouth, nor let your heart be hasty to utter a word before God, for God is in heaven and you are on earth. Therefore, let your words be few" (Ecclesiastes 5:2, ESV).

There is, however, more than one kind of apophatic theology. Some of what passes for apophatic theology is more akin to agnosticism born of Enlightenment philosophy around epistemological limits. We have no sensible experience of God, according to Kant, and so no real knowledge of God. This approach to the limits of theological language is, it seems to me, simply a denial of revelation; that is, that God can effectively make God's self known through Jesus of Nazareth. Apophatic theology of this sort may not be about humility but rather an attempt to press revelation into a theory.[50]

Negative theology, in the history of the Christian church, is less sanguine where it comes to speech about God. It is often accompanied by a more kataphatic confidence; that is, while we cannot say everything about God, we can truly, but never exhaustively, speak of God by grace. It affirms that we cannot *finally* capture who God is in our formulations; but also that this is a joy, not a reason for silence. The inability ever to reach closure in our speech about God,

> doesn't lead them to conclude that nothing can be said of God. What they affirm is that no form of words, however true as far as it goes, is going to be fully adequate; there is always more to say (even in heaven). This is a theology that is hopeful because

49. Luther, *Luther's Works*, vol. 33, 24.

50. For a detailed discussion of differences between "classical apophaticism" and its modern Kantian versions with examples, see Turner, *Darkness of God*, cited in Pardue, *Mind of Christ*, 178.

of the conviction that there is always more, and that this 'more' is always more compelling and wonderful.[51]

And so, we speak of God as those who have heard and are provoked to praise. We pray for deliverance and take up practices to temper our carnal affections and worldly disquietudes and, like Basil, we scan the world in search of analogical language that may be worthy of God. In Christian theology, we take up the invitation "to conceive of the infinite Being whose immensity and omnipotence surpass all the efforts of the imagination." And so we pray . . .

> Ineffable Creator, Who out of the treasures of Thy wisdom hast appointed three hierarchies of Angels and set them in admirable order high above the heavens and hast disposed the divers portions of the universe in such marvelous array, Thou Who art called the True Source of Light and super eminent Principle of Wisdom, be pleased to cast a beam of Thy radiance upon the darkness of my mind and dispel from me the double darkness of sin and ignorance in which I have been born.
>
> Thou Who makest eloquent the tongues of little children, fashion my words and pour upon my lips the grace of Thy benediction. Grant me penetration to understand, capacity to retain, method and facility in study, subtlety in interpretation and abundant grace of expression.
>
> Order the beginning, direct the progress and perfect the achievement of my work, Thou who art true God and Man and livest and reignest for ever and ever. Amen.[52]

51. Williams, *Faith in the Public Square*, Kindle loc. 1408–14. See also the lucid treatment of apophatic and kataphatic traditions in Rigby, *Holding Faith*, 19–25. She makes the important point that discussion about God ought not to terminate here—at whether we can speak about God—but move to what it is about and how it matters to life.

52. Recited frequently by St. Thomas Aquinas, this prayer before study was published at the conclusion of Pope Pius XI, *Studiorum Ducem*.

2

Christian Mission

ROBERT S. PAUL

THE STORY OF CHRISTIAN mission, as told in the church where I grew up, was quite simple. The disciples of Jesus preached the gospel starting in Jerusalem, then St. Paul took over. He traveled about, got thrown in jail, survived shipwrecks, and started churches wherever he went. Thanks to Paul, the church was established in the Roman Empire. It later got a boost from Emperor Constantine, and then Protestant missionaries spread the gospel to the rest of the world. While this version of the story contains some important elements, it is a bit sketchy to say the least.

Happily, ignorance can be cured. The actual story of how the Christian faith spread around the world, I later learned, is more complicated but also far more interesting than my first simplistic understanding. It is a story full of fascinating characters, surprising plot twists, tragic setbacks, unlikely successes, and unexpected outcomes. It also invites thoughtful consideration because the history of Christianity puts both the best and worst instances of Christian mission on full display. An honest assessment should encourage a proper humility among Christians, but it also offers inspiration. The story is replete with examples of heroic sacrifice and it offers glimpses of how God works through flawed human beings, despite our missteps.

The study of Christian mission is a vital aspect of theological education. Greater understanding of how the Christian movement, from tiny beginnings, came to be a worldwide phenomenon helps to dispel myths about the role of missionaries, whether idealistic or otherwise. It also supports the church's theological self-criticism. To study mission is to examine what Christians have *done* to make the gospel known, not only what they *believe* in abstract terms. Thoughtful engagement with the subject is perennially important for the sake of a more faithful and fulsome witness to the gospel of Jesus Christ. In this brief introduction, we will seek to trace the contours of the subject, indicate some of the nuances involved, and point to resources valuable for further study.

WORLDWIDE EXPANSION:
A TWO-THOUSAND-YEAR JOURNEY

To get a sense of the current status of Christian mission, it is useful to begin about a hundred years ago, at the beginning of the twentieth century. Christian leaders in Europe and North America then were highly optimistic about the prospects for their mission to the world. Christianity was solidly established in the West and the nations of Europe exercised sovereignty over a vast network of colonial outposts that stretched around the globe. Telegraph communications linked the continents and travel was increasingly fast and common. A transatlantic crossing from London to New York by modern steamship took less than a week. Visionary leaders believed the favorable position of the church was a divinely orchestrated and unprecedented opportunity to fulfill the command of Jesus to "Go therefore and make disciples of all nations" (Matthew 28:19). They also believed that the blessings of the gospel and the benefits of Western civilization were meant to be shared with the entire world. When over 1,200 delegates of the Protestant missionary movement gathered in Edinburgh in 1910, their watchword was to "evangelize the world in this generation."[1]

The twentieth century, however, did not unfold as those visionaries imagined. Soon after, Europe plunged into one of the most destructive wars of all history. Armies of the German-Austrian-Hungarian alliance faced off against the armies of France-Russia-Britain, with Canada and the United States joining as well. In the conflagration that ensued from 1914–1918 (described as the "war to end all wars"[2]) at least sixteen

1. Mott, *Evangelization of the World in This Generation.*
2. The phrase is attributed to a book by Wells, *The War That Will End War.*

million people died in the fighting with another twenty million casualties resulting from disease and malnutrition. On both sides, the combatant nations understood themselves as representing the apex of Christian civilization.

From our viewpoint a century later, the bold vision expressed by Christian leaders in 1910 smacks of both naïveté and arrogance. Though born of deep faith in the power of God, the global mission they imagined was entangled with the idea that the Christian West stood at the forefront of human progress, and that a grateful world would embrace the Christian faith on that account. This was not the case. Other nations proved resistant to a religious message that came wrapped up in colonialism and the West's cultural hegemony.

Even so, the worldwide expansion of Christian faith those earlier leaders envisioned was not entirely off the mark, though it did not happen as they anticipated. Following the First and Second World Wars, the church's stronghold in Europe and North America deteriorated. Western cultures became increasingly secularized and the church declined in both numbers and influence. However, the Christian movement grew rapidly elsewhere, increasing more in the twentieth century than in any previous period, and more rapidly than world population growth as a whole. In 1950, some 80 percent of all Christians lived in Europe and North America, but by 2005 the majority lived in the southern hemisphere, in Asia, Africa, and Latin America.

The African case is especially striking, with growth from 9 million Christians in 1900 to roughly 393 million by 2005. Africa is on pace to become the most Christian continent in the world before 2030. There are remarkable Christian movements taking place in India, China, and across Latin America too, as well as other places. In 1900, the typical Christian was a white European. If there is a "typical" Christian today, we should think of an African, Latin American, or Asian who is more likely than not a woman.[3]

Entailed in this dramatic growth is a shift in Christianity's center of gravity from the North Atlantic nations to the Global South, the full implications of which remain to be seen. At the very least, these changes challenge those of us in North America and Europe to reconsider whether our cultures are really at the forefront of human history and to remember

---

3. See Jenkins, *Next Christendom*. See also Pew Research Center, "Future of World Religions," https://www.pewforum.org/2015/04/02/religious-projections-2010-2050/.

that the Christian faith was not a Western religion in the beginning, nor is it primarily so now.[4]

The book of Acts, by its focus on the missionary work of St. Paul, creates the impression that the trajectory of early Christian growth was primarily north and westward from Jerusalem, through Asia Minor to Rome and beyond. In fact, this was just one of several vectors of early Christian expansion. Starting from Jerusalem, the gospel message took root in major cities such as Antioch, Alexandria, Edessa, and Ephesus, and spread in all directions. It traveled eastward with merchant caravans along the Silk Road from Arabia and Persia, through India, and all the way to China. It moved south along the Nile Valley to the kingdom of Kush in the Sudan. It spread by merchant vessels across the Arabian Sea to India, and to North Africa by ships that crisscrossed the Mediterranean—the *mare nostrum* ("our sea"), as the Romans called it—as well as Italy, Gaul, and the Iberian Peninsula.

Until quite recently, histories of the church written in the modern era were thoroughly Western-centric. These have begun to be supplemented by accounts that take a more comprehensive view of Christian expansion.[5] Christian communities were formed in Rome long before St. Paul arrived there, and were established in Egypt and the Nile Valley within the first century CE. The apostle Thomas was preaching in India at the same time that Paul preached among the cities of Asia Minor, according to respected ancient traditions. In the second century CE, the strongest churches were in the eastern part of the Roman Empire and worshipped in the Syriac language. By the end of that century, there were Christians living all around the Mediterranean, north to the Danube, in Britannia, and to the eastern edge of the Persian Empire. By the seventh century, Christians could be found as far east as China and as far south as Nubia.

This expansion obviously was not the exclusive work of St. Paul and the other apostles, as important as they were. Most of the early "missionaries" were merchants, artisans, pilgrims, and refugees who embraced the gospel and carried it with them to far-flung places. In its early stages, the movement was facilitated by the Jewish diaspora and the wide influence of Hellenistic culture. Early Christian writers followed the example of the Jews in Alexandria who had translated the Hebrew Scriptures into

4. See Sanneh, *Whose Religion Is Christianity?*

5. The three-volume series by Irvin and Sunquist, *History of the World Christian Movement*, is exemplary in this regard.

Greek around 250 BCE, the language used in trade and commerce from the Pyrenees to the Himalayas. Christian expansion was a peoples' movement, conveying a message about a God who had compassion for the poor, the downtrodden, women and children, and even slaves. In a world dominated by rich and powerful men, this message not only promised life after death, but transcended ethnicity, politics, and social class. Early Christian communities were notable for how they differed from the prevailing social order.[6]

THE DYNAMICS OF A MULTICULTURAL MOVEMENT

Envisioning how the Christian message spread points to a central puzzle in the story—namely, how it could be that non-Jews came to see Jesus, proclaimed as the *Jewish* Messiah, as being relevant for them. The earliest followers of Jesus, all of whom were Jews, were not of one mind about the phenomenon. The account offered in the book of Acts narrates the steps by which Gentiles heard and responded to the message and the conflicting opinions this created among Jewish followers of Jesus. Eventually, Gentiles were accepted into the movement, but not without controversy. The crux of the issue was whether they were required to adopt Jewish customs (especially male circumcision) in order to be considered part of Israel's covenant community. The resolution that was reached established cultural flexibility, not conformity to Jewish customs, as the guiding principle of a movement that increasingly diverged from Judaism, and which eventually became known as "Christian."[7]

To explore this principle of cultural flexibility further, it is useful to contrast Christianity with Islam, a religion that designates one language, certain sacred locations, and particular practices as indispensable requirements of the religion. The Arabic language has special status in Islam, being the language in which the holy prophet Muhammed received the divine revelation. The Qur'an, though it has been translated into other languages, is regarded as authoritative only in Arabic. Prayers must be said in Arabic as well, regardless of a person's mother tongue, and always facing towards Mecca, the central place of sacred importance to Muslims. The *Hajj* pilgrimage to Mecca likewise is mandatory for Muslim adults at

---

6. See Irvin and Sunquist. *History of the World Christian Movement*, vol. 1, 47–48; and Robert, *Christian Mission*.

7. See especially Acts 6–11.

least once in their lifetime, provided they have the means and health for
the journey. Restrictions on diet, known as *halal*, are mandatory for all
Muslims everywhere, regardless of local cultures, customs, and cuisines.

By contrast, Jesus challenged the customs associated with keeping
the Jewish Sabbath in his time, and he did not require his disciples to
observe the clean/unclean rules that separated the "righteous" from the
"unrighteous." The movement he launched was nonconformist and con-
troversial, as evidenced by disputes with scribes and Pharisees, especially
where the keeping of certain laws and traditions was considered essential
to a person's standing before God. To be sure, worshipping in the temple
and observing Torah laws and traditions concerning diet and other
practices persisted among the earliest Jewish followers of Jesus, but these
practices ultimately did not carry over as a requirement of Christian
faithfulness. Among the apostles, Peter and Paul notably claimed freedom from their own Jewish traditions, and Gentiles were not required to
become culturally Jewish in order to be Christian.[8]

Christianity does not have a central site that functions in the way
that Mecca does for Muslims. Christian shrines exist in many places and
some are revered as destinations for pilgrimage, but none of that is an
obligatory part of Christian practice. Neither does the Aramaic language
that Jesus spoke have the authoritative status that is attributed to Arabic in Islamic theology and practice. Instead, the Christian message was
translated into other languages from the beginning, starting with the
writers of the New Testament documents, who opted for *koine* (common) Greek rather than Aramaic or Hebrew. The desire to communicate
in understandable terms, rather conformity to primitive origins, was the
operative principle of Christian expansion.

This is exemplified by the importance of Bible translation in the
work of Christian missionaries across the centuries, to whom it seemed
obvious that the gospel should be translated so people could understand
it in their mother tongue. Numerous linguist-missionaries have devoted
their lives to deciphering languages and committing them to written
form for this purpose, an effort that often involved educational initiatives
to promote literacy. The result in many instances has been the preservation of ancient oral traditions and Indigenous languages that otherwise
might have been lost in the midst of cultural change and the wider forces
of modernization. Contrary to common misconceptions, missionaries

8. See Acts 15:1–35.

who engaged in these efforts demonstrated profound respect for local cultures and served as agents of cultural preservation and renewal.[9]

As Lamin Sanneh puts it, the Christian faith has not advanced by the hegemonic *diffusion* of fixed cultural forms, but serially from one cultural context to another through *translation* into vernacular languages. The essence of the faith is not its outward forms, but the core message of Jesus Christ. Those who receive it in their mother tongue may interpret its meaning for themselves and respond to it in forms apropos to their own context. This is not to say that Christian missionaries or church officials always refrained from offering their own interpretation of the Bible, or from attempting to conform new converts to their own traditions. Nevertheless, in the long run the receptors of the message have been more determinative of its outworking in different contexts than the missionary transmitters. As a result, the most striking feature of worldwide Christianity after two thousand years is not its uniformity, but its cultural diversity. The one faith of the apostles has been translated, interpreted, and assimilated again and again in different situations and contexts, resulting not in a monolithic religion, but in "multiple Christianities" around the world.[10]

THE DARK SIDE OF THE STORY

The preceding assessment of Christian expansion may raise eyebrows in some circles since the missionary enterprise is not universally regarded with favor. For some, the term "missionary" conjures images like that of Nathan Price, the fictional protagonist of Barbara Kingsolver's novel *The Poisonwood Bible*. In his efforts to evangelize Africans in the Congo, so the story goes, the missionary tried to baptize his converts in a river filled with crocodiles, not understanding what he was doing. Price is a metaphor for gross cultural insensitivity—a white man determined to convert bewildered natives to his religion. The caricature resonates with those who feel that "mission" implies a kind of aggression that seems incongruent with Jesus, as portrayed in the Gospels, and a spiritual exclusivism that is indefensible in the face of the world's many religions and diverse cultures.

9. See Sanneh, *Translating the Message*.

10. See Sanneh and Carpenter, eds., *Changing Face of Christianity*.

Caricatures aside, any honest account of Christian mission must acknowledge the reality that the church and its missionary agents have not always respected cultural diversity nor personal freedom. Christians have resorted to coercive and even violent methods at times, practices made all the worse for being done in the name of God. This tendency, however, did not begin in the modern era, nor was it instituted by missionaries.

In 772 CE, the king of the Franks, Charles the Great (*Charlemagne*), conducted a military campaign to subdue Saxon tribes on his northeast border. They had defied earlier efforts to bring them under Charles's rule and persisted in raiding Frankish settlements, so he resolved to settle the matter. It was a brutal campaign. At one point the king personally oversaw the mass execution of four thousand Saxon prisoners of war, a demonstration that his rule required utter submission. Among the laws he imposed in the aftermath, Saxons were forced to undergo Christian baptism or face execution. Capital punishment also was imposed as the penalty for failing to have one's children baptized. This was the first full-scale use of lethal force to compel conversion to Christianity, and it set a precedent that other Christian kings would follow.[11]

Eight years after subduing the Saxons, Charles was crowned emperor of the Holy Roman Empire by Pope Leo II in St. Peter's Basilica in Rome. Historians regard this as the event where "Christendom" began—the alliance of political and military power with the Christian church. The church gave divine sanction to the authority of kings and rulers, including the use of force, while kings in their turn provided protection and advantages to the church and its officials.[12]

The Christendom arrangement assumed a territorial concept of Christianity, in which the religion of the king became the mandatory religion for all in his kingdom. Christian territories could be defined as those under control of a Christian king. This concept was in full play in 1095 CE when Pope Urban II called for a military campaign "under the sign of the cross" (thus, a *Crusade*) to wrest control of formerly Christian territories from Muslims, whose expansionary armies had taken them in the seventh and eight centuries. Christians were not excluded from these territories under the Islamic dispensation, but when a new Muslim dynasty, the Seljuk Turks, took control of Palestine, they cut off Christian pilgrimages to Jerusalem. When a Christian army recaptured the city of

---

11. Irvin and Sunquist. *History of the World Christian Movement*, 336–37.

12. See Brown, *Rise of Western Christendom*.

Toledo in Spain from Muslim control, the pope saw an opportunity. He called upon Christian kings throughout Europe to organize armies to reconquer the Holy Lands. The Crusades that followed achieved varying results, but the legitimization of "holy violence" as a means for Christian expansion and control had long-term consequences.

One such consequence is the opposition and antagonism that persists today between nations traditionally defined as "Christian" or "Muslim." Although it is anachronistic and misleading to categorize most modern nation-states in terms of religion, international relations are haunted by the history of religiously defined conflict. Another consequence of the territorial idea was the acceptance of coercive violence as a legitimate form of discipline within Christendom itself. Those deemed to be heretics and nonconformists within Christian territories were treated brutally in "a reign of terror that lasted for centuries directed by the hierarchy of the church."[13] Jan Huss, for example, was burned alive in 1415 by order of the Council of Constance for contesting the authority of church hierarchies. The same council also condemned John Wycliffe as a heretic though he had died thirty years earlier. They ordered his bones dug up and burned anyway. Many other instances of gruesome capital punishment would follow.

The unholy alliance of political and ecclesiastical power is where we find the roots of the Spanish Inquisition and so-called religious wars in Europe. It is evident also in the oppression of Indigenous peoples when the kingdoms of Christendom extended their control to the Americas and beyond. The actions of Spanish conquistadors and the British tolerance of the Atlantic slave trade are egregious examples, but more subtle forms of coercion were also utilized in the early American colonies. Groups such as the Puritans in New England and the Baptists in Rhode Island, among others, emigrated from Europe in search of "religious freedom." The freedom they sought, however, was not for the sake of promoting religious tolerance. They wanted to organize their own communities how they believed God commanded, without outside interference. Most of them "came to these shores not to establish religious liberty, but to practice their own form of orthodoxy."[14] In the quest for a holier manner of life they were not averse to using coercion and violence to punish

13. Irvin and Sunquist, *History of the World Christian Movement*, 410.
14. Murrin, "Religion and Politics in America," 20.

nonconformity. This impulse, sadly, cannot be dismissed as an unfortunate and long-gone artifact of history.

A more recent example is the central role that churches took in implementing the residential school system for Canada's Indigenous population. Established in the nineteenth century, these schools were part of the government's effort to force Indigenous people to assimilate to the dominant Euro-Canadian culture. Very young children were forcibly removed from their families and home communities and placed in residential schools, most of which were operated by Christian denominations.[15] The practice continued for 130 years and led to horrific abuses. Thousands of children died, and thousands more were injured and traumatized. All this has been documented and acknowledged in hindsight as a form of "cultural genocide," and the social and psychological damage done is extensive and long-lasting. The ongoing process of "Truth and Reconciliation" is aimed at righting these wrongs, but it remains far from complete.[16]

LOOKING FOR LIGHT IN THE DARKNESS

In view of this dark history, it is fair to ask how or why Christian mission can claim any legitimacy in the twenty-first century. It is not a question that permits glib answers but calls for thoughtful consideration and meaningful corrective actions.

A starting place is to observe that the period of most rapid and extensive growth of the Christian faith globally did not take place during the era of European colonialism, at the height of Western missionary activity. As noted previously, as recently as 1950 some 80% of all Christians lived in Europe and North America, but by 2005 the majority lived in Asia, Africa, and Latin America. This is to say that the period of rapid Christian growth outside the West corresponds to those decades when national liberation movements displaced the older colonial system. This presents a puzzling paradox: Why did formerly colonized people, who eagerly claimed national independence after the Second World War, not

15. Roman Catholic, Anglican, United, Methodist, and Presbyterian churches were the major denominations involved in the administration of the residential school system. The government's partnership with the churches remained in place until 1969. Most of the schools had closed by the 1980s, but the last federally supported residential schools remained in operation until the late 1990s.

16. See *Canada's Residential Schools.*

jettison the Christian faith of their oppressors when their hour of liberation came?

Christian mission in the modern era (broadly from the sixteenth
through mid-twentieth centuries) was entangled with European imperialism in many respects, and so the sunset of Western colonialism cast
a long shadow over the missionary enterprise. By the mid-twentieth
century the European nations were depleted by two successive wars. Thy
had neither the will nor the means to sustain their colonial hegemony
and their empires collapsed like so many dominoes. India achieved its
independence from Britain in 1947, Burma followed in 1948, and China
expelled all foreign missionaries from the country following the Commu-
nist takeover in 1949. Ghana became the first African nation to achieve
independence in 1957, and all the rest of the African nations quickly followed in the 1960s.

This shift of political power unleashed a backlash against colonialism in which the Christian missionary effort could not avoid its share
of the opprobrium. In postcolonial critique, it became commonplace to
dismiss missionaries as nothing more than the religious arm of European
colonialism, or to condemn them as insidious purveyors of oppression
who promoted "cultural imperialism" by propagating a foreign religion.[17]
Negative reaction against missionary complicity with colonialism became so acute that even some Christian leaders called for a "moratorium
on missions."[18]

The entanglement of Christian mission with colonialism cannot
be denied, but there are reasons to see the matter in another light. The
collapse of colonialism also presented an opportunity to disentangle the
gospel from the church's long affair with coercive violence. Part of this
process has involved studies that move beyond generalities to more refined examinations of missionary practices in the midst of colonialism.
As Andrew Walls notes,

> Missionaries had a double identity. They were representative
> Christians trying (and in the process demonstrating all the el-
> ements of human fallenness and all the limitations of human
> vision and foresight) to do Christian things . . . and more than

17 See, for example, Comaroff and Comaroff, *Of Revelation and Revolution.*

18. The idea of a "moratorium" was proposed at a World Council of Churches conference on "Salvation Today," held in Bangkok in 1972/73.

any other group of Westerners . . . were trying to make Christian choices and live in a Christian way.[19]

Missionaries, Walls is suggesting, were not merely colonialists. Although they arrived in foreign lands carrying the assumptions of their home cultures, exposure to the realities of colonialism in the field caused many missionaries (though not all) to become sharp critics of European imperialism and thorns in the side of colonial administrators. Their engagement with Indigenous languages pioneered new methods of research into other cultures and opened new fields of study. Early anthropologists, in fact, were often dependent on missionaries to gain access to remote tribal groups, and their research benefited from the work missionaries had done in linguistics and in deciphering cultural patterns. In the postcolonial period, anthropologists repaid the missionaries for their help by becoming some of their sharpest critics.

With time, though, scholarly discourse came to recognize both missionaries and their converts as "postcolonial subjects," rather than simplistically juxtaposing them as "Westerners" and "natives," or as "oppressors" and "victims." Closer examination of the matter revealed that the interaction between missionaries and Indigenous people was not one-sided but often involved a mutual interchange that promoted "hybridity."

> Both missionaries and their early Christian converts were chief agents of the transfer of knowledge and technologies from one culture to another. As such, they participated in both the globalization of knowledge and the re-creation of local identities that emerged from interaction with global modernity. In postcolonialist discourse, therefore, the long-term effects of missions and missionaries undercut a simplistic equation with cultural imperialism.[20]

The relationship between missionaries and colonial administrations was a carryover of the Christendom arrangement between the church and state power. However, the way in which particular missionaries engaged with Indigenous people could be radically different from the attitude and manner of colonial officials or merchants. Where missionaries were most *dependent* on colonial power, the faith they represented was most likely to be seen as a foreign entity alien to Indigenous cultures. Where missionaries were relatively *independent* of colonial power and engaged with

19. Walls, *Missionary Movement in Christian History*, xviii.

20. Robert, *Christian Mission*, 96.

Indigenous people in more personal terms, the result often was different. The efforts of missionaries in language translation, literacy, education, and health care left a legacy that supported rather than hindered movements of national independence and cultural renewal, with long-lasting positive effects.[21]

Those missionaries who were more deeply engaged with Indigenous people as fellow human beings, rather than with the apparatus of colonialism, made prodigious efforts to learn local languages and adopted local customs, cuisines, and patterns of social interaction. The message of Christ they conveyed, though associated with colonialism, was not identical to it. Indigenous receptors of the gospel were quite able to differentiate between the message itself, with its themes of hope, healing, and liberation, and the oppressive mechanisms of the colonial project. Indeed, they found in the Bible a rich resource to aid in their struggle for liberty and justice. As the colonial system was deconstructed, millions of people around the world bid good riddance to the oppression but retained the gospel as their own.

Historically, the poor, the oppressed, and the disadvantaged often have been more receptive and responsive to the gospel than the rich, the powerful, and the privileged. Modern Westerners often assume that the relative decline of Christianity in the West is because we are a scientifically advanced culture that has discarded old superstitions. Disaffection with religion, however, may have as much to do with the habits of power and privilege. Economic comparisons between the "developed" versus "less developed" (or "developing") parts of the world, for example, may lead us to assume that we are more "developed" culturally, morally, and spiritually as well; that is, more advanced, or superior. Many Westerners, for example, regard the traditional politics of sexuality and gender in African societies with a sense of disdain that scarcely disguises an insidious attitude of cultural superiority (or racism). This has nothing to do with being religious. Being rich, powerful, and privileged tempts one to think that other cultures are primitive and must eventually catch up with the "enlightened" liberality of the West.

It should be obvious that the habits of relying on power, and the attitudes of cultural superiority this tends to breed, are contrary to a gospel that speaks of God's reconciling purpose towards all people, and which calls us to love one another as Christ has loved us. Missionaries in the

21. Woodberry, "Reclaiming the M-Word." Also, Dilley, "Surprising Discovery," 34.

modern era traveled on the same vessels as colonial forces and sometimes relied on the military and political power this afforded them. Even so, the gospel message they proclaimed was not so distorted or compromised as to be incomprehensible to those who received it. Indeed, the remarkable expansion of Christian faith in the *post*colonial period was overwhelmingly the achievement of Indigenous leaders, who found in the message they received a deep affirmation of their identity and liberation that derives from God. This suggests that the gospel, rather than being dependent on the coercive power or cultural status afforded by the Christendom alliance, flourishes far better without that kind of assistance.

THEOLOGICAL EDUCATION AND THE STUDY OF MISSION

I began this essay by speaking of "the story of Christian mission." In considering how mission relates to theological education, it is helpful to recognize why the study of this story is a multifaceted undertaking.

First is simply that it is a story about real human beings. The term "missionary" is faceless on its own and vulnerable to fictional caricatures such as that of Nathan Price. By contrast, *non*fictional stories of Christian missionaries resist caricature because they are about actual human beings in all their particularity. Historically, missionaries lived and worked in many different places and times, spoke various languages, and were shaped by various cultures. That remains the case today. Every missionary must be considered in his or her particularity, rather than reduced to a general category.

The study of mission, in this sense, is about real people with names such as Peter and Paul, Lydia and Timothy, and Priscilla and Aquila in the biblical record; and later figures like Patrick of Ireland, Jeanne d'Arc, Hudson Taylor, Adoniram Judson, Mother Teresa, Helen Rosaveare, Oscar Romero, Manche Masemola, Esther John, and Bernard Mizeki. The list goes on and on. Part of the wonder of Christian mission is found in the biographies of people who devoted their lives to making Jesus Christ known to others, some at the cost of their own life. As Tertullian noted long ago, "the blood of the martyrs is the seed of the Church."[22]

The story is not only about individuals, however. From its beginnings, Christian mission has been a collective enterprise of the church.

22. *Apologeticus*, ch. 50.

Whether Roman Catholic, Orthodox, Protestant, or otherwise, the church has provided organizational support to missionaries and has imposed controls upon them. This has been a source of some tension virtually from the beginning. As Lamin Sanneh puts it:

> Two impulses, running on concurrent lines, developed quickly as a result of the impact of the preaching and ministry of Jesus and by virtue of apostolic faithfulness. One was the urge to spread the message with every available facility. The other was the desire to regulate the emerging community of believers . . . [23]

Tensions between church leaders and missionaries arose very early in the question of Gentile inclusion. The church in Jerusalem held *de facto* authority in the early years because of their direct ties to Jesus and his brother, James (see Acts 15). Yet Paul and Barnabas, and Peter before them (Acts 11), testified that the Spirit of Jesus had led them beyond the sociocultural boundaries that separated Jews from Gentiles, and that Gentiles were responsive to the message concerning Jesus and manifested signs of the Spirit's presence. This sense of Spirit-led connection with new people in unexpected places can be found again and again in the history of missionary activity. The missionary impulse to cross customary boundaries has put them at odds with ecclesiastical authorities more than once, but it also has led to innovations that brought change and renewal to the church itself. Some examples may be given, albeit briefly.

First is the prominent role of women in missionary activities in contrast to the limited roles traditionally allowed to them in the church. In the nineteenth century and the first half of the twentieth, at the peak of the modern missionary movement, almost no Christian church allowed the ordination of women to the priesthood or clergy. The majority of Catholic and Protestant missionaries, however, were women. In foreign mission fields, women were free from the restrictions that applied in their "sending" churches. Many provided exemplary leadership in fields as diverse as education, medicine, care of orphans, the liberation of girls and women from sex slavery, advocacy for women's rights, and evangelism. Women missionaries enacted and demonstrated Paul's vision of gender equality—that "in Christ Jesus" "there is neither male nor female" (Galatians 3:28, NASB)—long before the established church was prepared to embrace it.[24]

---

23. Sanneh, *Translating the Message*, 35.

24. See Robert, *Christian Mission*, 114–41; also Robert, *American Women in*

We can also point to the significance of missionaries in struggles against racism, the abolition of slavery in the British Empire, and the end of apartheid in South Africa being prominent examples. In these struggles, some missionaries advocated for justice in the political realm, but the influence they exercised by propagating the gospel through evangelism, preaching, and education was an equal or greater contribution. Societal change required government action, but changing laws was not sufficient on its own. The deep sociocultural issues at the root of these practices needed to be engaged at ground level, and for this the work of Indigenous leaders was indispensable. Many Africans who became powerful advocates for social reform and justice were armed for the battle by the deep conviction that the gospel itself required it. Archbishop Desmond Tutu, for instance, is famous for his work in relation to apartheid.

African Christians also were crucial to ending the transatlantic slave trade. While Europeans challenged the morality of the practice in their courts and assemblies, Indigenous leaders were required to confront the problem in its African strongholds, where slavery existed long before Europeans exploited it. The proclamation of the gospel was a key weapon in this task. European missionaries who introduced the gospel in Africa, and established schools where many Indigenous leaders acquired skills and resources to confront the evils of colonialism, deserve some credit for their contributions.[25]

A third example is the seminal role of the mission enterprise in the modern ecumenical movement. At the 1910 world missionary conference in Edinburgh only a handful of non-Westerners were present, but they were harbingers of the coming reality that worldwide Christianity could not remain within structures of Western control. Those who envisioned evangelizing the world "in this generation" foresaw the need for ecclesial structures capacious enough to embrace a worldwide church (*oikoumene*). The International Missionary Council (IMC), formed in 1921 to coordinate missionary efforts around the world, was a predecessor to the formation of the World Council of Churches in 1948.[26] The study of ecumenical relations is incomplete if it fails to appreciate how the missionary movement showed the way forward.

Mission.

25. Sanneh, *Abolitionists Abroad.*

26. Numerous sources document this ecumenical process. Lesslie Newbigin's autobiographical memoir is particularly illuminating (Newbigin, *Unfinished Agenda*).

Implicit in these examples are several reasons why the study of mission is a crucial part of theological education in the twenty-first century. It is important in the first place for an accurate understanding of church history, and the contemporary church as well. The movement that came to be known as Christianity grew out of the apostles' conviction that they were commissioned to bear witness to Jesus "in Jerusalem, in all Judea and Samaria, and to the ends of the earth" (Acts 1:8). Their faithfulness to this task gave rise to a "Christian" identity that was multicultural rather than confined as a sect of Judaism. One of the central themes of twentieth-century theology was to clarify that "mission" is not merely one of many activities or programs of the church, but is the essential identity, nature, and *raison d'être* of the church itself—the "missional" church as it is sometimes called.[27]

This has great relevance in our world where technology and the relentless process of international commerce and immigration virtually have eliminated the distance that once separated people of different languages and cultures. In the city of Vancouver, for instance, dozens of languages other than the official English and French are the mother tongue of a substantial portion of the population. Similar linguistic diversity may be found in many urban centers around the world.[28]

Language and cultural diversity go hand in hand. To illustrate, we might consider what commonly occurs as immigrant families enter Canadian society. Simply stated, the children of new immigrants tend to assimilate into the surrounding culture faster and more fully than their parents, in part because they are faster language learners. This process creates some tension between generations within families and ethnic communities. Chinese or Korean churches in Vancouver that were formed by first-generation immigrants, for example, often divide into separate congregations as time passes, the differences between generations becoming a source of cultural divergence. Politics also breed cultural diversity as identity groups cluster together for mutual support, or to advocate for one cause or another. All these factors contribute to a cultural milieu that is complex, fluid, and prone to social conflict.

Christian mission has much to offer in this milieu because it long has been at the forefront of intercultural encounter. Indeed, no other movement in human history has sustained this engagement as long or

27. See Bosch, *Transforming Mission*; also Guder, ed., *Missional Church*.

28. Minsky, "Vancouver at the Crossroads."

as widely. Within the history and corporate memory of the church is a treasure trove of experience and wisdom about how otherness can be navigated with mutual respect. Some of this wisdom is found in libraries, archives, and among missionary veterans, but one can also look to the students who now populate our classrooms. Increasingly, our theological students are as likely to come from Indonesia, Korea, Taiwan, Africa, or Brazil as from Canadian provinces or the United States. Even those who have grown up in Canada are ethnically diverse, including Indigenous students, whose ancestral families have inhabited these lands for ten thousand years. Such diversity makes for challenging conversations, but it is a richly rewarding environment for the education and preparation of Christian leaders.

Ultimately, Christian mission is part of the theological curriculum because Jesus is the original missionary. The term "missionary" derives from the Latin *missio* and refers to the act of sending, or to one who is sent. It is notable that the word does not appear in the Bible primarily in reference to Peter or Paul or any of the other apostles, but to Jesus. He is the one "sent" by God into the world for its salvation, an action born of the infinite love of God for the world (John 3:16). His mission is the beginning point and foundation for the mission of the church, which bears witness to what God has done in Jesus Christ. *Sicut misit me Pater, et ego mitto vos.* "As the Father has sent me," Jesus said, "so I send you" (John 20:21).

Through all the seasons and variations in the two-thousand-year story of Christian mission, the core message has remained remarkably consistent. As Andrew Walls puts it, "the person of Jesus called the Christ has ultimate significance."[29] Jesus is proclaimed as "the image of the invisible God" (Colossians 1:15), the singular figure in human history who reveals the character and purpose of God in relation with humankind; who indeed is God incarnate, acting for the sake of the world's salvation.

Seen in this light, the study of mission is a crucial aspect of theological education for more than historical and practical reasons. The subject draws us into deeper reflection about our calling as followers of Jesus, the purpose of the church, the character of our lives, the manner of our witness and proclamation of the gospel, the respect and service we owe to people of all kinds and cultures, the need for repentance over things done and harm caused in the name of Christ, and the possibility of redemption

29. Walls, *Missionary Movement in Christian History*, 6.

and spiritual renewal. All of this is rooted in the same source: the contemplation and worship of God as revealed in Jesus Christ, whose life and work are attested in Scripture and by the Holy Spirit as the fullest and truest expression given to humankind of the very character of God.

3

The Importance and Nature of the Study of Liturgy for Theological Students

THERE IS A MODEL that we teach lay and clergy Anglicans and Episcopalians in a comprehensive congregational development training in the US and in Canada called The College for Congregational Development and The School for Parish Development respectively. That model is called the "Sources of Transformation" model (see Figure 3.1).

One of the points of the model is that those dimensions of congregational life shown in the model all contribute, with God's help, to the transformation of a Christian in terms of their ability to live out their baptismal identity and purpose. Another point of the model is that each of the different dimensions depicted influence one another; in a parish system none operates on its own. And finally, in the above version of the model we teach Anglicans, at the center of the model is Worship and Prayer, which means that Anglicans believe that the Eucharist, that some form of the daily prayer that we call the Divine Office, and that some form of personal prayer, be it intercession, contemplation, adoration or other forms of prayer, is at the heart of how Anglicans enlarge their capacity to be the body of Christ in and for the world.

My colleagues and I have had many discussions about whether this model looks the same for Christians from different ecclesial traditions. Some have argued that one specific tradition would put Study and Learning at the center of the model while another tradition would place Christian Action at the center. Regardless, however, of where a given ecclesial tradition would place it, liturgy, the structured communal life of prayer of a faith community, is clearly one of the most powerful ways that Christians are challenged, supported, and formed in their lives in Christ.

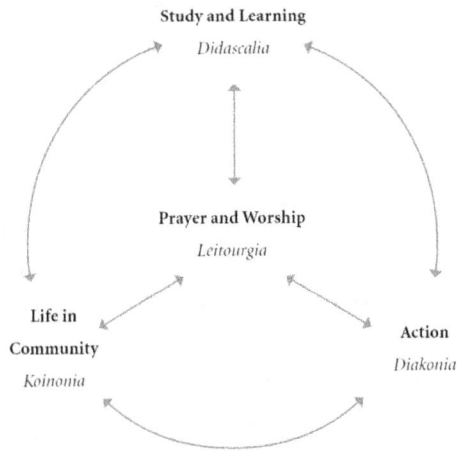

Study and Learning

Didascalia

Prayer and Worship

Leitourgia

Life in Community

Koinonia

Action

Diakonia

Prayer and Worship: Holy Eucharist, Daily Office, and Personal Prayer

Study and Learning: Mind, Heart, and Practice

Action: Stewardship, Service, and Evangelism

Life in Community: Conversation, Food, and Silence/Listening

Figure 3.1. Sources of Transformation model.[1]

---

1. As found in Skelton and Diocese of Olympia, *College for Congregational Development; Manuals Year A and Year B*, 34.

THE IMPORTANCE OF THE STUDY OF LITURGY
FOR THEOLOGICAL STUDENTS

And so, it seems to me, that the importance of the study of liturgy for theological students is obvious if those theological students are headed towards congregational leadership that seeks, with God's help, to foster the formation of Christians of all ages and circumstances toward greater Christian maturity at the congregational level. The question, it seems to me, is this: what, in particular, makes the study of liturgy important within theological education? And how can the study of liturgy best contribute to students' formation for leadership in congregations?

Why is the study of liturgy important for theological students in formation for congregational leadership? My answer is simple: liturgy has the potential and power to engage the entire human person in both preparation for and the enactment of the Christian life that all other areas of theological study point to. In liturgy, all other areas of theological study show up or do not show up. In liturgy, all other areas of theological study take on flesh or do not take on flesh.

Consider this: where else in the life of the church are all these things happening simultaneously?

* The gathering of people in which some groups of people are present, and some are not.

* The intentional use of the space within which the liturgy is happening.

* The use of art in the space or in the liturgy.

* The use of sound and the kind of music listened to and participated in.

* The presence of objects in the space in a way that suggests importance of the actions associated with them.

* The words that are spoken and the words that are not spoken.

* The presence of leaders and their influential energies.

* The use, or not, of silence.

* The nature, quality, and flow of activity.

* The degree to which those gathered use their bodies and their senses to participate.

* The flow and order of liturgies over the yearly calendar that suggest the order of and emphasis within the life of faith.

Each of these things and all of these things collectively are a part of the experience we call liturgy and each of these things and all of these things collectively have formational power—some of it conscious to those being formed and most of it unconscious.

And so, to follow on this, what might we in a congregation learn about ethics not only from a sermon on the topic of homelessness within the context of a Sunday liturgy but also from the experience of being in relationship to the homeless who are with us in that liturgy? What might we learn about a theology of God not only from the language used for God in liturgical rites but from what we absorb about God by worshipping in a space that communicates the immense mystery of God or God's intimate nearness? What might we learn about the history of the church not only through the participation in liturgical rites that trace their roots back to the early days of the Christian church but also through being surrounded by the faces of the saints in icons and in stained glass and in textiles? What might we in a congregation learn about pastoral care not only from a sermon that treats a question from a pastoral point of view but from the presence of a liturgical leader that is centered, available, and compassionate? In fact, how else might we learn about the power of prayer to lift up, to unify, to enflame our desire for God, and to open us to the God's desire for us except through the rhythms of shared said prayer, communal singing, and the shared silences that make up the liturgy?

Which brings me to questions about how best to engage theological students in the study of liturgy. As one who has herself taught liturgy to Anglican and Episcopal theological students, these questions have weighed on me as I have looked at students' faces and as I have thought about their potential to affect those who come to the worship they create and lead—those who come regularly, those who come occasionally, and those who by happenstance find themselves in a worship service only because someone else wanted and needed them to be there. Will these people encounter the God who seeks after all human beings with a dignifying love that will not be stopped? Will these people encounter a God immense enough to be trusted with their deepest thoughts, their most profound regrets, and their most exquisite yearnings to be the human beings they were created to be in relationship to God and to other human beings?

From my own experience in teaching liturgy to Anglican students, I have felt under tremendous pressure (pressure I put on myself) to "get everything in" in the basic course in Anglican liturgy: Anglican liturgical history, orientation to the range of authorized liturgies in a given part of the Anglican Communion, liturgy as prayer, and the many dimensions of liturgy (use of language, liturgy as pastoral care, liturgy as Christian formation, and on and on.) All of these matters were not only important but essential for students. And I would say, right along with this, in my view, we as theological educators need to find new ways to raise awareness about and teach students how to create and lead liturgies that engage these three fundamental questions:

1. What can congregational leaders do to create and offer liturgies that express a theology of God that is Trinitarian and, with God's help, has the power to form people through their experience of the Trinity in liturgy?

2. What view of Christian maturity is operative in the liturgies we create and offer as we seek to foster Christian maturity through our liturgies? In what way do the liturgies we create or offer allow us to practice some of what we believe are the elements of Christian maturity?

3. What do liturgical leaders need to attend to outside the liturgy and, therefore, bring to the liturgy that will assist in furthering the aims embedded in questions 1 and 2 above?

EXPLORING HOW LITURGY CAN ASSIST THE ASSEMBLY IN EXPERIENCING THE TRINITY

Some Assumptions about the Trinity

In speaking about the Trinity and liturgy, I am assuming that at the heart of the Trinity is a dynamic relationship of love among equals who are distinct and at the same time are one. I'm also assuming that in any exploration of the Trinity, it is difficult to speak about the persons of the Trinity as entirely separate entities or persons, that the dynamic energies of the persons of the Trinity are woven together in a way that will mean that the distinctions I will make are artificial at best.

Within the relationship of equals, God the Creator and Father (Jesus's "Abba") is "that without which there would be nothing at all."[2] God the Creator creates, loves, and sustains all there is. In accounts within the Hebrew Scriptures and in the Christian Testament, God as Creator and Father (Jesus's "Abba") relentlessly desires and seeks after humanity, whose image, though tarnished, reflects its Creator, with all its potential for dignity and dignifying action, with all its potential for compassion, with all its potential for the good, with all its potential for justice-making, with all its potential for creativity, with all its potential for healing and wholeness, and with all its potential for liberty.

God the Holy Spirit is God who, through praying in us, draws us to the source of being who is God. In being drawn to God we become adopted children who occupy and travel within the space that Jesus has opened for us. As Sarah Coakley puts it, "God the Holy Spirit is the perpetual invitation and lure of the Creator to return to its source, the Father, yet never without the full and suffering implications of incarnate Sonship."[3] God the Holy Spirit, then, is essential in the spiritual life and in the experience of prayer within and outside the liturgy. I would also add that I understand God the Holy Spirit to be a holy "*esprit du corps*," an energy that moves among human beings and works towards deepened relationships and unity within the body of Christ, a unity that does not obliterate distinctiveness or difference.

The second person of the Trinity, Jesus Christ, is the incarnate Son whose life, death, resurrection, and ascension open for us, through the Spirit, what Sarah Coakley has called the potential for our becoming adopted children of God, who through their bodies and in their lives share in Christ's own solidarity with and suffering in the world. As a part of this sharing in the life of Christ, we participate in the paschal mystery throughout our lives, losing life in order to find life, dying in order to live.

Some Admissions about Myself

Whereas I have experience teaching in theological schools with students from a number of different ecclesial traditions and while I have participated in liturgies prepared and offered within different ecclesial traditions, I am at my core an Anglican. What this means is that I am

2. Coakley, *God, Sexuality, and the Self*, 4
3. Coakley, "Spirit in the Trinity."

of a tradition of worship that is eucharistically centered and that makes use of the full range of potential elements in the liturgy in terms of the formation of participants in the liturgy. These elements include language, speech and silence, music, the visual arts, movement, liturgical objects, the liturgical space, and the use of the senses in liturgy.

Experiencing God as Creator in the liturgy

Perhaps the best place to start in exploring what we do might do to assist theological students as they prepare to create and lead liturgies that will, with God's help, assist those participating in experiencing God as Creator, is to invite students to consider these questions, questions that are meant to get at the theology of God that our liturgies may be expressing:

4. Do those experiencing the liturgies we prepare and offer experience a God of mystery and power or do they meet a God who is merely one among many other competing categories? Connected to this, do those experiencing the liturgy have the possibility of feeling awe, reverence, and wonder in the liturgy? What particular elements within the liturgy best bring participants into the presence of a God of mystery and power who evokes a sense of awe, reverence, and wonder in them?

5. Do those experiencing the liturgies that we prepare and offer make actual contact with the materials and things of creation with all their magnitude or plenteousness, their depth, their texture and power, or are materials and elements of the creation omitted or somehow fenced out of the liturgical experience?

6. To borrow a line from the Song of Songs (2:3–4, KJV), do those experiencing the liturgies we prepare and offer, from their welcome prior to the liturgy through the movement of the liturgy to its culmination and sending forth, discover that "his [sic] banner over me [is] love"; or, put another way, do participants in the liturgy discover in the liturgy a Creator who desires them, who seeks after them and, with the Spirit's help, is forever drawing and enticing them back towards God's very self?

7. In terms of language for God, do the liturgies, both spoken words and the sung lyrics, offer a range of images and language that do not allow the liturgical participant to settle into an idolatry around

particular images or language that overly defines God, that robs the assembly of an experience of the mystery of God?

While students, of course, are to answer questions such as these for themselves when they experience or plan liturgies, what I can share from my experience is that is that the range of things that affect my responses to these questions have been: the size, particularly the height, of the liturgical space; liturgical art in the space that points beyond itself to a greater mystery; the use of local materials (wood, stone, metal) in the space and the generous use of water, oil, fire, in liturgical action; the use of silence in the liturgy; the use of language and music that does not domesticate or overly identify the Creator with a certain language system; the use of music that expresses the longing of the human heart for God as an answering love; the avoidance of what Aidan Kavanaugh refers to as affecting a kind of "loose informality" when leading the assembly in worship; the adoption of a tone of solemnity in the liturgy.[4]

Experiencing the Holy Spirit in the liturgy

In approaching the experience of the Holy Spirit in liturgy, I would pose the following questions to theological students:

1. Are those leading and participating in the liturgy prayerful? Is the liturgy itself prayerful? Within this, do those leading the liturgy bring an available and nonanxious presence to the liturgy as a part of their prayerfulness?

2. Does the liturgy allow those leading and participating to enter into times of shared silence? Do these silences open a receptive space for the movement of Spirit in the lives of people and in the collective life of the assembly?

3. Does the music, to include the lyrics in liturgies, assist those singing it or listening to it to experience the desire of God for them or to inflame their desire for God? Do the liturgies have enough love songs in them?

4. Is the liturgy done in a way that allows people to function as one in terms of shared gesture, shared speech, and shared singing? Another way of asking this question is this: is the assembly of people

4. Kavanaugh, *Elements of Rite*, 99.

connected in a way that is the fruit of their awareness of and ability to "listen" to each other? Does the assembly of people listen to other voices and blend their voices with them? Do they notice others' gestures and harmonize their gestures with them?

5. Is beauty and its power to entice people toward God nurtured and protected in the liturgy?

While most of these questions simply assume an affirmative answer as the "right" answer, let me just say that the cultivation of a tone of prayerfulness on the part of those leading the liturgy and on the part of those participating in the liturgy is, in my view, an essential element when it comes to assisting others in their experience of the movement of the Holy Spirit in liturgy. One of the fruits of this prayerfulness is a spirit of surrender, a spirit that, I believe, is critical for the Spirit to do her work within us and among us as we yearn for reunion with God. This prayerfulness and surrender enable the members of the assembly to put aside their needs to overshadow others and allows the assembly to function as one in terms of gesture, singing, speaking, and sharing silence. It is in this shared experience of accord that the assembly can be drawn back towards the accord that is at the heart of the Trinity itself.

Experiencing Jesus Christ in the Liturgy

Finally, we come to the questions for theological students related to experiencing the second person of the Trinity in liturgy. I suggest that those questions might be:

1. Are the liturgies we prepare and offer earthy, or are these liturgies heavily weighted toward the abstract, conceptual, the analytical, and the logical? Are the liturgies and liturgical spaces where liturgies are offered rich with images, smells, sounds, music, the opportunity to touch something or someone and to move? Is the preaching in liturgies rich with story and images?

2. Do the liturgies we prepare and offer assist us in entering the "Jesus space," a space in which we are able to identify with our own suffering and the suffering of the world? Do homilies deal with pain, brokenness, and the lives of the poor and the marginal in real ways? Do homilies deal with the pain of listeners in ways that are real and

would evoke a "that's me" response from listeners, an experience that prepares the way for the gospel to be preached?

3. Do the liturgies that we prepare and offer assist us in developing our capacity and willingness to lose life in order to find life, to understand Jesus not as a "past figure to emulate" but "the life into which we step"?[5]

4. Do the physical spaces, art, or objects in the space and the actions associated with the objects, an does the observation of the liturgical calendar and the enactment of important liturgies, especially in Holy Week and Easter, enable us more fully to enter the "Jesus space" and live out of that space?

Again, while students will need to answer these questions for themselves, out of my own experience I would offer the following as elements in the liturgy that support participants experiencing Jesus Christ in the liturgy: a sensory-rich liturgical experience to include the use of incense, the use of high-quality, colorful vestments, the use of candles and flowers that are real versus objects that are masquerading as real; the opportunity those participating have to do something—to bow, to cross themselves, to light a candle, to touch another person's hand or make a gesture towards them, to sing, to hold silence with others; and the opportunity to experience sermons that are essentially narrative in nature.

In terms of liturgies that assist us in entering the "Jesus space," I would offer the following as important elements of our liturgies that can assist with this: a font in the space that is large enough for a person to lose their life in and that is filled with an abundance of living water; bread, wine, and oil that are real, fragrant, and speak of the sense-filled nature of the incarnate life and the generosity of the sacrament; images of the crucified one in the space (as opposed to the empty cross); the full observance of Palm Sunday and Holy Week and Easter liturgies to include Maundy Thursday, Good Friday, Holy Saturday, Easter Vigil, and Easter Sunday; within the Holy Week liturgies, the full observance of foot-washing, the veneration of the cross, and the entire experience of readings and psalms within the Easter Vigil liturgy; the observance of devotional practices such as the Stations of the Cross; praying the Rosary, praying the Angelus; preaching that highlights and invites us over and over again to give

5. Coakley "Spirit in the Trinity."

ourselves to the paschal mystery, that is, "in order to come to fuller life and spirit we must constantly let go of present life and spirit."[6]

EXPLORING NOTIONS OF CHRISTIAN MATURITY

Underlying What We Do in the Congregation and in Liturgy

Now that we have described some of the ways in which the liturgies we prepare and offer might express the triune God, how might we describe the Christian maturity we seek to foster in our liturgies? In what way do the liturgies we create or engage in allow us to practice the Christian maturity we seek to foster? These are the key questions for theological students studying liturgy and for anyone who plans and offers liturgies on a regular basis. While the totality of congregational life has as one of its aims the fostering of Christian maturity, liturgy must play an important role in this aim.

As I think about Christian maturity, one of the first descriptions that comes to mind is found in Henri Nouwen's book *Reaching Out: The Three Movements of the Spiritual Life*,[7] in which Nouwen describes three different poles between which our lives move back and forth or are held in tension. These poles Nouwen describes as the polarity between loneliness and solitude (a polarity related to our relationship with ourselves), the polarity between hostility and hospitality (a polarity related to our relationship with others), and the polarity between illusion and prayer (a polarity related to our relationship with God). These three polarities, it seems to me, offer a valuable description of the areas of life that Christians seek to attend to along their ever "beginning-again," and yet ever deepening maturity. Awareness about and movement along these polarities, then, are part of what liturgy seeks to foster.

To move from loneliness to solitude is to move from the compulsive craving of others' company or of outer things as way to fill up what is empty to a place of solidity and comfort with our aloneness and the ability to abide in what Nouwen calls the "garden of solitude."[8] According to Nouwen, it's from this position of solitude, especially the solitude of the heart, that allows a person "to perceive and understand the world from

6. Rolheiser, *Holy Longing*, 145.

7. Nouwen, *Reaching Out*.

8. Nouwen, *Reaching Out*, 32.

a quiet inner center,"[9] leading both to a receptivity to others and to God and to the creation of a space where a person can hear the voice of what Nouwen calls "our inner necessity," or vocation.[10] Finally, for Nouwen, solitude allows community to flourish in that we are not grasping for others. Such solitude, it seems to me, is needed if one is ever able to live in community with others in a way that does not grasp but both allows the other to be who they will be and allows the self to flourish grounded in its own createdness in the image of God.

To move from hostility to hospitality is a natural movement that follows on the movement from loneliness to solitude. In this movement, Nouwen describes our moving from seeing and responding to the world out of fear, defensiveness, suspicion, and aggression towards the stranger and moving towards the "creation of a free space where the stranger can enter and become a friend instead of an enemy."[11] Nouwen goes on: "Hospitality is not [about] changing people, but [instead] offers them space where change can take place . . . the paradox of hospitality is that it wants to create emptiness, not a fearful emptiness, but a friendly emptiness where strangers can enter and discover themselves as created free; free to sing their own songs, speak their own languages, dance their own dances; free also to leave and follow their own vocations."[12] Nouwen goes on to outline forms of hospitality, including within this the relationship between parents and children, teachers and students, healers and patients, all of which are grounded in receptivity but also contain the ability to draw appropriate boundaries.

Finally, Nouwen describes the movement from illusion to prayer, a polarity and a movement that Nouwen says is both hard to grasp and is essential to the spiritual life. Nouwen's describes this polarity as moving from living out of the illusions that tempt us to seek our own security and safety and moving towards a way of seeing and responding to the world that relies on what is trustworthy, opening ourselves and extending ourselves toward God. In this movement, we go from what we believe we know to what is unknown. The effect of this is to open our vulnerability to the pain of the world and to open our hearts to love God and the world more deeply and in a more costly way. The effect of this is that we

9. Nouwen, *Reaching*, 36.

10. Nouwen, *Reaching Out*, 38.

11. Nouwen, *Reaching Out*, 72.

12. Nouwen, *Reaching Out*, 72.

are moved to prayer while at the same time more and more aware that prayer can only be received as a gift. According to Nouwen, this movement comprehends experiences of both the nearness of God and God's absence. Activities that facilitate this movement include "a contemplative reading of the word of God, a silent listening to the voice of God, and a trusting obedience to a spiritual guide."[13] Finally, we experience prayer in the gathered community, whose words, gestures, and silence acknowledge a God who is present and also a God who is desired and waited for.

Drawing on these three movements, then, this in part describes the Christian maturity we seek to foster in liturgy. It is a maturity that assists people to settle down in themselves and to get comfortable with their aloneness before God through the liberal use of silence in liturgy. It is a maturity that sees the practice of hospitality within the liturgy as core to its way of being, not just important to a congregational growth strategy. It is a maturity that places contemplation and prayer as touchstones to return to over and over again and seeks to "catch" from the prayerfulness of those leading the liturgy and the prayerfulness that has been cultivated in others participating in the liturgy.

But there is yet another way to understand the Christian maturity liturgy seeks to foster. This way is different from what Nouwen describes. We find it in the Benedictine way of living that embraces a process of stability, obedience, and conversion of life.

As a reminder, Benedict's Rule in all its pragmatism sought to assist the monk or nun to embrace a way of life that rested in a stability of place and relationships, and engaged in obedience, which had to do with listening and responding to important and reliable sources of authority (Scripture, the Abbot, the experience of prayer), all in order to inform a new turning to Christ that would typically mean change (conversion of life). In translating these touchstones or ways of living into today's world, stability can be seen as the ability to recognize and experience God in the here and now of one's current life and circumstances; obedience can be seen as the ability to listen and be informed by trusted sources of wisdom (Scripture, prayer, mentors and friends, family, the body itself), all in order to respond and act toward a conversion of life, that is, the turning toward the horizon of a new and deepened humanity that is Christ.[14]

13. Nouwen, *Reaching Out*, 137.
14. See De Waal, *Seeking God*.

It seems to me, then, that our liturgies should foster this spirit of continual discernment in the human person. Liturgy should deepen our awareness of the presence of God in the here and now, in the very moments of the liturgy in order to school our awareness of the presence of God in the here-and-now moments of our everyday lives. Our liturgies should deepen our ability to listen deeply—to Scripture, to music, to the homily, to the prayers of our own hearts, to the church's and others' prayers for the world, to God in silence, all for the purpose of stirring some response or action. And this action, this response, is meant to be a turning to Christ in a new way which, of course, leads to a new stability. And the cycle begins again.

This, then, is another understanding of the process of formation and discernment that a congregation is meant to foster. And, of course, liturgy should play an important part in this overall congregational aim.

EXPLORING WHAT LITURGICAL LEADERS MIGHT ATTEND TO OUTSIDE OF THE LITURGY

Given the interconnectedness of all parts of a congregational system, the final area, in my view, that is essential to teaching liturgy concerns actions congregational leaders might engage in outside the liturgy that affect what participants experience in the liturgy, especially in terms of the two areas already touched on in this chapter. What activities are the best investment of leaders' and congregants' time if they wish to strengthen the capacity of the liturgy to express the triune God and to foster Christian maturity

The first activity that leaders and congregants can engage in is prayer outside of the liturgy. In an Anglican tradition, this can be teaching and supporting people in the praying of the Divine Office, the saying or singing of the Angelus, engaging in centering prayer or other forms of meditation, or participating in other forms of personal prayer that deepen the capacity to listen deeply to Scripture, especially the Psalms, to sit in silence before God and to wait on the action of the Spirit. Examples of this in my experience have been: the chanting of the Rosary for a full hour in a Chaldean Christian community prior to the beginning of the Eucharist; engaging in what Indigenous peoples in Canada and in the US call "Gospel-Based Discipleship," which is a form of the Divine Office that embeds a *lectio divina* exercise at its center; and in my former parish's case, the simple creation of teams of people who together led and participated in a simplified daily Evening Prayer that included times of silence, done on weeknights, with the teams sharing responsibility for reading, officiating, and participating; and, finally, in the same parish periodically leading classes in which, based on their personality type, parishioners explored different kinds of personal prayer with the goal of finding which methods most supported them in developing a habit of personal prayer. The message in all the encouragement to pray needs to be, as Sarah Coakley has said, simply to tell people to "Pray as you can, and not as you can't. Just pray."[15]

Regardless of the specific methods people used, the effect of prayer either directly before or at another time entirely, on a principal Sunday liturgy was profound. Learning to pray and praying outside of a principal Sunday liturgy, especially when that prayer had a deeply reflective element (silence or times when participants made connections between Scripture and their lives), created a more prayerful environment in the Sunday liturgy. Prayer outside of liturgy deepens the capacity to pray within the liturgy, deepens the ability of people to hold silence and use silence as a time of receptivity, and deepens the ability of leaders themselves to bring prayerfulness to the liturgy.

The second activity that leaders might engage in that can most affect the experience of the liturgy is any formation around and practice among those leading the liturgy in a) doing whatever they do with competence, grace, flow, beauty and dignity; and b) practicing their ability to bring a centered and nonanxious presence to the liturgy. Both of these components—competence in a particular role and grace in enacting that role along with the cultivation of a nonanxious liturgical presence—are essential if the liturgies we offer seek to impart and form others for the same. Part of this, is, of course, rehearsing for liturgies, not just for special once-a-year liturgical events but for Sunday after Sunday after Sunday.

The third and final activity I would offer as important in affecting the power of liturgy to express the triune God and to assist the development of Christian maturity is time spent in liturgy planning that has as its goal creative seasonal and occasional variation, led by an openness to the Spirit with the aim of helping participants engage the rhythm of the church year and its important occasions with openness and, through the power of the Holy Spirit, come to a deeper experience of God. Liturgy

---

15. Coakley, "Spirit in the Trinity."

planning must also focus on concrete and sustained support for the continuance and deepening of the fundamental approaches to liturgy described in this chapter.

Fundamental strengths in liturgies do not stay put all by themselves. Instead, in my view, what is required is steady oversight (exercised by one or, better, many) that protects and enhances the use of silence in liturgy, for instance, and at the same time takes risks related to making space for the surprising and challenging movement of the Spirit, who is forever seeking to find new ways to entice us into a deeper relationship with God within the prayer of a community that is liturgy.

A FINAL WORD ABOUT LITURGY
AND THEOLOGICAL EDUCATION

As I survey what I have written here, I am struck once again by what an ambitious task it is to form theological students in becoming liturgical practitioners. This is because, of course, I am suggesting that to be the kind of liturgical practitioner that the church needs today, we need practitioners who are grounded in broad theory about the nature of worship, schooled in the history of Christian worship and the history of liturgy within a particular ecclesial tradition, and attentive to the role that liturgy can play in the formation of Christians in a congregational setting. But, drawing on all of this, what makes liturgical practice have the potential, with God's help, to "sing" in terms of God's own transformation of the human person is nothing less than the sensibility, presence, and touch of a liturgical artist—a liturgical artist who sees their role as clearing a space for the presence of the triune God, a liturgical artist who cares deeply about the actual experience of people in the liturgy, a liturgical artist who both cultivates their own life of prayer and attends to their presence and the presence of other liturgical leaders in the liturgy. This and nothing less is our task as theological educators in the field of liturgy. This and nothing less continues to be our ongoing vocation as liturgists in the church.

4

Denominational Formation for Ministry

Grant Rodgers

THE CHRISTIAN APPROACH HAS always been comprehensive, inclusive of the practical dimension, and rooted not just in the intellect but in that deeper, mysterious dimension we refer to as "heart" or "soul," as well as in the actual life of the community.

"What do you do when . . . ?"

The Facebook page "Things They Didn't Teach Us in Seminary" describes itself as "a group for those who have graduated from an accredited seminary who want to share the things that we have experienced in the Church that were not necessarily covered in seminary . . . " The page is fascinating because (as I know from over thirty years of experience as a pastor of the church) there are countless scenarios clergy face for which there is no preparation, not even a warning:

How to respond to an invitation from a member of the parish to help round up steers, for instance? I didn't know how to ride a horse very well, let alone how to round up big, fast, agile steers. And then came the inoculating, branding, and neutering! No one in my seminary could have prepared me for that day—but in a larger sense they did.

One professor had taught me that in the realm of theology you're always in over your head—that it's all right to be confident that you know enough, but important to remain open to new learning and experience, because you can never know everything. I learned that I should be prepared to meet God in apparently unlikely places and people.

Another taught me to see the church in holistic terms, that it is about the whole people of God, not just about the clergy, and not just about church buildings—that the people are the church and their lives are their vocations.

Another suggested that looking foolish is not the worst thing, since there is much precedent for it in the history of the Christian church, going back at least as far as St. Paul.

Perhaps most importantly, I learned that love is the ultimate virtue and criterion. The author of *The Cloud of Unknowing*, perhaps in reaction to the intellectual complexities of the medieval Scholastic era, said:

> The One whom neither humans nor angels can grasp by knowledge can be embraced by love. For the intellect of both humans and angels is too small to comprehend God as God is.[1]

All these insights and more were applicable and reliable in my everyday pastoral encounters. In a society in which there is not only a disconnect between science and faith, but in which spirituality has come to be seen as separate from religion, that kind of reconnecting of head and heart, analysis and practice, is an important contribution.

It's interesting that when Jesus was faced with a theological question about how to inherit eternal life, his response was the Parable of the Good Samaritan, and the question he returned was, "Which of these three . . . was a neighbor?" (to the man who had been assaulted and robbed) (Luke 10:25–42). Ministry is always about the relationship between theory and action, theology and morality, being and doing.

When I left seminary, I was as equipped as I needed to be to face into situations of marital conflict, theological disagreements, management issues, programming priorities, building-related problems, cattle herding and countless more. Thankfully, as our tradition so wisely teaches us, we are saved not by our acquired competencies but by the grace of God, through faith, and, thanks in good part to my theological education, I knew that too.

---

1. Johnston, ed., *Cloud of Unknowing*.

THE IMPORTANCE OF PASTORAL THEOLOGY

Denominational formation programs tend to be focused on the doing of theology, the "love the Lord with all your strength" part of the formula. That has tended to be dismissed or deemed secondary, although recent thinking and experience point to the important task of integrating the various streams of learning.[2]

In an article called "It Is Time to Get Past the Snobbery against Pastoral Theologians," the Rev. James Heft, Alton Brooks Professor of Religion at the University of Southern California, said:

> I think the highest level of theology is, indeed, pastoral theology. Why? Because to be a good pastoral theologian, you have to be well acquainted with doctrine, be able to put it in its historical and biblical context and acquire a genuine understanding of what ought to be said to someone confronted with a complex human situation. In other words, competent pastoral theologians understand that all these subspecialties need to be integrated . . . Moreover, pastoral theologians not only need to pay attention to doctrine, Scripture, tradition and ethics, they also need to be attentive to the *sensus fidelium*, the actual experience of believers trying to live their Christian lives in the push-and-pull of their own time and place.[3]

An analogy of our place in the theological enterprise might be the relation between the Letter of James and, say, the Letter to the Romans. In Martin Luther's mind, one was sublime and the other was "straw."[4] Yet the two letters are more closely related than it appears initially, and the New Testament is better for both of them being there.

Formation for ministry may well be the "James" dimension with its emphasis on the doing of theology, putting theory into practice. Formation necessarily involves an emphasis on the practical. James would say "Show me your faith," show me your carefully crafted credal statement, your theological arguments, and I will show you by my actions what my faith means and how it applies. According to James, faith has to be tested in real-life situations for it to be valid.

The Anglican Church of Canada, in its document "Competencies for Ordination to the Priesthood in the Anglican Church of Canada,"

---

2. Osmer, *Practical Theology*, 222.

3. Heft, "It Is Time."

4 See Luther, *Luther's Works*, vol. 35, 395–97.

says the following: "A priest is one who is able to translate the rich tradition of Christian and Anglican thought into the real life of the actual communities and contexts where we minister."[5]

Eileen R. Campbell-Reed and Christian A. B. Scharen use the term "pastoral imagination":

> Now more than ever, pastors and ministers need to recover the distinct value of practical, embodied, and relational wisdom in order to lead faith communities and movements through the challenges of our time. They also need that kind of wisdom for the everyday work beyond parishes, including work in hospitals, homeless ministries and many other faith-based nonprofits. "Pastoral imagination" is the term we use to describe this practical wisdom for ministry needed for everything from the ordinary to the visionary.[6]

WHAT IS FORMATION?

In the late nineteenth century, an exasperated Presbyterian area minister by the name of James Robertson, working to establish the church on the Canadian prairies, wrote "I would far rather have a man [sic] know less Latin and more horse."[7] Even in an era that we associate with institutional obedience and conformity, this man was expressing frustration with a rather fixed and nonadaptive approach to formation and looking for a more creative and relevant response.

We don't require Latin anymore, and for the most part clergy don't need to know much about horses either, but we are constantly reflecting on what people do need to know in order to be faithful, informed, and effective servants of the church and society. Formation is not just about how we do things but also why we do them.

Formation is not and probably never can be a fixed format, as the word "formation" could suggest, some existing and ideal pattern into which we mold people for some well-defined purpose or role, or a program by which we train people toward a desired end, with the church (and perhaps society) understood as a kind of constant.

5. Anglican Church of Canada, "Competencies for Ordination," 7.

6. Campbell-Reed and Scharen, "Are Your Graduates Ready?," 2.

7. Anger, "Historical Vignettes," https://presbyterianarchives.ca/2014/06/09/historical-vignettes-snapshots-from-our-history/.

For instance, clergy of the Anglican tradition were once all male, all English, all white, all educated and cultured in a particular way. Their experience and even their education were somewhat narrow, steeped in assumptions that they did not feel the need to examine or critique. Surprisingly, this male-dominated, Anglocentric model persisted well into the twentieth century and has even now not completely disappeared.

As a recent national church document suggests, the church acknowledges that God is calling us to greater diversity of membership and wider participation in ministry and leadership. As we continue to seek to come to terms with the legacy of colonial domination, and the suppression of Indigenous wisdom and culture, we are also doing our best to integrate emerging insights relating to gender, sexuality, ecology, and socioeconomic injustice, seeking "a stronger resolve in challenging attitudes and structures that cause injustice."[8]

Various crises and challenges the church has faced in the last fifty to seventy-five years have obliged us to be critical and even suspicious of some of the old norms and assumptions. In a book called *If You Meet George Herbert on the Road, Kill Him,* Justin Lewis-Anthony spoke of how he "felt increasingly alienated by the way a *false* memory of [seventeenth-century priest and poet] Herbert was being used to keep the clergy of the Church of England today, now in the twenty-first century, in a Babylonian captivity, a fantasy of what we were, what we are, and who we ought to be."[9]

Scandals relating to the abuse of authority in all forms of religious organization, from televangelists to megachurch evangelical icons to countless clergy in the Roman Catholic, Baptist,[10] and other denominations, have intensified scrutiny upon the church in general and especially upon would-be leaders of the church. The sexual predation scandals, the revelations of what went on in the residential schools, accompanied by the emergence of a more negative approach to "institutional religion," in addition to other developing social and theological issues, oblige us to ask harder questions and find new ways and different kinds of leaders to fulfill the mission of particular churches. Therefore, the idea of leadership itself, and the kinds of images or metaphors we have used to describe or define ministry, have had to be reexamined, and educational processes

8. Anglican Church of Canada, "Our Beliefs."

9. Lewis-Anthony, *If You Meet George Herbert*, 217.

10. "The Southern Baptist Convention must enact tough reform on its sexual abuse crisis."

adapted to new experience and awareness of needs. Students are encouraged to become very aware of who they are and what are their interpretive principles. Given the controversies around ministry in our time, it is almost a matter of training people how *not* to be clergy.

There are no scripts or fixed formulae for guaranteed success. Indeed, as we now know, "success" in one generation may be seen to be (or even cause) failure in a subsequent generation.

The Association of Theological Schools (ATS) reveals something of the enormity of the task:

> ATS schools have gradually added to their degree requirements.
> The impetus to do this has come from several sources:

> - ATS itself requires a more global perspective for MDiv programs, necessitating additional content.

> - The core disciplines of theological scholarship have developed new knowledge, approaches, and methodologies that need to be covered in the curriculum.

> - Constituent churches want coverage of leadership theory and skills not historically part of the MDiv curriculum, including community organizing, financial literacy, fundraising, volunteer management, risk management, strategic planning, and project management, all the while demanding improved preparation in fundamentals such as doctrinal theology and preaching.

> - MDiv candidates come from increasingly diverse backgrounds and it has become nearly impossible to maintain any expectations of prior preparation for many schools. Schools utilize various strategies to fill gaps but they all require time.

> - At one time the vast majority of MDiv candidates were preparing for local church ministry but it has become increasingly difficult to predict where students' careers will take them. The curriculum has to be adapted to this reality.[11]

All of that impacts formational training, so small wonder that formation more than ever needs to be fluid and responsive, as more variety and new challenges continue to emerge. We are training people not just to take up the torch handed on from the past, but to prepare them for

---

11. Association of Theological Schools, "Educational Models and Practices."

the future, and, in a sense, there is no program for that. Certainly faith becomes an essential part of this process at an early stage!

The earliest models probably looked a lot like apprenticeship, with people interested and showing signs of promise attaching to prominent church leaders and accompanying these mentors for a time, just as the disciples had accompanied Jesus. Monasteries aided in the process of formation for many. Eventually, universities came to play a role in the process. A lively relationship between training and the church was central to it all.

In the liturgy of ordination there is this exchange:

> *Bishop:* Will you do your best to pattern your life (and that of your family) in accordance with the teachings of Christ, so that you may be a wholesome example to your people?
> *Answer:* I will.[12]

Ministry is never a matter of merely imparting information; it is never simply a matter of techniques and formulas. Ministry is never done in isolation, and it is not something done to people, but among people, with people, for people. So the integrity of our own being, the specific ways in which we embody the gospel and relate to others in the contexts of ministry, authenticates the knowledge we are so eager to share. We live in a time when the concept of public service and personal accountability seems to have deteriorated on all levels. However, it is especially in the light of the worldwide scandal of abuse in the churches and the accompanying drastic loss of credibility and members that the issue of exemplary lives takes on a new and urgent sense of importance for people training for leadership in the church—in fact, becomes one of the essential aspects of formation and preparation. Students must be aware of the damage that has been done to people (there are now recovery groups for former church members), the impact of that loss of credibility, the continuing potential for abuse, and the accompanying need to be a different kind of leader in a different sort of church.

Various dioceses and national church committees around the world have produced criteria which in turn help set the agenda for training. The Anglican Church of Canada, in its document "Competencies for Ordination to the Priesthood in the Anglican Church of Canada," says the following:

---

12. Anglican Church of Canada, *Book of Alternative Services*, 647.

Any statement of Competencies will be limited. For example, it:

- Does not constitute a set of standards. A standard is something by which a competency is measured. The understanding, interpretation, and application of the competencies will vary appropriately from context to context.

- Does not advocate a single-path approach. There will be multiple paths by which candidates may come to maturity in these competencies.

- Does not provide a list of all skills that might be needed in all circumstances . . .

- Competency alone is not enough. Passion in ministry is an essential ingredient. Charism, call and character . . . are the foundations, and need to be brought into dialogue with what is offered here in the Competencies. While competency without passion, character and call is ineffective, passion without competence can be destructive. These two parts of ministerial formation are intended to be brought together in every step in the life of ministry.[13]

VOCATION AND CONTEXT

In my class on vocation, I have typically asked the question, "Whose calling is it?" A person's vocation is not simply between themselves and God (or their idea of God); it has to do with how that calling may serve God's people. So often, both the sense of call and the process of study and formation become an individual matter, and thus the ordained person's sense of church and ministry is focused largely on themselves. Robin Greenwood writes, "it is the nature of the Church itself that determines the nature of its ministry . . . Training for ministry should have in mind the needs of the Church as a whole, rather than considering the particular minister in differing situations."[14] So formation necessarily involves an active dialogue and relationship between the seminary/theological college and the church.

13. Anglican Church of Canada, "Competencies for Ordination," 6.
14. Greenwood, *Transforming Priesthood*, 56.

Given that vocation to ministry must always be a somewhat nebulous thing, and wary of the possibility of turning vocation into merely an aspect of church program, thus losing the potential for new and diverse kinds of leaders to emerge, it can be helpful to paint at least some of the broad strokes. ATS names the following core criteria:

- Knowledge of religious heritage
- Understanding of the cultural context
- Growth in spiritual depth and moral integrity
- Capacity for ministerial and public leadership[15]

With the awareness of all these realities, VST's Readiness for Ministry (RFM) criteria[16] and self-examination become more important than ever. The RFM criteria create behavioral/attitudinal/ethical expectations and norms and establish an ongoing dialogue between the student and the community, a process of growth of self-awareness, reflection, and accountability, engaging the help of the Directors of Denominational Formation (DDFs), the faculty and, in a sense, the whole community, in a process of growing self-awareness and transformation.

The Anglican Diocese of New Westminster (DNW) articulates criteria that have been identified in relation to its mission, as a way of saying these are the kinds of people and these are the kinds of personal characteristics we need at this time:

> **A person who is a gatherer and builder of community:** We seek a person who is gifted in gathering diverse people into a community and then building and developing that community over time. We seek those who can help groups of people come together around shared values and a sense of purpose . . . [17]

Not just the experience of community, but more importantly the reality of being in communion, is an essential dimension of a comprehensive approach to theological education, formation, and ordained leadership. Formation enables future church leaders to see themselves in context. Students in training toward ministry are already creating templates for their ministry and the kind of church they will help build.

---

15. Association of Theological Schools, "Educational Models and Practices," 38.

16. *Vancouver School of Theology Student Handbook: 2019–2020* (https://vst.edu/wp-content/uploads/2019/08/Student-Handbook-2019-20-.pdf), 33.

17. Diocese of New Westminster, "Discernment Process for Holy Orders," 3.

The religious, educational, and social activities in which they participate, the relationships they form, and the giving and receiving of support they experience all generate a capacity to be present, and an ability to share the journey with others, that can make them much more effective pastors and leaders.

One of the great values of studying in a diverse theological environment like VST is that students have their eyes opened to other ways of thinking about things and other ways of doing liturgy, community, ethics, etc. Rubbing shoulders with people of other faith traditions who at times may be curious, confused, critical, or simply indifferent about the ways we tend to think and do things can be very instructive. If there is an atmosphere of mutual respect, and a genuine encouragement to encounter the other rather than a sectarian mindset, it can lead to a broader perspective about one's tradition in living context, and a better ability to articulate why we believe and act in the ways we do, as well as more willingness to explore change.

The Diocese of New Westminster also seeks:

> A person who has a pattern of spiritual practice that is rooted in a Christ-centered, Anglican approach to spirituality: We seek a person who is committed to a life of prayer. We seek a person who is regular in the Daily Offices, faithful in their participation in the Eucharist, and active in the practice of personal prayer . . . [18]

One of my seminary professors, himself a priest, told us that, in light of the constant demands and stress involved in being clergy, we would have to "Learn how to do nothing, and do it well."

Conflict, isolation, lack of coherence, disappointment, doubt, burnout, and even PTSD can all be aspects of a pastor's experience. Studies have repeatedly indicated that clergy who maintain a meaningful spiritual practice fare dramatically better in dealing with the inevitable challenges of ministry. Meaningful spiritual practices that encourage us to pause, step aside, and be still are sustaining in ministry, because they connect us to the Source, renew our ability to relate to others, and enable us to accept ourselves as we are (not as we idealize ourselves).

> . . . a person who has a sense of presence and who is emotionally and relationally mature: We seek a person whose presence grounds, encourages and inspires others. We seek a person who

18. Diocese of New Westminster, "Discernment Process for Holy Orders," 4.

is working on their self-awareness and who nurtures authentic
and productive relationships with others . . . [19]

Relating to people and motivating and leading people requires a
very high level of ability or social intelligence. As Heft says, "One of the
gifts of competent pastoral theologians is their ability to understand the
people with whom they work."[20]

> . . . a person who can exercise leadership that carries authority
> and can live productively in relationship to those in authority:
> We seek a leader who is comfortable exercising a style of leader-
> ship that is both relational and carries authority . . . [21]

This speaks to the importance of experiences of leadership and also
of being led, and not just in the context of the church. One's mentors
are often a huge influence in this area, and field education (e.g., parish
and institutional placements), clinical pastoral education, as well as the
daily behaviors modeled by faculty and others create opportunities for
students to develop as servant-leaders in their own right.

Bearing authority without being authoritarian, manipulative, or
coercive is a big challenge for some, yet absolutely essential for the time
in which we live. "To embody such an authentic contextual wisdom requires a daily immersion in the practice of leadership on a long arc of
learning ministry."[22] In our context, gifts of reconciliation, mediation,
conflict resolution, and peacemaking are important gifts to cultivate.

> . . . a person who listens and loves to learn: We seek a person
> who is open and intrigued by the learning process and who sees
> God as moving and active in Scripture, tradition, reason, learn-
> ing from other disciplines and in the wisdom of the community
> . . . [23]

So how do you "prepare" someone or form them for meaningful ministry? Make sure they are open, flexible, adaptable, resourceful,
imaginative, creative, willing to go on learning, and, above all, confident
in the presence and guidance of the living God.

---

19. Diocese of New Westminster, "Discernment Process for Holy Orders," 4.
20. Heft, "Snobbery."
21. Diocese of New Westminster, "Discernment Process for Holy Orders," 4.
22. Campbell-Reed and Scharen, "Are Your Graduates Ready?," 2.
23. Diocese of New Westminster, "Discernment Process for Holy Orders," 4.

THE SUMMONS OF THE FUTURE

Once, clergy of historic mainline churches could expect to be included and consulted as important partners of the professional and cultural establishment. Though that may still occur, it is on an individual, ad hoc basis, and people training toward ministry need to expect to occupy a different kind of place in society, one more on the margins and in many cases at odds with the values and power of the elites. Clergy today often feel like pariahs, not prelates, and it can be very deflating to the ego. Leaders today must truly be people foolish enough to believe in the truth of the gospel, and to recognize that God's power is actually perfected in weakness(See 2 Corinthians 12:9).

Once, the church provided a stable and long-term "career" with a decent salary and benefits. Now, people in training for ministry are reconciling themselves to the strong possibility of serving part-time situations, shorter-term ministries, and the need to find other ways to make ends meet. Finding compatible part-time work is a difficult prospect partly because of the expectations that clergy must be available "24/7." New clergy will need to shift from the model of doing things by themselves to deliberately doing things in collaboration with the members of the parish, become adept at training lay people to be doing much more of the real pastoral ministry of the church, and be willing to cooperate with other clergy. Hence the importance of learning opportunities (like our formation retreats) in which students are able to get to know each other and form trusting relationships that lend themselves to future collegiality.

The old mainline churches are often characterized by a maintenance mentality and so people training for ministry need to bring different skills to guide people out of stagnation into new priorities and more meaningful life in community, with a view to creating a new generation of disciples.

Many historic, traditional denominations are obliged to pay homage to the past; some more than others are tied to the past. It is interesting to attend ordination services and to hear how much is being said to the newly ordained about fidelity to the past, to traditional ways of doing things, and how little is said about the future, as if doing what we have always done will automatically end up creating different results. God willing, the church has a much longer future than its past.

Simply to be able to look at all that and acknowledge that it is true is a step forward, so that the expectation is that the solutions that may be needed are to be found at least as much in looking forward as in dwelling on the past. Rather than being held captive by the past, some theologians have suggested a different perspective: that we are being pulled toward the future, or the Omega Point, as Teilhard de Chardin put it.

Part of formation necessarily involves changing people's expectations. The ways in which clergy of the future will be serving are not necessarily the ones that they have experienced to this point in their lives. Just as more and more people in seminary have limited experience of the specific denomination, as Kyle Roberts writes, "more and more seminarians envision their future vocations outside of the institutional church— in social justice work, community organizing, social entrepreneurship, and other fields [chaplaincies for instance]."[24]

The old mainline churches could once afford to adopt a passive approach to being Christian, just setting up shop on the corner and waiting for people to come—not only that, but also simply trusting that the liturgy, the preaching, and perhaps Sunday school would be sufficient tools for formation.

Future clergy are going to have to know how to balance expertise in traditional ways with being change agents, and develop skills in goal-setting, consultation, and collaborative and inclusive approaches to decision-making, rather than simply finding effective ways to impose their own agenda. Clergy will need to be able to discern between merely institutional self-preservation and the larger mission of the church, so their time and energy (and training) are not expended on things of very little consequence.

In future, churches will need to put more focus on formation, including spirituality, discipleship, community, evangelism, and mission. Clergy themselves can't be content to be siloed, associating only with like-minded people, but willing to get out and connect, ask questions, listen, and learn.

This approach will require the church to be supportive not just in principle but in practical ways—offering incentive, special training, and financial support to those who are coming up with new models. Seminary is certainly a place people can expect to explore possibilities, but the church as a whole needs to embrace its role in this development. There is a great difference between merely adapting and discerning the kind of church and mission that need to emerge to meet the needs of God's

24. Roberts, "Six Tensions in Curriculum Revision."

people in the future. We can teach adaptive behaviors and encourage students to develop skills in marketing, promotion, facilitation, mediation, conflict management, self-care, systems theory, etc., but whether or not the existing church is willing to welcome creativity and change is another matter, and is a major aspect of the crisis of faith we now experience.

Ultimately, we believe we serve a God who says things like this:

> From this time forward I will make you hear new things,
> hidden things that you have not known.
> They are created now, not long ago;
> before today you have never heard of them,
> so that you could not say, "I already knew them." (Isaiah 48:6–7)

Christianity is a "good news" story premised on the idea that God at least occasionally (if not constantly) initiates new life, and theological colleges and the church are distinct in that there are always certain questions lurking just below the surface, such as, "To what degree are we a faith enterprise?"

So how can we best address the functional atheism of our time and not only encourage people toward God but reveal to people what it means to live in the presence of God? We can put programs together that enable people to adapt to current conditions and challenges. But the deeper question for me is: Where does God fit into our plans? In my view, the pull toward ministry and the gifts for it originate in God, so the nurturing and understanding of that Source and connection is essential to those who would be serving God in more than a token way (as more than just a "job option" or career). What kind of spiritual disciplines are necessary for the formation of pastors who are familiar with the realm of the Spirit and capable of leading people out of the desert?

Rilke's phrase "live the questions" has become almost cliché. What we might ask is: Are we living the right questions? Are we prepared to discern the *Missio Dei* for our time?

Campbell-Reed and Scharen put it this way: "With pastoral imagination, ministers are oriented toward seeing the fullness of their situation—with all its complexity and holiness. Just as importantly, ministers with a robust pastoral imagination are poised to collaborate with the Spirit to respond with fortitude and grace. A pastoral imagination opens up a range of leadership responses that draw fully on knowledge, skill, spiritual sense, and relational insight."[25]

---

25. Campbell-Reed and Scharen, "Are Your Graduates Ready?," 2.

A key dimension required for those discerning toward ministry is a sense of hope, rooted less in our ability to fix the problems than in the redemptive, gracious, and compassionate nature of the God whom we seek and serve.

5

Questions with No Right to Go Away
A Course in Spiritual Formation

Janet Gear

I OPEN MY FIRST class at VST every autumn term by asking each student to articulate, as well as they are able, the question that brought them to the school. In the words of the poet David Whyte, I inquire about the "questions that have patiently waited for [them], questions that have no right to go away."[1] We fill a blackboard with the questions the students have brought. Some are weighty and worthy questions. Others are on their way to ripening. It takes time and courage to form a good question—years, most often.[2]

And on the blackboard every year, inevitably, there are questions to do with what a life is for—whether it means or amounts to anything in the end. There are questions about love—how to love and what to love. There are questions about suffering; the why of suffering, and what to do about suffering. There are questions of purpose; the quest for some way to spend life in the direction of something larger or more meaningful than what one was doing to that point. Some are even bold enough to ask

---

1. Whyte, "Sometimes."
2. Parks, *Big Questions, Worthy Dreams.*

God questions: who and whether God is, and what God is calling them to be or do.

Each year more and more of the questions are set in the context of what is happening in the world. The students are aware that these times are both difficult and dangerous. They frame their questions in the context of not only ecclesial matters but global ones: climate change, poverty, war, and other stresses of globalization including mental illness, addiction, loneliness, and the disintegration of community life. Lately the blackboard also contains the words "xenophobia," "nationalism," and "tyranny" all bound up in the questions they bring about suffering, God, church, service, hope, meaning, and purpose. We begin our term together by gathering the questions that "have no right to go away."

I make no promises that the course will answer those questions. They serve a more important purpose than that. The questions we carry set the direction of our inquiry. I believe theological study must be grounded in what matters deeply to each of us, must be poised on the threshold of what troubles us as well as what enlightens, enlivens, or emboldens us.

In this volume, each of us has been invited to introduce our disciplines, the areas we teach. One of areas of the curriculum for which I am responsible is formation. What we mean by that quite simply—though it is not simple at all—is the consideration of how all the other disciplines taught here, from Bible to history to theology to practice of ministry, land within us. In other words, formation is about the form we take on, individually and corporately, the shape *we* become, when experiences and knowledge filter into our fiber and begin to shape us from the inside out. It is about the way our experience and knowledge are teaching us about what it is to be human, about what the poet referred to as "the making of a life."[3] We can become who we are by accident or we can take on the work of being human with intention. Spiritual formation is the rigorous, intentional work of becoming human as we have been divinely created and called to be human.

SPIRITUAL FORMATION

All the questions that come into the classroom are spiritual questions, by which I mean they are questions related to the depth and breadth of our humanity. By definition (Scottish Council of Churches), spirituality

3. Whyte, "Sometimes."

"concerns itself with the exploration into what is involved in becoming human." It refers to growth in "sensitivity to self, others, non-human creation and God who is within and beyond this totality."[4]

The term "spirituality" nonetheless can be as suspect among the theological disciplines as it is among fervent materialists. The word has successfully escaped religious life and belongs to public life. This is not at all a bad thing but it is not always a good thing either, as evidenced by the commodification of spirituality in everything from warm drinks to home décor. The work of spiritual formation, of becoming fully human in the image of God, can be judged even in schools of theology to be at best a "soft science" and at worst a narcissistic preoccupation. At VST, spiritual formation is recognized as the ancient traditional practice of taking up the question of how to live in the image of God. In Christian terms, formation is about growing in likeness to Christ. More ecumenically, we speak of human flourishing—a flourishing that in contrast to individual or even collective prosperity, has to do with reconciling all that is within and beyond the self.

Every religious tradition offers the world a path to becoming human—whether we call that the path of awakening, illumination, oneness, compassion, sanctification, or salvation. We tend to think about religions as having to do entirely with God. Religions, of course, also have to do with human life—what it is and how to live it. Spiritual formation, then, in every way, is the discipline that concerns itself with the exploration of questions like those that fill the blackboard on the first day of my class each fall. What is it to have hope? What does suffering teach us? What is salvation for myself, for the planet? How, then, shall we live?

Those large questions the students bring inevitably tug in two directions: *inward* to the heart of what life is about and *outward* toward how it is lived. Inside the question of what it is to be human is a hunger in both those directions, inward and outward. We often distinguish those two streams by calling one "reflection" and the other "action." What we discover in the work of spiritual formation, however, is that the path to becoming human always takes us in *both* these directions *simultaneously*. There is no genuine awakening of the heart that does not turn it *from* the self and *toward* all that is beyond it; inward turns outward. And there is no radical self-offering to the *world* that does not test and polish the

4. Quoted in McFague, *Blessed Are the Consumers*, 18.

human *heart*; outward leads inward. On the path to becoming human, the spiritual and the ethical become one.

One characteristic of religious traditions is that the spiritual path is entered across three thresholds or doorways: one each for the mind (study), the body (community), and the heart (lived experience).[5] Religious traditions have academies where the faith is *learned*. They also have institutions or communities (a church, a mosque, or a temple) where the faith is *practiced* in a particular way so that our love for God becomes animated, brought to life among others. And religious traditions acknowledge spiritual *experiences* that do not come second hand through books or sermons but firsthand in the ordinary and extraordinary experiences of human life, experiences that open us to the way in which our lives are held in God, experiences that awaken us to the sacred reality or "divine milieu,"[6] in which we live. The apostle Paul wrote that "we live and move and have our being" in God (Acts 17:28). We know this, in part, because we *experience* it.

Much of Protestantism is suspicious of individuals' "spiritual experiences." There are good reasons to be suspect of certain claims of mystical union of any kind. Harm has been done in the name of so-called direct knowledge of God. Of course, harm also has been done by certain interpretations of Scripture, tradition, and community norms. None of these thresholds is foolproof. That is why we need all three.

SPIRITUAL EXPERIENCE

Many years ago, I found a teacher who, though she was both a church-woman and an academic, preferred to teach through the third door, the door of spiritual experience, because, she believed, it was the widest, the least exclusive. Anyone can walk through this third door whether or not they are baptized, whether or not they are a doctor of theology, she insisted. Dorothee Sölle spoke about the democracy of mysticism, by which she meant that every human life includes experiences of a felt sense of our belonging to something beyond ourselves. That to which we belong goes by many names and by no name: the Source of Life, the Ground of Being, the Fountain of Love, the All-in-All; the one Jesus and his followers, our ancestors in faith, and our church call God. She insisted, as I

5. Sölle, *Silent Cry*, 1, 49–50.

6. Chardin, *Divine Milieu*, 44.

do, that this experiential entry into religious life is not a door *instead* of the church and academy; rather, it is a door *with* the church and academy. This is a doorway through which many both within and outside the church and academy encounter God. Though she is no longer living, I believe Sölle was prescient in her commitment to thinking about Christian life through the teaching and example of Christian mysticism. She perhaps could see before many of us how pressing the question of what it is to be human would become in our time, how much would be at stake, and how much a path through this doorway to human flourishing would contribute to spiritual and ethical life in this century. If there is anything these times call for, it is spiritually mature and awakened individuals and communities, formed to align their lives with the creator and sustainer of life in all its fullness, for the sake of all living things.

At the heart of Christian faith we hold, paradoxically, two things to be true: that God is closer to us than we are to ourselves, in the words of Augustine,[7] *and* that God is mystery; God becomes and God unbecomes, in the words of Eckhart.[8] God is intimately close *and* the closer we get (the more intimate), the more mysterious God becomes (unknowable). These insights are important in considering the experiences of God we have in ordinary life. We must remember that intimacy does not mean knowledge. Something can be close to us but retain its unknowability. Think of a newborn, for example. Nothing is more intimate than a life that is carried within a mother and yet nothing is more unknown than that new life. Likewise, that something has mystery does not mean it is remote. Quite the contrary. That God is "above all knowledge" does not make God distant. The revelation of God holds both intimacy and ineffability. So we do not need to worry when we speak of having an experience of proximity, intimacy, or oneness with God in our ordinary lives—on a forested walk or in a time of prayer—that we have reduced God to the equivalent of the scent of fir trees or a flickering candle. God is irreducibly God. Intimacy does not undo mystery or unknowability. These profound experiences of life in God in the ordinariness of our own human lives become the bedrock of spiritual formation, alongside the teachings of the church, the revelation of Scripture to communities of faith, and knowledge of the world.

---

7. Augustine, *Confessions* 3.6, 108.

8. Walshe, trans., *Complete Mystical Works of Meister Eckhart*, 293.

Students of Christian theology implicitly or explicitly consent to venture through each of these three doorways of religious life—academy, community, personal experience—onto the wide plain of exploration into what it is to be human in likeness to Christ. In the Christian tradition, the incarnation confronts us with a physical manifestation of divine intention, namely, flesh. We are never human in the abstract. Spiritual formation drives this home; we cannot be spiritual without a body, a body that does something in the world. For this reason, no matter what question troubles them into my classroom that first day, none of my students leave asking a disembodied or theoretical question, nor a purely internal, private question. Rather, they recognize that they are asking a physical, material, concrete, incarnate question. Such a question begins on the ground and ends on the ground, is lived and informs their living. A spiritual question is always a concrete and public question because we do not live theoretically; we live concretely, and we live together. Thomas Merton wrote:

> Humans have a responsibility to their own time, not as if they could seem to stand outside it and donate various spiritual and material benefits to it from a position of compassionate distance. Humans have a responsibility to find themselves where they are, in the history to which they belong.[9]

SPIRITUAL LIFE

From the outside, religion looks light and lofty. It isn't. It is gritty and grounded. It has to do very concretely with life, with what is real. The features we associate with the spiritual life are to do with being awake and engaged within and around us. What is it to find ourselves where we are, on this planet, in this country, in this city or town, in this neighborhood, among these people, with my intact or fragmented family, in my well or ailing body? These are *always* the concrete foundations to our spiritual formation, the quest to live faithfully our God-given humanity.

When we think about those whom we would consider contemporary spiritual leaders, whether Mother Teresa, Dorothy Day, Bishop Tutu, Mahatma Gandhi, or the Dalai Lama, this becomes so very evident. Without hesitation, we can picture them in their physical surroundings. Why? Because their spiritual lives took on the shape of their context and

9. Quoted in Wheatley, *Perseverance*, 12.

were lived out right where they were. The spiritual task of becoming human (in Christian terms, by becoming more capable of love as Christ was capable of love) is concrete and particular. It begins by finding ourselves in the time and place to which we belong. More than that, it *involves* us in the time and place to which we belong.

This is quite a different notion of spiritual life or experience than we may have considered before. Though it is absolutely true that there is a personal dimension to the experiences we have of God, in the sense in which we are speaking of them here, spiritual experience does not leave the world out, does not leave it untouched. "It is impossible," Mary Jo Leddy taught, "to have a spiritual awakening and leave the world as you found it."[10] A spiritual awakening is simultaneously a path to the flourishing of our own life and a way of siding with life as it struggles to flourish for all.

Irenaeus of Lyons, a first-century church leader, gave us a beautiful image. He wrote that the glory of God, the fullness of God, the presence of God, "is every creature fully alive." If this is true, it means that, as creatures made in the image of God, we are somehow fashioned to come to life by becoming part of the flourishing of the whole of life, created to flourish within when we participate in the fullness of life around us. We might think of this as becoming part of God's own life by living life in a way that fosters life, that befriends it.

Yet the connection between the inner and outer life is not self-evident. How, students ask, can we be centered, well, peaceable, and grounded—those things we associate with a prayerful life—*and*, at the same time, be invested in the state of the world and engaged in the struggle for justice—those things that demand the relentless self-sacrificing efforts of the activist life? These two inclinations seem mutually exclusive. We feel forced to choose either contemplation *or* action, not both. If, however, we are to become human, for example, in the way of Jesus, in the image of God, we experience our humanity both as a thriving of our own life and as a siding with all of life. It is not that we look inward, get ourselves sorted out (whatever that means), and then do a good deed or two in the world. Nor does it mean that we give and give and give and then take a retreat to fill our tired souls for heading back out into the fray. These are false and distorted versions of Christian life, of spiritual life. It is harmful to us to be on either of these roads. Rather, it is one event, one motion,

10. Leddy, *Radical Gratitude*.

the way breathing is one motion though it is both inhalation and exhalation. Spiritual vitality is exactly the same. Such vitality is a single fluid rhythm calling us to life, an inward and outward motion that sends us out and pulls us deep. The word we use to point to this is two-fold gesture, this choreography of the human soul at work, is *love*. So, our love lands in the world and brings us to life all in the same breath. Why would we be made any other way? We are fashioned, our tradition assures us, to be human in a way that flourishes and lets flourish:

> Blessed are the man and woman who have
> grown beyond their greed and have put an
> end to their hatred and no longer nourish illusions.
> But they delight in the way things are
> and keep their hearts open, day and night.
> They are like trees planted near flowing rivers,
> which bear fruit when they are ready. (based on Psalm 1)

SPIRITUAL PRACTICE

Wisdom traditions, including Christianity, teach a path to becoming human, a path of spiritual formation. Though there are many variations, there is a common thread. We discover that the essential posture of a spiritual life is to pay attention. Though it is difficult to master, it is in no way difficult to learn in everyday terms the way in which paying attention brings the human heart to life and offers it to life.

Each year in my introductory class to spiritual foundations for ministry, we walk through a version of this path of attentiveness together. I ask the students very simply what were the events in their lives that woke them up, if and how they stayed awake, and what difference it makes to how they live. And there is a pattern in their responses. This pattern matches patterns in ancient spiritual traditions; echoes the pattern of the masters, saints, and mystics in our tradition; and resembles the narratives in Scripture and in literature. The pattern is this: it is life itself that awakens us; it takes discipline to remain awake; and it is to our belonging to the whole of things, to God and to one another, that we are awakened.

The students tell of the way their own lives have been thread with *waking-up* experiences—from the day they saw the Grand Canyon to the year they lost their sibling to the afternoon their first child was born. Our life experience, in its beauty and its tragedy, provides all we need to be stirred or pried open to life beyond the borders of our own skin. Next, we explore the spiritual practices in our own tradition designed to keep us awake to the depth and breadth of wonder and vulnerability that tethers us to mystery and to the heart of God. We learn that everything from a rule of life, a labyrinth or pilgrimage walk, or a daily examen to Scripture reading, worship, silence, and song are spiritual practices that are training the heart to remain open. It takes *intention and discipline to stay awake* because our distractions are myriad and our temptations to deny what is real are great. The awakened state makes us vulnerable because it is unselective—awake to beauty and to pain, to our loved ones and to strangers. Above all, however, it keeps us *awake to our life in God and to our belonging to the whole of things.* This is not something we *do* but something we *experience.* There is, as a result of seeing things as they are and being open to how the "divine milieu" beckons us in the direction of life's flourishing, a radical conversion from the self at the center of one's life to an understanding of one's place in the integrity of the whole, a conversion from subject/object relationships to a genuine posture of intersubjectivity. In other words, there is a way in which we learn to love, to become human in the image of God.

Awakening, seeing, connecting—most every student recognizes this pattern. They can trace it in their own lives and they recognize that in their own tradition, whatever it may be, there are spiritual practices that in whole or in part are aimed at these movements. Anyone who has a contemplative practice (prayer or mindfulness) will recognize this path. Activists may know it too, though not as a taught discipline so much as a practiced experience of attentiveness, surrender, and solidarity.

Every year we bring teachers into the classroom, teachers of this pattern—a pattern honed through the simple yet nearly impossible practice of attentiveness. We host a public school teacher, a public servant, a therapist, a minister, a priest, and a counselor of street youth—ordinary people with extraordinary discipline. Each of them tells the story of how they came to be doing what they are doing, their *formation.* They speak (though it is often difficult to articulate) of the deep sense of connection they feel to God, to the source and purpose and pleasure of their humanity, and to the whole of things in which they feel a part. In each unique story the pattern emerges: *awoken,* as Annie Dillard wrote, "to mystery, rumors of death, beauty, and violence"; kept awake by the constant discipline of *letting go* of pretense, false consolation, and distraction; and convinced of their belonging in God and felt kinship on the earth through an experience of union with God through union with what God does—God who is of love and for life. Each of these teachers engages the lifelong practice of formation, crossing the thresholds (intellectual, communal, experiential) again and again in the work of becoming human. Through suspect eyes, spiritual life appears self-serving and self-indulgent. It is the opposite. Awakening to the world, to the self, and to Godz is the only way to proportion the self in relation to others. The unexamined self is large and self-involved. Awakening is always both an outward and inward gesture that situates us in relation to others and attunes us deeply to the world and to God. The poet Rumi put it this way:

> Out beyond ideas of wrongdoing and rightdoing,
> there is a field. I'll meet you there.
> When the soul lies down in that grass,
> the world is too full to talk about.
> Ideas, language, even the phrase each other
> doesn't make any sense.[11]

That, we discover, is where the work of spiritual formation leads. It leads toward an experience of human life in union with all things such that the phrase "each other" does not make any sense. It leads toward an ethics and a spirituality of our shared life in God from which compassion, wisdom, service, and praise arise and triumph. No one arrives at such a place in one semester. Few of us, if any, arrive there in a lifetime. Formation is a lifelong practice, not a graduate school achievement. It begins wherever and whenever we choose to take seriously the questions that have patiently waited for us.

11. Barks, *Essential Rumi*, 36.

6

Reading the Ancient Past

*A World Behind the Text, In the Text,
and In Front of the Text*

PATRICIA DUTCHER-WALLS

IMAGINE THE FOLLOWING SCENARIO. One day, you heard of a demonstration in a city near your home being held to support a recent wave of refugees and migrants and to confront the political leaders of the city, province, and federal governments to create supportive measures for immigrants, especially for refugees who came to the country desperate for safety and well-being. Curious, you attended the demonstration and saw a platform full of leaders from various religious traditions—Christian, Jewish, Indigenous, Muslim, Buddhist—speaking eloquently in favor of positive action. All around you were people from all types of backgrounds, some wearing religious or cultural clothing or symbols that identified their faith. Intrigued, you listened in. You heard many ethical declarations from the religious leaders about why people and governments should take action to support refugees and exiles. And you were deeply moved by a Christian pastor who spoke about welcoming the stranger; they quoted Jesus, using a verse from Matthew: "I was a stranger and you welcomed me" (Matthew 25:35). That seemed to make sense, a Christian quoting Jesus.

However, you really started wondering when the pastor went on to quote several verses from the Old Testament. You knew of the Old Testament, of course, but thought it was pretty much full of violent and archaic stuff. But here was this pastor referring to the prophet Isaiah as one who said the Lord welcomes foreigners, even though foreigners were usually not considered worthy of worshipping at the temple at that time. The pastor read an Isaiah passage saying, "And the foreigners who join themselves to the Lord . . . and hold fast my covenant—these I will bring to my holy mountain, and make them joyful in my house of prayer" (Isaiah 56:6–7). You were really surprised when the pastor quoted Leviticus, because you always thought that ancient law book had nothing nice to say. But the passage they quoted certainly seemed relevant to the purpose of the demonstration, "The alien who resides with you shall be to you as the citizen among you; you shall love the alien as yourself, for you were aliens in the land of Egypt: I am the Lord your God" (Leviticus 19:34). The point the pastor drove home was that the audience was called to take "'prophetic action' to extend 'radical hospitality' to immigrants and immigrant communities."[1] When you finally went home, you had a lot to think about how all the religious leaders, and especially that pastor who had quoted the Old Testament, had made their religious values and sacred texts so relevant for a current political issue.[2]

Helping you think well about an interpretive situation like that described in this imaginary but realistic scenario is one of the goals of a course introducing the Hebrew Bible.[3] Questions such a course can raise and begin to answer include: How can we read the Hebrew Bible well? What do we need to know as readers to understand the text?

1. Burke, "Evangelical Lutheran Church in Americ," para. 2.

2. This scenario is imaginary, but the issue about welcoming refugees was inspired by the August 2019 vote of the Evangelical Lutheran Church in America to become a "sanctuary church body." See the article quoted in the previous footnote and the following: Northeastern Pennsylvania Synod, "ELCA Sanctuary Background and Recommendations."

3. This chapter will use the term Hebrew Bible for the sacred text also known as the Old Testament for Christians and as the Bible for Jews.

A WORLD *BEHIND* THE TEXT, *IN* THE TEXT, AND *IN FRONT* OF THE TEXT

For a modern reader, the Hebrew Bible can seem foreign and complicated because there is such a gap between when it was written and today. The writers—storytellers, psalmists, prophets, poets, sages, and scribes—were living in social structures and environmental, geographical, and political settings in the ancient world that can seem very different from anything a modern reader knows. And yet the stories and poetry of the Bible might seem familiar to some readers, especially if they have been involved with a church. Little about that perplexing combination of strangeness and familiarity make it straightforward to describe how the Hebrew Bible might be interpreted today. Whether a reader identifies as a member of a group that looks to the Hebrew Bible as Scripture or as a sacred text, there are many reasons to do good interpretation today—for preaching in a service of worship, for teaching in a church or community context, for giving consolation in times of difficulty, for praying with and for the community and the world, as a source for spiritual insight, for grounding and motivating mission, for joining with other religious leaders in compassionate action for the world.

We might think of the situation of ourselves and the ancient text this way, picturing three "worlds" behind, in and in front of the text.[4] A picture of the world in which all the storytelling and writing of the Hebrew Bible occurred can be described as "the world *behind* the text." That ancient reality can be examined and recreated by fields of knowledge like history, archaeology, sociology, anthropology, geography, and economics. Of course, there is a limit to how much anyone can know about life three thousand years ago, but we can understand some of the ways of life and patterns of behavior then. As well, there is also "a world *in* the text," a description of events and experience portrayed by the story or poetry. This "story world" or "poetic world" is accessible through methods that study the narrative artistry, poetic imagination, and persuasive or rhetorical skillfulness of the writing. This reading is sensitive to the way texts create and intersect with theological insights and commitments. Finally, we as readers today stand in "the world *in front of* the text." We are interpreters of the text; we are located in our own times, spaces, and contexts that shape how we see and think and the assumptions we make about life, the universe, etc. Methods that take seriously the world of interpreters

4. To understand the meaning of "worlds," see Ricoeur, *Interpretation Theory*.

include approaches that appreciate how the Bible was interpreted in the history of the church, or methods such as feminist, liberation, and post-colonial readings, reader response theory, and other approaches that recognize that our own "world" might shape how we understand the world behind the text and the world in the text.

Any given biblical scholar or interpreter will approach their task making assumptions about what one or combination of these worlds they most want to emphasize or pay attention to. Some interpreters will be up front about their assumptions and inform their readers of their approach; others will write as if their approach is the only way imaginable to understand the Hebrew Bible. Readers of biblical interpretations do well to be aware of various ways authors and other interpreters like preachers and teachers approach the Hebrew Bible. *In this chapter, we will take the approach that knowing more about the world behind the text and the story world in the text can aid us as interpreters in understanding more about what the texts say to us today in the world in front of the text.*

In this introduction, we will focus first on *the story world* of the Hebrew Bible so that we accomplish a simple review of how the Hebrew Bible relates an ongoing story about God's people in ancient times. For readers unfamiliar with that story, this will be helpful orientation. We will weave that together with an appreciation of *the world behind the text.* What realities, knowledge, and environments were parts of the unspoken background that the biblical writers took for granted? We will highlight several of the most significant aspects of the world of the Hebrew Bible—land, households, states and empires, and religion. This survey will also provide reference to some of the major historical moments of the biblical story as the texts themselves portray it, without making any particular commitments to whether events happened exactly the way they are described. The intriguing questions and issues about *the world in front of the text* we leave for later consideration.

THE WORLD BEHIND THE TEXT: LOCATED ON LAND[5]

A very general description of the geographical world of the Hebrew Bible locates the context of the biblical books in a time and place: a time period

---

5. Much of the material in the following sections of the essay is drawn from Dutcher-Walls, *Reading the Historical Books.*

of about one thousand years long, from about 1200 BCE to about 100 BCE, in an area called the ancient Near East. This area runs from Egypt in northern Africa, through the eastern seaboard of the Mediterranean Sea, eastward through the vast valley of the Tigris and Euphrates Rivers in ancient Mesopotamia (modern Iraq and Iran) and northward up through modern Turkey and Greece. One word of explanation about the term "Israel." In its most general usage, that term identifies the whole people and community that is the focus of the Hebrew Bible, as in the phrase "people of ancient Israel." However, Israel was also the name of the northern state of the two states that developed in the land. In this more specific usage, Israel is often mentioned with Judah, the southern state. The stories contained in the Hebrew Bible are situated on the strip of coastal plains and mountains along the eastern seaboard of the Mediterranean Sea, in an area known in the ancient world as Canaan or Palestine:

> . . . the hill country of the Amorites as well as into the neighboring regions—the Arabah, the hill country, the Shephelah, the Negeb, and the seacoast . . . (Deuteronomy 1:7)

This quote lists various geographical zones that generally run north-south, from east to west: the "Arabah" or rift valley of the Jordan River and Dead Sea, the central ridge of hills and mountains, the "Shephelah" or foothills between the central hills and seacoast, and the generally low and flat seacoast. The Negeb was the southernmost dry wilderness area.

THE WORLD IN THE TEXT: ANCESTRAL ORIGINS

The story line traced in the narrative books of the Hebrew Bible was grounded in a foundation tradition that recounted the ancestors of the people coming from the East and traveling to a land promised by God:

> 1Now the Lord said to Abram, 'Go from your country and your kindred and your father's house to the land that I will show you . . . 5Abram took his wife Sarai and his brother's son Lot, and all the possessions that they had gathered, and the persons whom they had acquired in Haran; and they set forth to go to the land of Canaan. (Genesis 12:1, 5)

The stories of the ancestors found in the book of Genesis follow the families of Abraham and Sarah, Isaac and Rebekah, Jacob and Leah and Rachel, and show their lives as pastoralists following their herds, and interacting with peoples in the land in Canaan.

The remembered foundation tradition continued with the story of the ancestors seeking refuge in Egypt during a time of famine and how that sojourn in time became oppression under slavery in Egypt. The suffering of the people under state slavery and God's response to their cry for help became a sacred story of deliverance that resonated throughout later writings of the Hebrew Bible.

> 23After a long time the king of Egypt died. The Israelites groaned under their slavery, and cried out. Out of the slavery their cry for help rose up to God. 24God heard their groaning, and God remembered his covenant with Abraham, Isaac, and Jacob. 25God looked upon the Israelites, and God took notice of them. (Exodus 2:23–25)

The story took a dramatic turn when the people, under the leadership of Moses and Aaron, made a daring escape from Pharaoh's armies through God's intervention and power; these stories are related in the book of Exodus. A time of sojourning in the wilderness was remembered before the people were led back to Canaan:

> 6When I brought your ancestors out of Egypt, you came to the sea; and the Egyptians pursued your ancestors with chariots and horsemen to the Red Sea. 7When they cried out to the Lord, he . . . made the sea come upon them and cover them. . . . Afterwards you lived in the wilderness for a long time. 8Then I brought you to the land of the Amorites . . . (Joshua 24:6–8)

The historical books of Joshua and Judges picked up this story line and related stories of the emergence of the people of Israel in the hill country inland from the Mediterranean seacoast after the escape from Egypt. Numerous stories and traditions that lay behind these books chronicled the interactions of their clans and tribes with the peoples who lived there, remembering both warfare and local treaties.

> Joshua turned back at that time, and took Hazor, and struck its king down with the sword. Before that time Hazor was the head of all those kingdoms. (Joshua 11:10)

> Manasseh did not drive out the inhabitants of Beth-shean and its villages, or Taanach and its villages, . . . or the inhabitants of Megiddo and its villages; but the Canaanites continued to live in that land. When Israel grew strong, they put the Canaanites

to forced labour, but did not in fact drive them out. (Judges 1:27–28)

THE WORLD BEHIND THE TEXT:
LOCATED IN HOUSEHOLDS

In some ways, the family-based context of the Hebrew Bible is an invisible background because the texts usually just assume that their audience understands how the families, social roles, groups, and institutions were structured in ancient Israel.[6] The most basic social unit in the world of ancient Israel was the family. From what we know of ancient Israel, when a person reported who they were, they did not first report their individual identity the way a person today might. Rather, they thought of themselves first and foremost as a member of an extended family. Look at how this individual was introduced:

> 1 There was a certain man of Ramathaim, a Zuphite from the hill country of Ephraim, whose name was Elkanah son of Jeroham son of Elihu son of Tohu son of Zuph, an Ephraimite. (1 Samuel 1:1)

This man is identified by his family of origin, tracing his lineage back several generations and placing that family on its ancestral land in the highland hill country. The primary context for the people's livelihood in agriculture, socialization, education, crafts and manufacturing of goods, and health was the family household. Households consisted of the elder generation, usually the patriarchal head of the household and his wife or wives (polygamy was common), their unmarried children, their married sons and their wives, and any grandchildren. Daughters married out into their husbands' households. This family unit usually lived together in a compound of connected or adjacent houses and that household was the primary economic production unit of the society.

Every household was nested inside a larger structure of the clan, a group of households related by blood or marriage, living in geographical proximity and providing an association for the families. Beyond that,

6. Sociological studies about ancient Israel and Judah include: Fritz, *City in Ancient Israel*; McNutt, *Reconstructing the Society of Ancient Israel*; King and Stager, *Life in Biblical Israel*; Carter and Meyers, eds., *Community, Identity, and Ideology*; Chalcraft, ed., *Social-Scientific Old Testament Criticism*; and Schloen, *House of the Father as Fact and Symbol*.

larger familial and generational connections linked the clans into tribes, and finally the tribes were part of the state as a whole.[7] The patriarchal heads of families were accorded honor and status and were responsible for adjudicating disputes among families, representing the family in the decisions of the village or town, and carrying the families' interests into decisions by the clans.

The family household functioned as the basic economic productive unit of the society. Much of the agricultural and household craft production was accomplished by both men and women who divided work among the married partners, brothers and sisters, and cousins of the extended household.[8] While women were under the protection and control of the males of the family—their fathers, brothers, or husbands—they also had significant economic status and roles in the household livelihood. For example, in 1 Samuel, Abigail, the wife of a powerful sheepherder in southern Judah, is portrayed as commanding knowledge of the economic resources of the household, is obeyed by the hired men of the household, and acts independently of her husband in coming to the aid of David, who was a tribal chief fighting for leadership of the tribes at the time.

> 18 Then Abigail hurried and took two hundred loaves, two skins of wine, five sheep ready dressed, five measures of parched grain, one hundred clusters of raisins, and two hundred cakes of figs. She loaded them on donkeys 19and said to her young men, "Go on ahead of me; I am coming after you." But she did not tell her husband Nabal. (1 Samuel 25:18–19)

The livelihood of the whole household was dependent on the land and its crops, especially wheat, grapes, and olives, in the largely agrarian society of ancient Israel. A variety of crops provided a varied diet and allowed the household a measure of protection against agricultural risks of drought and blight, which endangered food supplies and the household's ability to pay its taxes and debts. Crop damage from "blight, mildew, locust, or caterpillar" (1 Kings 8:37) brought risks to harvests. Drought was a constant threat that could result in starvation for the poor, who had no other protection when their crops failed. During a drought, the prophet Elijah was sent to a poor widow who described her plight:

---

7. King and Stager, *Life in Biblical Israel.*

8. See especially Meyers, *Discovering Eve.*

12But she said, "As the Lord your God lives, I have nothing baked, only a handful of meal in a jar, and a little oil in a jug; I am now gathering a couple of sticks, so that I may go home and prepare it for myself and my son, that we may eat it, and die." (1 Kings 17:12)

In several other passages, the importance of land for the peasant farmers of ancient Israel is traced. Another prophetic story depicted the response of an Israelite land holder when King Ahab asked to acquire his vineyard, which was near the palace. The man is portrayed as being unable even to conceive of giving away his ancestral land: "But Naboth said to Ahab, 'The Lord forbid that I should give you my ancestral inheritance'" (1 Kings 21:3).

The land of ancient Israel was also organized socially to fit the needs of the people. Household lands were distributed around the land of a local village, which might contain several extended families and their land holdings in fields, vineyards, orchards, and pastureland. The next level of organization would have been towns, where other households also lived but which contained a local market for the area and were perhaps protected by a defensive wall. The largest social habitation were cities. Though small in population by our standards, with a population in only the thousands even for a substantial city, the cities were protected by major defensive walls and included significant marketplaces, cisterns for water storage, as well as governmental, commercial, and military buildings. This environment of households on the land can also be described politically, that is, as land that is divided up into territories associated with respective tribes of the people or the states of Israel and Judah. The last section of the book of Joshua (chapters 13–21) shows how the text's description of the boundaries of the areas allotted to the tribes reflects a combination of geographical and political awareness about the land. The writers of the Hebrew Bible were deliberate in conveying information about the political entities that inhabited and controlled the land. The presence of the clans and tribes and then later the monarchies of the states of Israel and Judah on the land, and their various fortunes in holding the land or losing the land, occupy much of the stories recounted and are reflected in the poetry of the prophetic books, wisdom literature, and the Psalms.

THE WORLD IN THE TEXT: KINGS AND STATES

The books of First and Second Samuel relate the rise of the monarchy and how a more organized state slowly developed from the early villages and clans, as political changes both within and beyond the local area affected the people and their institutions in the time period around 1000 BCE. The account of the reign of the first king, Saul, recounted how he and the northern tribes he represented did not hold on to power when David, a rival leader, secured the support of all the tribes. The biblical story is shaped to highlight the theological aspects of David's rise and eventual kingship, but we see as well that the story portrayed his power and ability to unite the northern and southern tribes.

> 3So all the elders of Israel came to the king at Hebron; and King David made a covenant with them at Hebron before the Lord, and they anointed David king over Israel. . . . 5At Hebron he reigned over Judah for seven years and six months; and at Jerusalem he reigned over all Israel and Judah for thirty-three years. (2 Samuel 5:3, 5)

As the story line continued in 2 Samuel and 1 Kings, David's long rule was riddled with political intrigue and conflict, but he passed on a united kingdom to his son Solomon. Solomon is recounted as a wise and rich king, best known for building the temple in the capital city of Jerusalem. However, the story relates how his policies of heavy-handed use of forced labor to build the monumental architecture of the temple and city cost the kingdom its unity when his son Rehoboam came to the throne.

> 1. . . all Israel had come to Shechem to make [Rehoboam] king . . . . 13The king answered the people harshly . . . 14"My father made your yoke heavy, but I will add to your yoke . . . 16When all Israel saw that the king would not listen to them, the people answered the king, "What share do we have in David? . . . To your tents, O Israel! Look now to your own house, O David." . . . 19So Israel has been in rebellion against the house of David to this day. (1 Kings 12:1, 13–14, 16, 19)

The rest of the story of the monarchies in the books of Kings related the stories of the separate states of Judah in the south, with its temple and dynasty located in Jerusalem, and Israel in the north, with its capital in Samaria. The history writing in the books of Kings, paralleled extensively in the books of 1 and 2 Chronicles, interwove the stories of the two monarchies, switching back and forth between the reigns of contemporaneous kings over the two hundred years when both states existed, from around 928 to 722 BCE.

THE WORLD BEHIND THE TEXT:
NEIGHBORING STATES AND EMPIRES

The writing about the story of the monarchies, while focused on Israel and Judah, also situated these states in the international world of the day, because from early on neighboring states along the Mediterranean seacoast interacted with Israel and Judah. In time, states further away began to have a heavy impact on the people of Israel when the empires of the ancient world took over vast areas of land. The texts of the historical and prophetic books in particular show awareness of these neighboring states, especially when those states invaded the territory of Judah and Israel.

Besides the Philistines along the seacoast, who occupied the tradition's attention during the rise of the monarchy, there were several other small rival states in the area that interacted with the people of Israel. Ammon, Moab, and Edom were, like Israel and Judah, small agrarian monarchies along the seacoast of the Mediterranean. Two other neighboring states had a particularly large influence on Israel and Judah. The first was the group of seafaring and trading cities of Phoenicia, up the coast from Israel. Both Israel and Judah recounted interactions with Tyre and Sidon, two of Phoenicia's largest cities. The northern state of Israel was particularly tied in with Phoenicia because they were major trading partners, Israel supplying agricultural products to the coastal cities in exchange for lumber and luxury goods. The relationship of the northern state of Israel with its nearest north neighbor, Aram (sometimes referred to as Damascus, after its capital city), was a subject of frequent interest in the history writing in 1 and 2 Kings. The two states occasionally engaged in trade and usually in ongoing skirmishes and warfare over territory for over two centuries.

Around 750 BCE, the context of the biblical world changed drastically with the rise of the Neo-Assyrian Empire, which was the first of a series of empires that controlled the ancient Near East for most of the rest of the Hebrew Bible period. These empires changed the international politics of the whole area, including the domination and conquest of both

Israel and Judah. The impacts of these empires on the history and theology of ancient Israel are widely reflected in the biblical books from Kings to Psalms to the prophets.

THE WORLD IN THE TEXT: OPPRESSION BY EMPIRES

The story line of the Hebrew Bible remembers and theologically reflects on the impacts of these empires. For example, the Assyrians conquered and destroyed Israel and its capital Samaria in 722 BCE (2 Kings 17), an event also interpreted by the prophet Amos.

> 11Therefore, thus says the Lord God: An adversary shall surround the land, and strip you of your defense; and your strongholds shall be plundered. (Amos 3:11)

Judah escaped total destruction under King Hezekiah when the Assyrian forces withdrew from a siege against the city of Jerusalem, an account that received significant attention in the history writing (2 Kings 18:17—19:37) and in the book of Isaiah (chapters 36–39). Jerusalem was spared from further assault when Hezekiah became a vassal of the Assyrian Empire, a status that continued under his successor through the next six decades.

As the Assyrian Empire weakened in the last decades of the seventh century BCE, the next world power was Babylon, which conquered Assyria, inherited its vast territory, and asserted its own control as the Babylonian Empire. The prophet Jeremiah warned Judah that its imminent demise was tied to its arrogance and refusal to listen to God's commands.

> 8Take warning, O Jerusalem, or I shall turn from you in disgust,
> and make you a desolation, an uninhabited land. (Jeremiah 6:8)

The biblical history also chronicled the siege and conquest of Jerusalem:

> 1And in the ninth year of [Zedekiah's] reign, in the tenth month, on the tenth day of the month, King Nebuchadnezzar of Babylon came with all his army against Jerusalem, and . . . 10broke down the walls around Jerusalem. (2 Kings 25:1, 10)

The Babylonian Empire, like the Assyrian Empire before it, practiced a policy of deportation and resettlement of conquered peoples to control acquired territories. Second Kings reported this ruinous and final reality for the Davidic monarchy and its capital city, Jerusalem, when its elite population was deported to Babylon in 587 BCE, a time known as the exile. The land of Judah was left as a devastated area, with a remaining population of peasant farmers to carry on basic agricultural work.

> 11Nebuzaradan the captain of the guard carried into exile the rest of the people who were left in the city and the deserters who had defected to the king of Babylon—all the rest of the population. 12But the captain of the guard left some of the poorest people of the land to be vinedressers and tillers of the soil. (2 Kings 25:11–12)

A poet later raised a lament for the destruction of the city, voicing the city's cry of woe.

> 16For these things I weep; my eyes flow with tears;
> for a comforter is far from me, one to revive my courage;
> my children are desolate, for the enemy has prevailed.
> (Lamentations 1:16)

After fifty years, the Babylonian Empire fell to the new power in the east, the Persian Empire. The Persian Empire provided the context for the history writing recorded in the books of Ezra and Nehemiah, as well as prophetic materials in Isaiah, Haggai, and Zechariah. The accounts in these books focused on the community that returned from exile to a restored Judah, the rebuilding of the temple, and the development of a religious hierarchy under Persian rule:

> 2Thus says King Cyrus of Persia: The Lord, the God of heaven, has given me all the kingdoms of the earth, and he has charged me to build him a house at Jerusalem in Judah. 3Any of those among you who are of his people—may their God be with them!—are now permitted to go up to Jerusalem in Judah, and rebuild the house of the Lord . . . (Ezra 1:2–3)

In addition, the two-hundred-year time period during which Persia held sway over the ancient Near East saw the development of many of the institutions and theological commitments that shaped how Judaism survived, both as a religion centered in its land, Judah, and temple city, Jerusalem, and as an increasingly scattered people, with communities developing around the ancient world. The reality of developing Judaism as a religion centered in law and sacred texts is reflected in accounts of the reading of the law under Ezra:

> 1All the people gathered together . . . . They told the scribe Ezra
> to bring the book of the law of Moses, which the Lord had given
> to Israel. 2Accordingly, the priest Ezra brought the law before
> the assembly . . . . 3He read from it facing the square before the
> Water Gate from early morning until midday, in the presence of
> the men and the women and those who could understand; and
> the ears of all the people were attentive to the book of the law.
> (Nehemiah 8:1–3)

Persia stayed in power as an empire for about two hundred years. The domination of the ancient world by Persia was challenged and eventually overthrown by the rise of Greece, which under the able military leader Alexander the Great conquered the Persian Empire and extended its own hegemony from Greece to Egypt to India. The resulting spread of Hellenistic culture and Greek language and customs changed the context of the families and institutions reflected in the stories and poetry of the later books of the Hebrew Bible, which itself was translated into Greek to meet the needs of Jewish worshippers throughout the Greek-speaking world during the second century BCE.

THE WORLD BEHIND THE TEXT: RELIGIOUS REALITIES

Moving to the religious context of the world behind the Hebrew Bible is not a big step because the political and religious realms were highly intertwined in ancient times. All ancient societies understood that they lived as a part of a cosmos that was controlled by a god or gods. Each state had its own pantheon of gods and goddesses and understood that the state, the dynasty, and the temple of that state were intimately connected with the cosmos in which the state existed. The king and dynasty representing the state looked to the gods for the legitimization of their power. The visible confirmation of the gods' presence and authorization for the state was the temple in the capital city, which was built by the king to give physical presence and honor to the gods that upheld the state.[9] Ancient Israel of course witnessed that only God was the creator and lord of the universe and framed its historical writing in that understanding,

9. For further understanding about the religion of ancient Israel, see the classic study Frankfort, *Kingship and the Gods*, as well as: Miller, *Religion of Ancient Israel*; Weinfeld, "Zion and Jerusalem as Religious and Political Capital: Ideology and Utopia"; **Hurowitz**, *I Have Built You an Exalted House*; and **Smith**, *Early History of God*.

but its understanding fit against this background of religion in its world and time.

THE WORLD IN THE TEXT: COVENANT AND KINGSHIP

The ancient storytellers and poets of course included religious reality in their writings. The foundation traditions of ancient Israel portray an understanding that the relationship between God and the people was one of covenant or promise. God says in Genesis 17,

> 7I will establish my covenant between me and you, and your offspring after you throughout their generations, for an everlasting covenant, to be God to you and to your offspring after you. (Genesis 17:7)

The foundation tradition continued with the crucial remembrance that after the people had escaped from Egypt and under Moses' leadership, they met God at a mountain in the wilderness. Here they received the teaching and law that would be the covenant constituting their community under and with God.

> 16 On the morning of the third day there was thunder and lightning, as well as a thick cloud on the mountain, and a blast of a trumpet so loud that all the people who were in the camp trembled. 17Moses brought the people out of the camp to meet God. They took their stand at the foot of the mountain. 20When the Lord descended upon Mount Sinai, to the top of the mountain, the Lord summoned Moses to the top of the mountain, and Moses went up . . . . 1Then God spoke all these words: 2I am the Lord your God, who brought you out of the land of Egypt, out of the house of slavery; 3you shall have no other gods before me. (Exodus 19:16–17, 20; 20:1–3)

Including the central Ten Commandments as well as commands of various sorts now found in the books of Exodus, Leviticus, and Numbers, the covenant was a set of laws that instituted the ways that the people had to relate to God and to each other to act out the grace they had received from God in the deliverance from Egypt. Later writers remembered this foundational event:

> 35The Lord had made a covenant with them and commanded them, "You shall not worship other gods or bow yourselves to them or serve them or sacrifice to them, 36but you shall worship

the Lord, who brought you out of the land of Egypt with great power and with an outstretched arm; you shall bow yourselves to him, and to him you shall sacrifice. 37The statutes and the ordinances and the law and the commandment that he wrote for you, you shall always be careful to observe." (2 Kings 17:35–37)

As the tribes made the transition to a monarchy under Saul and David, we see characteristic assumptions of the ancient world in the texts that kingship, dynasty, and temple were linked with God's presence and power. In a passage that portrays this central religious reality of the Davidic dynasty, 2 Samuel 7 reports the word King David heard from God about his decision to build a temple in Jerusalem. The story tells how, after David had built his own house (the palace) and wanted to build the house of God (the temple), the prophet Nathan spoke God's message about how God would build a house (dynasty) for David:

> 5Go and tell my servant David: Thus says the Lord: Are you the one to build me a house to live in? . . . 11. . . the Lord declares to you that the Lord will make you a house. 12When your days are fulfilled and you lie down with your ancestors, I will raise up your offspring after you, who shall come forth from your body, and I will establish his kingdom. 13He shall build a house for my name, and I will establish the throne of his kingdom forever. (2 Samuel 7:5, 11–13)

THE WORLD IN THE TEXT: TEMPLE, HOLINESS, AND WORSHIP

The temple in Jerusalem became the center of religious focus for Judah in the centuries after its founding by Solomon. And in the centuries after the exile, when the temple was rebuilt, it provided a center for the whole community of restored Judah, especially because the political dynasty could not be reestablished under Persian occupation. The temple had been built on a high point in the geography of Jerusalem and the hill it crowned was known as Zion, a term that occurs regularly in the poetry and prophecy of the Hebrew Bible. The temple symbolized the very presence of God's glory and name in the midst of the people. The spiritual and sacred quality of the temple was conveyed in the account about bringing the ark that had contained the tablets of the law into the newly built temple,

6Then the priests brought the ark of the covenant of the Lord to its place, in the inner sanctuary of the house, in the most holy place, . . . 9There was nothing in the ark except the two tablets of stone that Moses had placed there at Horeb, where the Lord made a covenant with the Israelites, when they came out of the land of Egypt. 10And when the priests came out of the holy place, a cloud filled the house of the Lord, 11so that the priests could not stand to minister because of the cloud; for the glory of the Lord filled the house of the Lord. (1 Kings 8:6, 9–11)

In addition to the intersections of divine and human realities in the political and religious realms, another basic religious concept of the context of ancient Israel was an understanding of "holiness." Holiness, a central concept of reality for ancient Israel, both expressed the ultimate revered and sacrosanct quality of God and the idea that God had ordered the cosmos into two states of being, that which was specially set apart to be holy or sacred, and the rest of reality, which was common or ordinary. Further, anything that was contrary to holiness was considered unclean or impure. In the same way that the cosmos was separated into distinct spheres of holiness or ordinariness, the created human realm was also understood as differentiated into different states, distinguishing purity from impurity, life from death, clean from unclean, order from chaos, and wholeness from partiality or mixture. The following quote from Leviticus expresses the basic ideal of holiness in the people's lives.

24. . . I am the Lord your God; I have separated you from the peoples. 25You shall therefore make a distinction between the clean animal and the unclean, and between the unclean bird and the clean; you shall not bring abomination on yourselves by animal or by bird or by anything with which the ground teems, which I have set apart for you to hold unclean. 26You shall be holy to me; for I the Lord am holy, and I have separated you from the other peoples to be mine. (Leviticus 20:24–26)

The daily rituals of life respected and embodied the distinctions of holiness, so that even ordinary actions like choosing foods, practicing healing and medicine, and ordering family relationships were supposed to reflect the distinctions of holiness and avoid impurity.

In addition to showing the connection between the divine realm and the political realm, and conveying the importance of holiness, religion in the ancient world also played an important role as the set of practices by which human worshippers expressed their reverence toward and dependence on the divine. For ancient Israel, their religious life had both a centralized and a local focus. The texts regularly express how the temple was the central focal point of worship for the people of the nation. Here the priests led worshippers in sacrifices and offerings, rituals that marked agricultural festivals and expressed reverence, thanksgiving, and repentance. The people participated through prayers, bringing donations for appropriate sacrifices, and contributing to support the temple and its personnel. These rituals embodied and symbolized the connections between the people and God and maintained the distinctions of holiness so that the people would be religiously acceptable to God. The book of Psalms contains in effect the prayer and song book of ancient Israel, from the centuries of the temple both before and especially after the exile.

> ¹Come, bless the LORD, all you servants of the LORD,
> who stand by night in the house of the LORD!
> ²Lift up your hands to the holy place
> and bless the LORD.
> ³May the LORD, maker of heaven and earth,
> bless you from Zion. (Psalm 134)

In addition to the central location of the temple in Jerusalem, for much of the period of the preexilic monarchy people in the towns and villages of Israel and Judah also worshipped at local sanctuaries. In these local cult sites, often on a hilltop near a village or town, a priestly family would maintain the small worship site and conduct sacrifices, burn incense, and hear prayers. This passage tells simply about the regular worship at such a site.

> 3Now this man [from the hill country of Ephraim] used to go up year by year from his town to worship and to sacrifice to the Lord of hosts at Shiloh, where the two sons of Eli, Hophni and Phinehas, were priests of the Lord. (1 Samuel 1:3)

In historical writings that emerged later in the preexilic period and in the postexilic period, such local sanctuaries were recognized as part of the life of the people but were condemned as "high places" that kept alive worship of the gods of the previous inhabitants of the land, the Canaanite god Baal and goddess Asherah.

THE WORLD IN THE TEXT: PROPHETS AND SAGES

The religious sphere of ancient Israel included another important aspect of life, the role of the prophets. The writings in both the narrative books that relate a historical account and the books of the prophets that contain collections of prophetic oracles, like Isaiah, Jeremiah, Amos, or Zechariah expressed the role of the prophets to be that of bringing a message from the divine realm to the leaders of the political and religious life of Israel and Judah, as illustrated in the call of the prophet Jeremiah:

> ⁴Now the word of the LORD came to me saying,
> ⁵"Before I formed you in the womb I knew you,
> and before you were born I consecrated you;
> I appointed you a prophet to the nations."
>
> ⁶Then I said, "Ah, Lord GOD! Truly I do not know how to speak, for I am only a boy." ⁷But the LORD said to me,
>
> "Do not say, 'I am only a boy,'
> for you shall go to all to whom I send you,
> and you shall speak whatever I command you.
> ⁸Do not be afraid of them, for I am with you to deliver you,
> says the LORD."
>
> ⁹Then the LORD put out his hand and touched my mouth; and the LORD said to me,
>
> "Now I have put my words in your mouth.
> ¹⁰ See, today I appoint you over nations and over kingdoms,
> to pluck up and to pull down,
> to destroy and to overthrow,
> to build and to plant." (Jeremiah 1:4–10)

This role also fits well against the context of the ancient world, where other societies also recognized the position of visionaries or seers who brought a word from the gods to kings and priests. Prophets often communicated their critique or support of actions and attitudes, and in this way the biblical texts showed how God intervened and communicated with the kings and other leaders of the state. The following passage shows such critical prophetic communication.

> 17When [King] Ahab saw [the prophet] Elijah, Ahab said to him, "Is it you, you troubler of Israel?" 18He answered, "I have not troubled Israel; but you have, and your father's house,

because you have forsaken the commandments of the Lord and
followed the Baals." (1 Kings 18:17–18)

Another social reality that is reflected in the stories and in prophetic
oracles was the fact that, as a typical agrarian society, there was a large
gap between the very few who were the richest members of the social
structure, the king and the governing elite, and the numerous poorest
members, the peasant farmers. Much of the economy was heavily influenced by the actions and control of the elites from the royal household
and its representatives through taxation, the acquisition of land, and the
imposition of duties on trade. The social and economic relationships between the rich and the poor often worked to the advantage of the wealthy
and powerful. The prophets confronted these realities with a word that
God did not approve of such actions.

> [4]Hear this, you that trample on the needy,
> and bring to ruin the poor of the land,
> [5]saying, "When will the new moon be over
> so that we may sell grain;
> and the sabbath,
> so that we may offer wheat for sale?
> We will make the ephah small and the shekel great,
> and practice deceit with false balances,
> [6]buying the poor for silver
> and the needy for a pair of sandals,
> and selling the sweepings of the wheat."
> [7]The Lord has sworn by the pride of Jacob:
> Surely, I will never forget any of their deeds. (Amos 8:4–7)

A final social group within the wider society of ancient Israel de-
serves attention. This was the class of learned and literate persons who
preserved a distinct stream of tradition known as wisdom literature, represented in the Hebrew Bible in the books of Proverbs, Job, and Ecclesiastes. As with other states of the day, this learned class acted as counselors
and sages for the royal house and government, and likely was conversant
with the international cultures of the day as ambassadors and envoys.
Wisdom traditions probably also had roots in the villages and towns of
the countryside, where prudent and resourceful learning and advice was
passed on from generation to generation.

> [8]Hear, my child, your father's instruction,
> and do not reject your mother's teaching;
> [9]for they are a fair garland for your head,

and pendants for your neck. (Proverbs 1:8–9)

In addition to practical advice for daily living about acting wisely, avoiding foolishness, and topics like careful speech, wisdom traditions also reflected on theological issues like the consequences of one's actions, the origins of evil, and unjust suffering. While the basic knowledge of wisdom came from careful observation of life and the teaching of elders, Israel's wisdom traditions also acknowledged the role of reverence before the divine.

> 10The fear of the Lord is the beginning of wisdom,
> and the knowledge of the Holy One is insight. (Proverbs 9:10)

SUMMARY

We have accomplished a review of some basics about the world *behind* the Hebrew Bible and the world *in* the storytelling and poetry of many types of biblical texts. In addition, the review included numerous quotes from the Hebrew Bible itself to show how the social, political, and religious contexts of the writing provided both the background for the stories, poetry, and prophecy as well as the material included in the texts themselves. These realities were the ordinary environment and backdrop of the writing, almost invisible, and yet they powerfully shaped the life of the people and the way that life was portrayed in the texts. Now that you are attuned to these worlds behind and in the text, you will be able to see them as they work in any Hebrew Bible passages you read. And you'll be ready to think about how the Hebrew Bible intersects with the world in front of the text today—in a whole range of situations, from a demonstration supporting refugees to a Bible study on the Psalms.

7

New Testament Study in the Service of Life

HARRY O. MAIER

WHAT ARE THE MARKS of a good conversation?[1] The ability to listen well? A capacity to speak clearly? Thoughtfulness? The search for mutual understanding and illumination? An ability accurately to translate what another person is saying into one's own words and to let the other know he or she is being accurately understood? What ethics do good conversations presuppose? What sort of character is required for fruitful conversation? Patience, honesty, prudence, temperance, goodness, trustworthiness, perhaps even courage and a commitment to values like justice and equity? New Testament study is an invitation to a conversation that implies all of these skills and virtues and several more. The formal study of the Bible entails a host of abilities and knowledge that aims to create thoughtful, engaged, and generous interpreters of Scripture.

The good news is that we are already in conversation with the Bible. Nobody can grow up in the Western world and not have already been shaped by the Scriptures. Even people who have never read or don't believe a word of what the Bible says can't escape from its influence. The

---

1. The approach to interpretation that guides this essay rests on my reading of Gadamer, *Truth and Method*. For a sustained theological engagement and application of Gadamer's methods to biblical interpretation and relation, see Thiselton, *New Horizons in Hermeneutics*.

Bible in general and the New Testament in particular have shaped what we take for granted when we talk about human rights, politics, economics, family relations, and even who we see when we look in the mirror. Whatever people believe or don't believe, scratch the surface a little bit and you will find the legacy of the Bible. This is because, as Northrop Frye once observed, the Bible is a "great code" that has shaped the Western imagination in ways of which we are usually scarcely aware.[2] But if the good news is that we are all already in conversation with the Bible, the bad news is that not all conversations are good ones. When someone either cannot hear or refuses to hear what the other is saying, when a person assumes from the outset what the other *must* be saying, when one cannot accurately reflect back to the other person what he is or she is saying—those are bad conversations. We have all been in those. Conversations can become shouting matches or willful misunderstandings. They can be life-bringing or death-dealing.

There are many different kinds of conversations. We can chat about the weather or discuss wedding vows. These are very different kinds of conversation because much more is at stake in the latter than the former. Similarly, New Testament study is conversation that can take many forms and degrees of earnestness. At times, reading and listening and responding to the New Testament is an act of devotion, used in prayer and worship. At other times, it is important to study the New Testament in an academic setting, treating it like any other historical document. This sometimes even includes taking a critical look at some of the assumptions we might find under the surface, uncovering incentives to violence and oppression, for example.

Theological conversation with the Bible has a distinctive set of features. At heart, at least for Christians, theological conversation is guided by the idea that through the words of the New Testament God has revealed and continues to reveal who God is for us: his people, her whole creation. Looking to the Bible for God's revelation is like going to a famous restaurant known for its outstanding food: there is food everywhere and restaurants all over the place, but *this* place is where you can legitimately expect *great* food. Formal theological study of the New Testament in a school of theology or seminary means learning what the ingredients of this great feast are, and then helping to serve the amazing food the chef has prepared, without dropping the plates on the way or spilling the wine.

2. Frye, *Great Code.*

Incarnational theological study proceeds from the assumption that God serves this banquet in flesh and blood—for Christians, in the Word made flesh in Jesus of Nazareth; the Word who comes to us to bring us life in the sacraments, worship, and discipleship; the Word continuing to be revealed to us in our immediate and lived contexts. This means taking account of our own flesh as well—where we are, our gender, our socio-economic status, our privileges, our theological heritage, and so on. The Word meets us where we are and engages us. This is the *sine qua non* of theological incarnational conversation with the New Testament.

LONG, NOISY, LIFE-GIVING CONVERSATION

There are a few important things to know when embarking upon a conversation with the Bible. The first is that the conversation has been going on for a long time. In the case of the Hebrew Scriptures, it has been running for over four thousand years—and longer than that if you include oral tradition; the New Testament, for two millennia.[3] And it will continue as long as God loves and desires to be in relationship with us and the whole of creation. The Bible begins the conversation with the word "let there be" and ends it with, "I am the Alpha and the Omega, the beginning and the end."

The second thing about this conversation is that it has been a raucous one. The kind of conversation the Bible invites us to imagine is not the measured exchange one might overhear in a university classroom, nor the hushed whispers of a church sanctuary, and absolutely not like the polite exchanges of strangers at a bus stop. No, the Bible's invitation to conversation is rather the kind that takes place at a noisy family meal with all the relatives around the table. There is the weird uncle and the quirky aunt, the strange cousin, the brother who drives you crazy, the sister-in-law you would rather never see again let alone talk to, the parent with the embarrassing stories. Everyone is talking at the same time; some people are trying *not* to talk to each other. Whatever time you arrive—whether late or early—you have a seat at the table and once there you are meant to join in with everyone else. In many ways the Bible itself is the outcome of a centuries-long conversation, first amongst the people who were parts

---

3. For a history of the origins, development, formation, and life of the biblical canon as well as extracanonical literature and then a history of interpretation in Jewish and Christian tradition, see Barton, *Bible*.

of the traditions that came to be written down, and then—after they died—between the people who gathered and edited and then circulated combinations of texts that eventually came to make up the Bible. Like the people around the table, the talk around the canonical table is also rowdy, sometimes with sharp disagreements, at other times with consensus, but always lively.[4]

The third thing to know about this conversation is that it is about life and death.[5] The best conversations are always like that—they matter and to take part in them is to be changed. They are risky conversations because we won't leave them the way we came into them. Some approaches to New Testament study are not risky. They are more like a scientific set of observations about the data without much depth of personal engagement. *Theological* study of the New Testament is not like that—it invites engagement, full immersion, and passionate encounter. Theological engagement with the New Testament does not come dressed in a lab coat; it is a "come as you are" kind of event that we are invited to enter with our commitments.[6] Theological study doesn't ask you to check your prejudices and past experiences at the door. It is these things that make us the conversation partners that we are. We enter this conversation from our unique context, but also expecting to be challenged, excited, angered, confused, and above all called and therefore changed. Christians and Jews believe that God uses the Bible to awaken life within us, to make us more fully human, and to live out what God is calling us to be in this particular moment in history. It is a life-and-death conversation and anyone who

4. The issue of theological diversity in the New Testament and debates on whether there is an overarching unity has furnished biblical scholars with innumerable hours of discussion from the second century onward; for a proposal that champions theological difference, see Morgan, "New Testament Canon and Christian Identity," 151–94; for a chronicle of discussion from the early church onward, see Barton, "Unity and Diversity in the Biblical Canon," 11–26.

5. For a lively treatment of social and existential engagement with the New Testament, see Ekblad, *Guerilla Gospel.*

6. This consideration leaves behind the idea that there is a singular original meaning of biblical texts or that the Bible has a purely historical meaning that we are to discover and then apply and rather sees biblical texts as living entities, generative of meaning—meaning arising from the contexts in which we live. For the relation of social location and interpretation, see Segovia and Tobert, eds., *Reading from This Place,* vols. 1–2. This is, however, more than sociology or autobiography; for Christians it arises from engaging with the biblical witness in the assembly of believers, who together are seeking after the will of God; for excellent theological investigation of this calling to believers, see Davis and Hays, eds., *Art of Reading Scripture.*

studies the Bible as a theologian is always in a process of living and dying, being called out to new horizons and exhorted to leave old ones. This means that this conversation is often messy—there is the mess of us, the mess of history, the mess of the world around us, and, yes, even the holy mess of God, who is revealed through all of the Bible as one who is for us. Nothing is neat and tidy; nothing is well ordered; life is often bewildering and confusing. No one can furnish the Archimedean point that will be the lever to move everything through *the* right interpretation of the New Testament. We will only know the New Testament's word for *us* when we attend to what living and dying are about.

The final thing about this conversation is that it is—to put it frankly—very weird. In the first place, it was first conducted in ancient languages that no one speaks today (Hebrew and Aramaic in the Jewish Bible and Greek in the New Testament; the modern versions of these are derivations of the ancient ones). When we translate things into English we lose subtleties and nuances of meaning, which is why having at least a preliminary acquaintance with ancient languages is a requisite of biblical study. English translations of the Bible tend to remove important aspects of this. For example, from an English translation you would never know that the Gospel of Mark and the book of Revelation are riddled with grammatical errors and ways of putting things that suggest the writers were either not writing in their first languages or not very literate. As Christianity emerged and spread across the Roman Empire, opponents such as the emperor Julian (reigned 361–363 CE) criticized the Greek of the New Testament as "vulgar, ordinary, and in every way trite."[7] Christians furnished a variety of responses to this kind of criticism, including that the Bible was written in a rustic style to reach the masses or even that the Greek New Testament was written in such poor form because God wanted us to look for the meaning behind the words and not get lost in the beauty of expression.[8] These are explanations of embarrassment, but there is a deeper truth to be found in the Greek New Testament's grammar. The way language is spoken has a certain effect on audiences listening to it: sometimes when you are around someone who speaks in a peculiar way, you end up picking up his or her expressions and turns of phrase and you start to sound a little foreign yourself. Weirdness wears

7. The quotation records the criticism of the emperor Julian (reign 361–363 CE) in the apology of Cyril of Alexandria, *Against Julian*, 7.21, as cited and translated by Ceulemens "The Septuagint and Other Translations," 39.

8. For example, Origen, *Philocalia* 4.1–2.

off on you. The New Testament's weirdness invites us to consider strangeness as a way of life: it keeps turning us toward what matters most and keeps that in front of you so long as you keep looking. Its strangeness asks us to consider all the things that matter: life, death, love, sex, even taxes and politics. And these things are expressed in ways charged with metaphors; they are conveyed through stories, and spoken of in ways we don't usually put things. To quote Emily Dickenson, it tells the world "slant."[9] So to be part of this weird conversation means learning how to be weird yourself, to be prepared to find yourself in foreign lands, with strange ways of naming and describing things. How often when you hear someone read a passage from the Bible in church are you not sure whether you should respond "Thanks be to God" when the reading is done or rather, "Say what?"

METHODS, MEANING, AND WHAT YOUR GRANDMA KNOWS

Wherever there have been words to read, there have been people theorizing about how to read them correctly. The problem of "right" methods of interpretation has challenged readers of the Bible for millennia. If I am in a conversation with someone, I can ask whether I am understanding him or her correctly by repeating what I think he or she is saying. There is a to-ing and fro-ing in lived conversation: "I thought you meant this when you said that." "No, you misunderstood me—I meant the opposite." Conversations with texts aren't like that. The person who wrote the text isn't in the room to let us know whether or not we are correctly understanding what she said. Even if she were, there might be things about what she wrote that even she didn't realize she was saying. So people who study the New Testament have spent a good deal of time thinking about what the best methods are for determining meaning in written texts.[10] There is a good deal of debate about what methods are best suited to New

---

9. Dickinson, "Tell all the truth but tell it slant" (1263): "Tell all the truth but tell it slant —/ Success in Circuit lies/ Too bright for our infirm Delight/ The Truth's superb surprise/ As Lightning to the Children eased/ With explanation kind/ The Truth must dazzle gradually/ Or every man be blind —." This model of interpretation is developed by Peterson, *Tell It Slant*.

10. For a sense of the magnitude of methods for biblical interpretation, see the over one hundred encyclopedic entries in McKenzie, *Oxford Encyclopedia of Biblical Interpretation*.

Testament study. Some argue that we should aim at what the author originally intended, and even that if we can get into the mind of the author
we can then determine what God intended when God inspired the writer
to write the words down.[11] Others say that this is a fool's errand—we can
barely know what we intend most of the time, let alone what someone else
did living centuries ago. We ought then to consider not what an author
intended but what the text says and what possibilities of meaning derive
from the text.[12] Another point of view seeks to look to Christian tradition
for the ways in which texts have functioned and been interpreted in the
shaping of theological tradition and the quest for divine illumination in
the church. The conversation is not with the author, but with the host of
witnesses who have been in an ongoing conversation with tradition.[13]
Each of these points of view has a different idea of what texts can mean.
Others contend that, while this is valuable, it can overlook the ideological
interests that helped to shape the mainstream theology of the Christian
tradition. In response, they seek to locate interpretation within the social
realities of those who are engaging in conversation. We ought then to begin with who we are: our socioeconomic status, our gender, what we take
for granted about how the world works, and so on.[14] Often this kind of interpretation has various forms of liberation as its goal. The starting point
is the conviction that in the church's conversation with the New Testament many voices over the centuries (LBTQ, Indigenous, non-European,
people of color, female, the ecological order, etc.) have been silenced by
powerful social and political interests that have used the Bible to violate
and destroy others.[15] New Testament scholars often use the word "criticism" to describe the kinds of things they do when trying to understand
the Bible. "Criticism" does not mean being judgmental; the term rather

11. For a classic exposition with a review of literature, see Kaiser, "Meaning of
Meaning," 27–46.

12. Barthes, "Death of the Author" presents a classic essay. A compendium of essays by various scholars takes up and challenges the pursuit of authorial intention as
the goal of interpretation in Breu, ed., *Biblical Exegesis without Authorial Intention?*

13. Louth, *Discerning the Mystery*; see also Byassee, *Surprised by Jesus Again.*

14. See Segovia and Tolbert, *Reading from This Place*, vols. 1–2, which contains a
host of essays that develop this approach.

15. For example, Botta and Andiñach, eds., *Bible and the Hermeneutics of Liberation*; Gross and West, eds. *Take Back the Word*; Horrell, *Bible and the Environment.*

is intended to communicate a set of objective and systematic methods to bring into relief the ways in which one seeks to read and understand.[16]

There are a variety of types of criticism New Testament scholars use to interpret texts. There is space here to name only a few of them. Since we don't have the original autograph copies of the New Testament, *text criticism* is about assembling from various surviving manuscripts both what the original text said and how differing people read it in ways that resulted in the text being altered over time. *Historical criticism* is a way of reading the Bible that tries to determine the social, culture, sociological, and anthropological contexts and events that resulted in the text being written down and then circulated and understood in certain ways. *Literary criticism* looks for the story the text tells as it crafts the world of the story, with characters, conflicts, climax, and resolution. *Audience-oriented modes of criticism* consider the ways things like the economics, gender, sexuality, religious tradition, and commitments of the interpreter shape how one gleans meaning from the New Testament. Other forms of criticism like *canonical criticism* seek to read a text in the light of the whole scriptural canon and to bring it into conversation with other texts, including those of the broader Christian theological tradition. *Post-structuralist forms of criticism* (something of a misnomer since post-structuralism contests the idea that the term "criticism" denotes in biblical studies) seek to examine the politics of meaning-making from texts, both amongst those who wrote them, within the stories they craft, and amongst the interpreters who seek to recover them. This represents only a few of the kinds of criticism one could name. Disciplined biblical study entails learning about these methods, how they operate, what they can and cannot do, and so on.[17]

Taken together, all this makes for a very eclectic mix of methods and approaches to New Testament study. There are purists who insist upon only one mode of study, but most New Testament scholars seek to be versatile and interdisciplinary. There are some methods that are best suited to one set of questions (for example, historical kinds of questions) and there are others that are better suited to others (for example, existential

16. For an orientation to the term and its meaning, see Barton, *Nature of Biblical Criticism.*

17. The issue of methods and their role in the academic study of the Bible has not escaped cross-examination; for a lively critique, see Moore and Sherwood, *Invention of the Biblical Scholar;* also, playfully earnest, Penner and Lopez, *De-Introducing the New Testament.*

kinds of questions, how we should live, what we should believe, who God is), and then again there are those that dedicated to issues of power and oppression. This is only a small taste of the kinds of questions and methods New Testament study engages. In keeping with the family table metaphor described above, we might think of this as the tools for cooking the meal and serving it up.

Students new to these tools often find them unsettling. Some students are scandalized by the results produced using these kinds of methods. They are challenged, for example, by the idea that not every word attributed to Jesus is something he actually said, or that not everything that purports to come from the pen of an apostle was actually written by him. They are told the Bible contradicts itself. They are challenged to reconsider traditional interpretations of biblical passages and to embrace new meanings. Some fear that studying the Bible at theological schools risks losing one's way and one's faith in God. Sometimes it even happens that after attending a few classes in New Testament a student returns to his church and tells people that what they've been taught to believe is wrong and naïve.

Then there is another kind of student who revels in questioning everything and who delights in the fact that everything should have a big question mark put over it: Isn't the story of Jesus a myth? Isn't the whole church just one big oppressive institution? Isn't agnosticism on most matters better than professions of faith?

There are two kinds of confusion going on in these students. The first is to confuse credulity with faith. Faith is not the ability, to quote *Alice in Wonderland's* White Queen, to believe "as many as six impossible things before breakfast." On the other side, neither is the capacity to be excited by skepticism faith. Faith is ultimately not what someone can or cannot believe. Like conversation, it is about a relationship, and finally it is about trust. The New Testament does not seek to argue that God is trustworthy and knowable; it simply assumes that. It is preaching to the choir. While methods and scholarly opinions are important in the theological study of the New Testament, far more important is the relationship of trust that the New Testament calls forth. It is because of the trustworthiness of God that the New Testament assumes that it is possible to be an engaged, thoughtful, and generous interpreter of Scripture.

This leads to a small observation about what your (well at least my) grandmother knows. Few people spend time studying the Bible in a systematic, academic way. For most people, the truth of the New Testament is found amidst the challenges of living everyday life. They are not very worried about when, where, and why the New Testament's writings were composed. They want to know what God is saying to them through the words of Scripture to help find a way through today. This brings about a certain paradox in that it is possible for someone who has never spent a moment of formal study of the Bible to know more about its contents than someone who has a PhD in it and has authored dozens of books about it. The person who desires to hear what the New Testament says is well advised to learn to listen to those who have walked closely with the Scriptures—especially those who have experienced times of suffering.

NEW TESTAMENT CONSPIRACY?
CONCERNING CANON AND SCRIPTURE

We have written of conversations, methods, meanings, and faith, but there is an elephant in the room that we so far haven't addressed. Why study the New Testament at all? Wasn't the New Testament created by a group of largely small-minded white men bent on securing their power by drawing up a list of books that conformed to their own prejudices, throwing everything else in the fire, and hunting down the people who opposed them as heretics?

There is a popular misconception about the emergence of the New Testament that the list of twenty-seven books that comprises the canon was drawn up in the fourth century, guided by an emperor (Constantine) who wanted to consolidate his rule by assuring that everyone would read a Bible whose contents he and the powerful bishops who controlled the church said were divinely inspired.[18] This is an entirely fictional account and, aside from fabricating history, it is mistaken in a number of important ways. In the first case, there never was a meeting in which the contents of the New Testament were settled at a church council of bishops, and certainly not by an emperor. The emergence of the New Testament came about through a long, organic process. The books that make up the New Testament were not so much decided upon as recognized by the fact that they were believed to be used universally across the church and were written in the first couple of generations after Jesus' death and resurrection.[19] This is not to suggest that the widespread usage of a set

18. A popular version of this can be found in Brown, *Da Vinci Code*.

19. For a thorough historical account, McDonald, *Formation of the Bible*, and

of writings did not emerge within a context of complicated social and local political circumstances, only to state that the process wasn't guided by a heavy-handed imperial process. A strict understanding of the term "canon" as a word to describe the set list of books that make up the Bible in opposition to others did not emerge until the seventeenth century.[20] In the earlier period "canon" (Greek *kanōn*) was a word that meant a measuring stick or ruler. As early Christian theologians came to use it to describe Christian thought and practice, it was used to indicate the limits of apostolic teaching and what did or did not conform to it. Canon here was a means of quality control rather than a set of fixed ideas or writings. This has resulted in some wide disagreement about what should constitute the writings we find in the Bible. Some Eastern churches to this day reject the inclusion of the book of Revelation. In his preface to the German translation of New Testament in 1522, Martin Luther famously called the book of James an "epistle of straw" and said that the book of Revelation was neither inspired by nor communicated Jesus Christ. The Roman Catholic Church and the worldwide Anglican Communion look to the Apocrypha for wisdom and preach on it. In all cases, canon as measure or guide of what is true is operative.

There is a second observation to make about this theory that an emperor and powerful male bishops set about to decide that only those things that supported their authority should be in the New Testament. The fact is, much of the contents of the Christian Bible are directly opposed both to totalitarian political rule and the absolute authority of church officials. This is a book where Roman authorities crucify its main protagonist, where disciples are at loggerheads with each other, and that describes the emperor as a beast and minion of Satan—a rather poor set of choices for a powerful elite wanting to assure mindless obedience to church and state. It would be more accurate to say that the biblical canon was formed *in spite of* the machinations of institutional church and state authorities.

Even so, there was of course a vast amount of literature produced in the first centuries of the Common Era that did not become part of what we today know as the Bible. Some of this literature is known as Christian Apocrypha (from the Greek word meaning "written outside or alongside

---

McDonald, *Formation of the Biblical Canon*, vol. 2.

20. These issues are taken up in the excellent essay of Gamble, "New Testament Canon." The volume of essays also offers orientation to the contemporary scholarly discussion (see McDonald and Sander, *Cannon Debate*).

of"). These include legends about the apostles, writings that describe the end of the world, narratives about Jesus' boyhood, and so on. (What did Jesus do between his infancy and his first appearances in the Gospels? There were plenty of people willing to offer an account!) These writings are often entertaining and they tell us much about what people in the early church believed and did. There is an entire discipline dedicated to the study of this literature.[21]

Aside from the apocryphal writings, there are a number of texts discovered in 1945 near the Upper Egyptian town of Nag Hammadi that are popularly known as Gnostic gospels—a misnomer because not all of them are Gnostic, nor are they all gospels.[22] The content of these writings help us to understand the diversity of early beliefs about Jesus and some of it even sheds important light on the teachings of the historical Jesus. Still, popular conspiracy theories abound around this literature—for example, that it contains things kept under lock and key (usually in the Vatican!) because the church wants nobody to know about them. Of course, it is impossible to prove that writings are *not* hidden away in some secret vault somewhere, but then it is also impossible to prove that *no one* has ever been abducted by an alien. The more important point here is this: over the centuries, the New Testament has been an irreducible source for productivity, reflection, and imagination. It makes us want to know more and it invites us to imagine more. Part of learning how to study the New Testament theologically is to harness imagination and to help others imagine what the world and life looks like when seen through the eyes of New Testament writings and teachings as well as other witnesses that represent the diversity of early Christ religion.

This brings us to the limits of the canon. Is the canon closed? Could it be emended and supplemented? Why can't we add new books to the New Testament canon? What if we discovered another gospel written by Jesus himself—would we want to include that in new editions of the New Testament? Should the New Testament include Martin Luther King's "I Have a Dream" speech? How about the American Bill of Rights, or the UN Declaration of Indigenous Rights and Freedoms? What about great poetry? Once one raises the question, a host of others follows What would be the criteria for including other writings? Would it be a form

21. For an excellent introduction to the vast primary literature and bibliography, see Burke, *Introduction to the Christian Apocrypha.*

22. For the primary texts with critical introductions, see Meyer, ed, *Nag Hammadi Scriptures.*

of cultural hegemony to include writing from one part of the world and not another? Who would decide this and what process would be used to determine it? Lurking behind the question of a closed canon is a popular misconception. The canon is *not* a closed list; it is rather the outline of a trajectory (or several of them). The two testaments say that if you want to talk and think about God, here are the parameters. God sounds like *this*; and so people who talk about God should sound like this too.

In an important sense, then, the canon is not closed—it is rather open-ended. In the ancient church Christians distinguished between "canon" and "scripture." "Canon" in the first instance described—as we saw—a measure of belief, circulated orally at first, then gradually gathered and recognized in particular writings, and refined in creeds. "Scripture," however, referred to a much more organic phenomenon, namely, what the Holy Spirit inspired and what was valuable for teaching, exhortation, and admonition. The canon may have been defined in a certain way, but scripture was far more organic.[23]

Today, the words "canon" and "scripture" are largely synonymous, but if we allow the ancient distinction, new possibilities arise. It would mean that the Scriptures remain open and are guided by a certain set of texts found in the Bible that act more like hedges or boundaries than strict rules. For Christians, this means that when, in the Holy Spirit, one proclaims what is in the Bible, one is continuing to generate scripture in this more open-ended, organic sense. Thus we might say that a great poem, speech, lost writing, and so on *can* be scripture, i.e., a means by which God reveals God's self to us. And we know this because it will sound like what we find in the Bible, or communicates the same set of meanings we encounter there. At the heart of these claims is that God wants to be known and wants us to know one another and ourselves in the light of what God is doing in the world. That is why we study the Bible theologically in the first place. God can use all sorts of things to reveal God's self to us and God doesn't always use words or things written down to do so.

---

23. Gamble, *New Testament Canon*, 15–19 furnishes an excellent account of the relation of the terms and their distinction as adopted here.

GETTING READY TO CHANGE

To study of the Bible is to engage in a conversation in the service of life. The New Testament in particular and the Bible in general reveal a God aching for conversation and longing for able interlocutors. Anyone who comes to the New Testament for theological study should be ready to join his or her voice in the raucous conversation about God's love for us and for the world, ready to be changed, ready to be turned away from death toward life.

8

Before Studying Homiletics and Biblical Hermeneutics

What You Need to Know

Jason Byassee

No one is ready for seminary. I certainly was not.

I say this because over the years I have often heard new students in theological schools worry that they are not ready. I most often hear it from second-career students who long ago studied something else that required much less reading and do not feel academically prepared. I sometimes hear it from students who have been marginalized in some way, whether because of gender or race or orientation, and understandably worry about getting marginalized again in graduate school. Sometimes folks are just naturally anxious about a new challenge. Honestly, I worry about new students who think they *are* ready. Reality usually hits them harder as they face new demands in quantity and sophistication of reading and writing and seminary can knock them right out of a fledgling vocation.

It is no new concern that students are not ready for seminary. It is no new fear to suffer from imposter syndrome either. One of my older professors in seminary spoke of an elderly New Testament scholar who taught him two generations ago. This teacher was concerned his incoming students only looked the part in their maleness and their uniform flattop haircuts and their whiteness and their formal suits. So he spent some two-thirds of his introductory class giving them the history of ancient Greece, Alexander the Great's bellicose wanderings around the ancient world, the empires he left behind to his generals, and so on. His earlier-career students used to arrive in seminary with something of a classical education. They had some preparation in Greek and Latin and ancient history. But those days were gone. This professor was worried about the lost foundation and tried to build it fast, single-handedly, before getting around to Judaism and Jesus and the Bible. You will not be surprised to learn that this did not work. When Jesus said those who do not listen to him or put his words into practice are like builders of a house on sand, he did not mean to learn your classical history first (go and check me on this: Matthew 7:24–27).

When I got to graduate school in the mid-1990s, I had majored in history. But US history hardly prepared me for theological education, with its heavy focus on the Bible, ancient languages, ancient history, ancient this and ancient that. I had an early conversation with my school's most renowned church historian, David Steinmetz. We met in church, and I asked him if he had any advice for a novice. He shook his head and sighed, heavily. "Lots of new students do not even know the differences between Plato and Aristotle," he lamented, doing me the favor of assuming I did. I laughed, repressing inner terror. Then I went home and looked up Plato and Aristotle. I mean, I knew their *names*, but I certainly didn't know the *differences* between them. Why didn't anyone tell me this was a prerequisite of some sort?!

In truth, it was not. Education in the liberal arts tradition is about learning how to learn, not about knowing everything already. Steinmetz himself made sure by the end of his church history class we knew *what the church thought* of both ancient Greek teachers, how we received them, what new purpose we put them to.[1] He did not reassure me at that first meeting. He did unwittingly scare me into the library. Which is no bad thing. I later came to understand the sort of education Steinmetz and some in his generation and before still came from. Scholastically inclined boys might start studying Greek and Latin *in secondary school*. Some

1. NB: it is a good thing to know whether the church was accurate in its reading of Plato and Aristotle as well, but one can really only learn one massive set of material at a time!

came from homes that still spoke German. By the time they got to Harvard or Oxbridge, they could keep up with classically trained professors. A very few people still study this way. I remember asking two teachers I admired if I should switch gears and study patristics. One told me she had learned Greek in high school. The other told me he learned Latin before kindergarten. The clear implication: I was too old to begin the training.

Here is what they did not tell me: university education has changed enormously. It was not my individual fault I did not know this or that language or huge swath of history. Fields of academic inquiry had mushroomed into thousands of alternatives from the day when being an educated gentleman meant Greek, Latin, and antiquities. I had studied something else, and done pretty well, actually, in modern US history at an expensive and elite school, thank you very much. But you may have heard that folks who like ancient languages and history have a bit of snobbishness about them. They like to foist this on unsuspecting neophytes. It can come across to hearers as a *moral* judgment. But not knowing something *before being educated* is no moral flaw. It is an educational opportunity. And a moral one. To dive for the first time into reservoirs of wisdom that have irrigated all of Western civilization for millennia can be a thrill. As long as we, the professorial gatekeepers, don't block you from taking the initial plunge.

I was not ready for seminary. You are not ready for seminary. And in truth, if you knew every language there is and all of ancient history, you would still not be ready for seminary. Because in this place we study the living God. We make no apology for demanding the study of history and languages. Every church and every religious group I know examines candidates for leadership partly on whether they know a body of material well enough. That knowledge is necessary, but not sufficient. To be a religious leader you have to be more than a living search engine. You have to love God and want to serve the world. The Abrahamic faiths believe that God acts in history. When we study history and language, we are searching for footprints, traces, patterns. Here is how God has acted before. The goal is to learn to detect how God might act anew. One of my teachers, the great preacher Will Willimon, lamented that in his generation seminary made students unable or unwilling to preach in a trailer park. They might have come from such people, but with their erudition they will not sink to such activities that are beneath them. But Methodism, the tradition he and I share, comes from lower-middle-class people. It was never designed to be a few privileged people in clerical collars navel-gazing and contemplating the blessed sacrament. Methodism does its work by ministering with the poor, by asking awkward questions in small groups ("Who sinned this week? *You* first!"), by preaching for conversion, not church membership. We are a revivalist sect. If we are not reviving anybody, then why are we there? I had to go to seminary to learn to talk like that.

The only times I showed up for church in Methodist land, I was bored out of my mind. It took a Baptist camp for me to have a personal conversion experience and begin to take God seriously (my colleague Rabbi Laura Duhan-Kaplan says you can ask a rabbi *where* they went to Jewish camp, not whether). I have since dived as far down as I can in seminaries on this continent, adjunct teaching at five and teaching full-time at another now. They are amazing places and I love them. And they are not enough. They were never meant to be enough. They are institutions that serve the church. And what does the church need from its leaders? Well, everything. There are very few moments when a church says, "We need this from our pastors," when the seminary can say, "Sorry, we don't do that." Bible and theology. Check. Scripture. Right. Pastoral care and preaching. Roger. Administration and leadership. Righto. Evangelism and church growth. Indeed. Finances and music. Of course. Seminaries have mushroomed in areas of academic expertise the same way all of higher education has. My own field, homiletics, is still not considered a proper field of academic inquiry in some quarters, especially in Europe, but of course we teach it—how could we not, future preachers? So we keep adding necessary things, but we have never dropped anything. And you only get three full-time years with us (often stretched out longer—appropriately—as folks serve churches or work to pay for it or to support family). There is no way for any institution to make you all expert in all those things. None of us faculty is expert in all those things. Maybe we are in one or two.

This is why I am committed to a liberal arts vision of theological education. We do not try to teach you everything you need to know. How could we? "Theology" is, etymologically, a word about God. We do not stop there; we teach about all the things God has made—creation. And we teach about the ways God is renewing all the things God has made, and how the church is to align with that remaking work. Anyone who claims full expertise in God and all things is either a liar or a fool. Saint Augustine, the late-fourth/early-fifth-century north African church father, who you'll come to learn a great deal more about, put it this way in one sermon: "If you understand it, it is not God."[2] We could understand an idol, a thing we make with our hands, but Israel's tradition is clear: things we make with our hands are not worthy of worship (check out Isaiah 44:9–20 on this; it is bracing reading—if, like me, you are trying to recover from idolatry). The definition of liberal arts is always changing, like all other created things (only God never changes). In classical antiquity and medieval Europe, the seven fields of liberal arts study were grammar, rhetoric, logic, and then, slightly less importantly, geometry, arithmetic, music, and astronomy. Augustine at one point wanted to write a book about all seven in light of his newfound Christian faith. He wrote a fascinating book on music and all the truths it relates to us about God, and then never made it to the other six.[3] Education is always incomplete. It is interesting what we still consider essential—grammar and math indeed; logic and rhetoric and music and astronomy are all elective now. (Note: I do rhetoric for a living.) When I was in college a liberal arts education was described as learning how to learn. There was no pretense to teach us all there is to know in arts and sciences. The goal was to teach us to be lifelong learners, students by disposition, people curious about all things, and committed to that learning being in service to others. This is a formerly Christian college that does not now know or care that that set of commitments is thoroughly steeped in its Christian heritage. But my teachers were fundamentally right. That is what we do here at VST. We teach you how to learn whatever you need to learn to lead where you're called.

I teach two fields that are often quite separate: homiletics and biblical hermeneutics. I have two words in my title that put off anyone without a master's degree. "Homiletics" means preaching. In some churches they speak of what the priest delivers as a "homily." It is the Greek-derived English word for the same thing as the Latin-derived word "sermon." Homiletics is the study of preaching. You will often be asked what you do by people you meet. I am told in some cultures this is almost considered rude—ask about someone's family and home before you ask how they make money—but we live in North America at least for now. When I am asked this, I am tempted to dodge. I remember one well-meaning relative asking what it meant that I study theology, and I reverted to psychology: I

---

2. Augustine, "Sermon 117.5," 211.

3. See Augusting, "On Music," 169–384.

am trying to help people adjust to their lives a little better. At other times we have tried to dodge into sociology: we want to understand society's problems and make things better. But I was studying theology. I wish I had replied, "I study God." I did not, because I know they would have been horrified. Is that not arrogant? Extremist? Dangerous? No, it is not; it is the most life-giving thing there is, or rather, God is the only source of life, and of all good things. Then we would be having an actual conversation, a step past small talk. You will respond that you study theology, so as to preach, teach, lead, advocate for social justice, whatever it is—say that. Claim it. It is weird. Delight in that.

One of the moments in homiletics that I value most from the last generation or two is a directive from Eugene Lowry, one of the deans of my field. He advised his students, when they are in the biblical text, to *look for the weird*.[4] Do not run from it or dodge it; run toward it, and bring your listeners with you. Not for salacious effect, the way we rubberneck at an accident on the highway. Augustine noticed that same disposition in his day and called it *curiositas*, venal and prurient interest, quite contrary to the sort of curiosity I'm encouraging in liberal arts education.[5] But look for the weird *because that's where God is at work*. The calling of Israel and the gospel of Jesus Christ are unutterably weird. When God wants to repair the world we have ruined, God calls a family through whom to bless all the other families on earth. When God wants to follow up and fulfill this calling to Israel and blessing of the world, God steps into history in person in Jesus of Nazareth. God in Jewish flesh died and resurrected to save. When God wants to renew us, God calls us into the church, alongside people we would never have chosen and don't want to be caught dead with, teaching us new languages we don't even know how to speak. That is what is genuinely weird—the God who works in love to save. Find that place in every passage of Scripture: God moving toward us to repair us and our neighbor, especially the neighbor we do not like. A campus-minister friend of mine here at UBC compares this to looking at the picture on the puzzle box. Each individual piece fits into a larger picture. We often lose that larger picture of the God who loves creation into being and redeems it at great personal cost. Show how each small piece fits into that larger picture. And then you have a sermon. Almost.

4. Lowry, *Sermon*, 95.

5. See here Griffiths, *Intellectual Appetite*, 19–22.

A sermon is a word filtered through the Scriptures. And every passage of Scripture is particular. Think of each as a part of the diet that God has arranged for the church. Something in each passage is essential to the health of the whole body. As a preacher, your charge is to offer the body that particular passage's health- and life-giving offering, without which the body will suffer. So, your work as an exegete is to notice the particular in the passage. What does it say that is not quite said anywhere else in Scripture? What will they only hear through that passage on that day? And of course you are eating too. "I am feeding you with what I am feasting on myself," Augustine tells his charges at one point.[6] A sermon is also aimed at a particular group of people at a particular time. Who is that group? Where are they headed in mission and ministry? What word do they need for this moment in time? A sermon is not a word in a vacuum, timeless, sealed off from other human beings. As a professor of mine used to ask, is "Deutero"-Isaiah right when it asks us to "Comfort ye, comfort ye my people" (40:1–11, KJV) or "First" Isaiah when it denounces us for "grinding the face of the poor"? (3:15).[7] Well, both are, depending on who *we* are, and what the living God of Israel wishes to speak to us at any moment in time. You study God, remember? You also study your people, but not like a pathologist studies a dead body; rather, like any leader who loves those she is charged to lead.[8] Notice what they need, what you need, what God is always offering. And of course what God is always offering is . . . more of God.

I accent this search for the weird partly because mainline Protestant denominations have a penchant for the Synoptic Gospels. A friend of mine reports on a rabbi friend of his saying mainline church sermons follow a pattern: "Something interesting happened to me this week . . . an op-ed in the *Times* said . . . a cartoon in the *New Yorker* said . . . but perhaps Jesus said it best _____."[9] In other words, Jesus is just an illustration of what all right-thinking, inclusive people already know. That sermon pattern depends on a text about Jesus overturning a supposedly hidebound convention (often preached with unwitting anti-Judaism). There

6. Augustine, "Sermon 339.4," 282. I was directed here by Harmless, *Augustine in His Own Words*, 156.

7. I am channeling a vignette from James M. Efird at Duke, with whom I took classes from 1996 to 1999.

8. It's David Steinmetz's image, often repeated in classes at Duke Divinity School while I was there (1996–2005).

9. This is Martin Copenhaver's vignette.

are less nefarious reasons: the lectionary has a sort of funneling effect where most sermons I hear and preach in these churches come from Matthew, Mark, or Luke. We tend to avoid John—the lectionary does. We tend to duck out of preaching on Paul—isn't he sexist and homophobic, and don't we know better now? Revelation is just scary. What are the Pastoral Epistles anyway? And the Old Testament is nearly eclipsed altogether. We know how *not* to approach Israel's scripture. Do not be supersessionist. Do not be naïve about historical-critical considerations. Do not impose meaning on the text that is not there—all professors have a mini-sermon against eisegesis, reading into the text, as opposed to exegesis, garnering out of it. With all those warnings we tend not to wander into that foreboding forest. The result, Old Testament scholar Ellen Davis writes, is the loss of the Old Testament to the church, a loss as tragic as the loss of a friend.[10] Friendships make us who we are—discipleship is ultimately friendship with Jesus Christ, one that makes us different, new, and even makes him different, new, as more members are added to his body. Friends, let me exhort you, preach from Israel's scripture. It will save your ministry and maybe the church. When the church becomes forgetful of Israel's Scripture, we tend to become forgetful of our Jewish roots. We can only wonder what if liberal Protestantism in Germany had remained in love with Israel's Scripture, as Dietrich Bonhoeffer and Karl Barth, each in their own ways, realized it had failed to do before the rise of Nazism. As you read Israel's Scripture you will find yourself with surprising friends because you will need help with interpretation—Jewish friends, with whom I hope you'll read Scripture, ask questions, get to know one another's families, and bless your community together.

My other obscure title is "hermeneutics," the discipline of reading texts. It comes from the Greek god Hermes, etymologically, the messenger god. But the discipline comes from the church. Friedrich Schleiermacher coined it in nineteenth-century Germany. Look him up and study him—almost all our debates have their footnotes to Schleiermacher, whom I confess I have never read carefully.[11] We're all still learning. The church in modern Europe was struggling to take into account new knowledges and

10. Davis, "Losing a Friend."

11. For a brief sketch, see the introduction in Ford and Muers, eds., *Modern Theologians*, 8–9. Ford and his fellow Cambridge theologian Sarah Coakley have been more careful to register their appreciation for Schleiermacher than some of their fellow Karl Barth–informed present-day theologians have been. Barth himself was careful to critique Schleiermacher only after noting just how much he had learned from him.

to say why Christianity is still true and worth following. Schleiermacher wrote for his friends, who were what he called the "cultured despisers" of faith. Sound familiar? Well-educated bourgeois Germans who thought they had outgrown Christianity. And he reduced Christianity to a feeling. A sense of awe before the All. There is something to that. Find me a human being without any experience of awe and I'll say you've found a corpse. A bridge is built there. But to what, and at what cost? Christian faith also claims to be about truth, reality, the way things are, and about morals, ethics, how we should behave in light of that truth. But look at what he was confronting. New biological data from Darwin and his disciples. New anthropological data from the Americas and Africa about people far different than Europeans had ever imagined. New biblical data about archaeology and other religions that seemed to cast doubt on the unique authority of the Bible. Trying to make sense of that avalanche of information birthed hermeneutics: the discipline of how to read any text at all. It is its own unique field now, with great contributors, some not so great. My own effort is to learn hermeneutics from the church fathers and mothers, those teachers closest to the incarnation up through the first eight centuries of the church's life. That's just what interests me; you will find what interests you—there's divine whimsy and serendipity in that; best not to fight it. G.K. Chesterton wrote that we moderns think of tradition and democracy as polar opposites. Actually, he countered, tradition is the most democratic thing there is. Because tradition means even dead people get to vote. It counters, in his matchless phrase, "the arrogant oligarchy of those who happen to be walking around above ground."[12] I am also guided by Alasdair MacIntyre's description of what a tradition is: it is an argument about the goods of the tradition.[13] Tradition does not only bear to us immutable facts that we must passively accept. It is no single voice—it is a cacophony of voices. Voices within the Scriptures not only disagree, but they fight against one another. Ancient Christianity tries to make sense of Scripture's strong claims that God is only one, and its claim that Jesus is (also?) Lord. Saint Augustine leaves unresolved what seem to be two conflicting claims: that God does all the work in human salvation, and also that we are expected to grow in holiness. The Reformation is partly a split in which Protestants and Catholics each take a portion of Augustine's thought and array it against another portion. The Vancouver

---

12. Chesterton, Orthodoxy, 39.

13. MacIntyre, Whose Justice? Which Rationality?, 12.

School of Theology enters this millennia-long debate at a specific point in history. In the early twentieth century mainline Protestant denominations were trying to grow toward one another ecumenically. This bore fruit in the creation of the United Church of Canada. At one point, Anglicans were anticipating joining in—so their being a founding denomination at VST represents a hoped-for conciliation that has not quite come yet (the sticking points were bishops and the Eucharist—pay attention in church history and worship and polity classes for more details!). Those denominations are all in distress now in the early twenty-first century across North America, and no one is sure of the way forward. Enter: you. Your calling and gifts and particular passions. What is God calling you to, that God can only do through you?

This conversation is not without barriers. All freedom happens within bounds; all creativity takes place within limits. The church will not go back on our confession that Jesus Christ is divine, *homoousion* with the Father, promulgated in 325 CE and our strongest ecumenical foundation across space and time ever since, over against Arianism (the alternative teaching that he is a very important person, but not divine). We will not undo our commitment to Jesus Christ being fully human, one of us, to save, despite efforts to say he only seems to be (Gnosticism), or there are really two persons in Christ, so that you can isolate when God acts over against when the person Jesus acts (Nestorianism). In mainline Protestantism we are not going back on our commitments to ordain women and be open to the stranger, nor on our commitment to ecumenism—being part of the one church for which Jesus prays in John 17. One great twentieth-century theologian, the Dominican Herbert McCabe, said we do not know what Christians will believe in the twenty-fourth century. We do know they will not be Arians or Nestorians![14] Those roads are closed off. But look at all these other roads we could try! Orthodoxy is freeing; heresy is limiting. It is good to know which ways lead to cliffs. We have almost gone over the side before. All these other ways are wide open. It is no curb on freedom to rope off a way that leads to death.

Theological debate is like the long-term disagreements, grudges, jokes, and delights of a great family. These are your crazy uncles and aunts, grandmothers and fathers. I know you'd rather choose somebody else besides the ones you have at times; who doesn't? But they make you you. You learn from them who to be and who not to be. And at some point you

---

14. Quoted in Owens, "Don't Talk Nonsense."

realize, hey, you have a voice too. You can push back, and influence them, not just the reverse. Within VST we have our own raucous debates. How much can and should we learn from evangelicals and Catholics? Does our commitment to openness to LGBTQ people, which we are not going back on, require us to forfeit that ecumenical commitment in which our institution was born? We have been committed to Indigenous studies for a third of a century. Often Indigenous Canadians are more evangelical than mainline ones. How do we remain genuinely open, and not open only to those as open as we are? Does VST's commitment to interreligious study mean a decentering of Christianity at this institution? Most institutions go that way—sliding from Christian specificity to religion in general. But we are a Christian institution, literally owned by the United Church, the Anglican Church, and, with our confederated college, St. Andrew's Hall, the Presbyterian Church in Canada. It is from our Christian commitment that we reach out beyond the walls of the church. This is no abdication of who we are; it is an expression of it. And we find that those who relate to Jesus also end up in relationships they wouldn't have chosen, that destabilize who they are, because the only stable center is him.

And, as you can tell, all of these doctrines have a bearing on how we preach. Theology is a servant of preaching. It is meant to help the church's teaching and preaching office know what to say, what not to say, even (as in my discipline, homiletics) *how* to say it. Take, for example, the Rt. Rev. Michael Curry's sermon at the royal wedding in the spring of 2018. The sermon was viewed by billions of people, many millions of whom may never have heard a Christian sermon in their lives. Few would have heard one that good. In just thirteen minutes, Curry gave a vision of love that doesn't just unite royals; it also overcomes hatred and violence. It is a love nurtured in the black church from days of slavery to freedom, demonstrating to the world that Jesus lives and reigns. It is a love conversant with modern problems and unafraid to speak to them (in front of the queen and Elton John, no less!). For a moment the world was captivated . . . by a sermon. Most of us will not have an opportunity quite that grand (but thank God Bishop Curry did not throw away his shot). But when we preach another audience is there, perhaps a grander one: all the angels and saints. The worst sinners imaginable, whom Jesus claims as friends. And the folks gathered you can see with your physical eyes. And you and me. That is good company.

That company lured me in to study. I realized the great teachers of the church were reading the same sources as me—principally the

Bible—and trying to figure out the Christian life in their light. When Thomas Aquinas writes about usury, lending money at interest, his intensity quickens. He writes angry. He is adamant, passionate, prophetic: no Christian should lend money at interest. The Scriptures are clear; the tradition gives no good counterargument; what more is there to say? Clearly this is a live issue in his time, and he is impatient with those who want a moral workaround.[15] It had other deleterious effects—it left moneylending as something Christians couldn't do, but needed doing, so Jews often stepped in, and we Christians then stereotyped them as money obsessed. History is no accumulation of ever-greater achievements—it is full of holiness and sin both, just like we are. Karl Barth reworks the doctrine of election against Augustine's view that God chooses some for salvation and some for damnation.[16] He finds a Jesus Christ–shaped hole in that doctrine. Who is this nameless, faceless God who arbitrarily sends some to heaven and some to fire? The God we have in Scripture has a name: Jesus. He has a face, and it is turned in love toward humanity. Barth suggests that God chooses damnation for himself in Christ's passion, and salvation for humanity in his resurrection. All the scriptural verbs are there, but they're moved around in the sentence. I'm still not sure Barth is right about that. But I'm utterly fascinated by it. It allows me to preach the doctrine of election as good news, not, as Luther countered, to muzzle it for fear it will cause despair. Barth had his own demons. We all do; we just can rarely see our own as well as we can see others, especially those long dead. But I think he may have been right on this. The reason these two and countless others, known and unknown, argue in similar ways is that they are doing theology in service to the church. They take God seriously. I was trying to do the same in the churches to which I was assigned, first as a summer intern then as a part-time rural pastor. I had a sense that whatever theology I did during the week at the university had better matter for the tobacco farmers and lawyers I was pastoring; and the life of faithfulness sought in the parish had better matter to the theology I was reading in the library and debating in the classroom. It was a catastrophe ever to sever the life of the mind from the life of worship, but sever it we have. Christ is presently mending back together every good thing we human beings have ruined, including this tear in the fabric of goodness. VST exists as a sign, instrument, and foretaste of that great work of repair.

15. For more on Aquinas and money, see Franks, *He Became Poor.*

16. See this famous section of Barth's doctrine of God: Barth, *Church Dogmatics,* II/2, 3–506.

Theology is also a servant of the church's worship. Pastors will get asked to baptize someone again who was already baptized as an infant. We will be asked if another name can be used in baptism. We will be asked to speak words at the holiest, most frightening, most human moments of people's lives: in the hospital room, the prison cell, the maternity ward, the grave, in front of the media. Let those be words of life. Ben Myers's terrific recent book on the Apostles' Creed argues that Jesus did not come to start a new religion, or to enlighten super-secret special people and not the *hoi polloi*. He is a remarkable teacher, but most of what he teaches (I'd argue all) is borrowed from his forebears in Israel. He came to bring life. His healings and exorcisms and self-offering are an undoing of the way of death. John's Gospel makes especially clear: what is in him is life, and that is light for all people (John 1:1–5). One tip from both hermeneutics and homiletics: speak of Jesus in the present tense. Don't imagine he is tragically unavailable, hidden behind archaic structures of the past. Don't speak hypothetically: if Jesus were alive today, he would think just like me. No, he is alive, and he judges all of us, and that judgment yields a verdict of grace, resurrection, new creation. And you, dear preacher, get to talk about that to whoever will listen.

And that is a life worth living.

9

Stick to Your Ticket:
Exegesis and Ethics

MARI JOERSTAD

EXEGESIS: WHERE DO YOU BEGIN?

WHEN I INTRODUCE STUDENTS to exegesis, I start by showing an early scene from the movie *Harry Potter and the Philosopher's Stone*. In it, Rubeus Hagrid accompanies Harry Potter to King's Cross Station, from where Harry is to take a train to Hogwarts School of Witchcraft and Wizardry. Looking at his watch, Hagrid realizes that it is later than he thought and that he needs to leave, so he gives Harry his train ticket and the following bit of advice:

> "Here's your ticket. Stick to it, Harry, that's very important, Harry. Stick to your ticket."

Harry looks at his ticket, a piece of parchment about the size of a bottle label, printed in gold and black, and screws up his face in confusion: "Platform 9]¾? But Hagrid, there must be a mistake. This says platform 9¾. There's no such thing, is there?"

When Harry looks up, Hagrid is gone. Harry is alone at King's Cross Station, pushing a trolley stacked with luggage and holding a caged owl, with no idea how to get to Platform 9 ¾.

At this point, Harry could have done a number of things. He could have panicked and cried, which is what I think I'd have done. He could have rounded up that unlikely platform number and gone looking for his train on platform 10. He could have asked for directions to platform 9 ¾, which he tries only to be ridiculed. He could have concluded that the ¾ was a typo, and gone to platform 9. None of these options would have gotten him to the right platform.

Fortunately for Harry, he overhears another family on their way to Platform 9 ¾, and with their help he is able to find it, board the train, and go to Hogwarts. All because he does what Hagrid says: he sticks to his ticket.

What does this have to do with exegesis? The analogy I discuss with my students is that sticking to your ticket is like sticking to the details of the text. All good exegesis, regardless of method, begins in this way, with noticing, gathering, and interpreting the specific words, grammatical constructions, images, and themes of a text. It sounds easy—all you are doing is noticing what is in front of you—but it is one of the most challenging aspects of reading the Bible. Part of the difficulty is that it is tempting, when reading Scripture, to correct what looks like nonsense. To round up to 10, to erase inconveniences, to assume that others know better than you, that the difficulty you see wouldn't be difficult if you were an expert with a long string of letters behind your name.

Instead of these options, I tell my students that they, like Harry, should stick to their ticket, however weird and unlikely that ticket is. Is your passage Hosea 1, and you don't know what to do about Hosea's marriage to Gomer and God's suggestions for baby names (Jezreel, a sign of the end of the house of Israel; *Lo-ruhamah*, no mercy; *Lo-ammi*, not my people [Hosea 1:1–9])? Don't write a paper about God's tender love. I have read multiple papers on Hosea 1 and God's tender love, but the text does not speak about love. It speaks about its absence. Or about love turned bitter, about anger. Sticking with your Hosea ticket requires finding a way to hold together the harshness of God's judgment, including the seeming use of an actual human family as a sign act of that judgment, and the message of God's tender love found elsewhere, including in Hosea. It is tempting to skip the hard work of thinking about the uncomfortable parts of the Bible, or the plain confusing ones (Zechariah 11, the whole chapter, stumps me!), but if you skip to an answer you already know, you will not, to return to the ticket vignette, get to Hogwarts. You'll just find yourself at platform 9 or 10, places you could visit any day.

EXEGESIS AND ETHICS
(OR WHAT WE'LL DO IN THIS ESSAY)

But the topic of this essay is interpretation and ethics: how do you get from reading a text and figuring out what it says to deciding what to do? To deciding how to live? Once you feel confident you have noticed and interpreted the details of the text, have you then automatically arrived at the ethics of the text? The short answer is no. In fact, your work has only begun. For the rest of this essay, we will look at the relationship between the details of the text, its ethical emphases, and how to turn these into ethics for modern life.

In this sense, deriving ethics from the Bible is different than Harry's ticket predicament. Once you have found platform 9 ¾, there's no question what you are going to do, right? You go to Hogwarts! But once you've figured out Hosea 1, then what? I can't even suggest what that might be because I still don't understand Hosea 1. I am sure the takeaway is not that you too should enter a loveless marriage and give your babies cruel names, but other than that, I don't know.

Maybe the difficulty starts even further back for you. Should we even look to the Bible for ethics? Isn't it outdated? When I tell people I study the Hebrew Bible, a common response is "I'm sorry," followed by reflections on the brutality and absurdity of Leviticus. I try to explain that, to me, Leviticus has much to say about the relationship between humans, animals, and land and reflects a seriousness about materiality that I think we've lost. Sometimes this leads to interesting conversations and sometimes just blank looks.

Or maybe you've been taught that the ethics of the Bible are obvious and we just need to get on with it. That the trouble isn't knowing what the Bible tells us to do; the trouble is that we're stubborn and unwilling. From this perspective, worrying about the details of the text and the nuances of its ethics is just equivocation, an attempt to dodge the demands the text makes on us.

What I hope you'll consider with me is that neither of these extremes pay sufficient respect to the text. Yes, the Bible is ancient, but that does not mean it is unwise or obsolete. And yes, we may be stubborn and unwilling, but that does not mean that getting from the details of the text to a sense of its ethics is easy.

The best way to show both the promise and challenge of looking to the Bible for ethics is to turn to a specific passage. To illustrate how to get from the words of the text to its ethics, let's look at a story that is less confusing than Hosea 1, though weird enough in its own right: the story of Tamar and the sons of Judah in Genesis 38. We'll begin by discussing some of the interpretive cruxes of the text (its details), and then turn to the ethical options these present us with. Finally, I'll suggest some general questions you can ask yourself and the text when you turn to Scripture for ethical guidance.

GENESIS 38: THE DETAILS OF THE TEXT

The story of Tamar and the sons of Judah begins with Judah's marriage to the daughter of Shua, who in quick order gives birth to three sons: Er, Onan, and Shelah. For the eldest, Judah takes as wife for him a woman named Tamar. Unfortunately, Er is "evil in the eyes of YHWH" and God kills him (Genesis 38:7). This leaves Er without descendants, so Judah instructs Onan to "Go in to the wife of your brother and perform the duty of brother-in-law to her, and raise up offspring for your brother" (Genesis 38:8, LEB). Onan realizes that children born by these means will not be counted as his own; they will not be his seed (Genesis 38:9), so "whenever he went in to the wife of his brother he would waste [his seed] on the ground so as not to give offspring to his brother" (38:9). Like Er's unspecified misdeeds, this too is "evil in the eyes of Yahweh," and God kills him (38:10, LEB). With two of his sons dead, Judah gets nervous (maybe Tamar is the problem) and tells Tamar to go back to her parents until Shelah is old enough for marriage, never intending to allow her to marry his youngest son.

People have long discussed what Onan does wrong. What is he punished for? Maybe a specific sexual practice? Many people read the story to indicate coitus interruptus, the practice of pulling out before ejaculation. Coitus interruptus is a form of birth control, though not a particularly reliable one.[1] People who have read the story in this way include

1. Out of a hundred couples who have unprotected sex with no form of birth control, eighty-five will get pregnant within a year. Out of a hundred couples who practice

the Midrash (the Talmud describes Onan's act as "unnatural intercourse," a less clear designation),[2] Augustine,[3] John Calvin,[4] and Pope Pius XI.[5] Others have identified the sin to be masturbation. For example, the title of a digest version of an eighteenth-century medical treatise on masturbation published by John Wesley is "Thoughts on the Sin of Onan."[6] In many modern languages, the word for masturbation comes from the word Onan—in German, for example, the noun is *die Onanie*. Modern exegetes have mostly argued against focus on any particular sexual act and have instead drawn attention to Judah's instructions and Onan's responsibility to his brother and sister-in-law, to the practice called levirate marriage.[7] According to this practice, Onan is obligated to provide offspring for his brother and continue his line, and by refusing to do so he claims his brother's inheritance as his own and leaves his sister-in-law without anyone to care for her. The problem with this interpretation is that elsewhere, in Deuteronomy 25:9–10, the punishment for failing to perform the duty of the brother-in-law is the loss of a sandal, being spit on by one's sister-in-law, and receiving, for one's house, the nickname "the house of the pulled-off sandal." A punishment, in other words, much less severe than death. Finally, some also suggest a pared-down version of this last interpretation: that what Onan does wrong is simply to disobey his father. His father asks Onan to provide offspring for Er, and Onan pretends to comply. He avoids doing what his father asks and is dishonest

---

typical (i.e., not ideal) coitus interruptus, somewhere between eighteen and twenty-seven (depending on what survey you consult) couples will get pregnant.

2. For an overview of Jewish interpretations of Onan, see Feldman, *Birth Control in Jewish Law*, 148–52.

3. Augustine, *Treatises on Marriage and Other Subjects*, 117.

4. Calvin, *Commentaries on the First Book of Moses*, ch. 38:9–10. Note that several editions of Calvin's commentaries omit his commentary on these two verses, the relevant portion of which reads: "Onan not only defrauded his brother of the right due him, but also preferred his semen to putrefy on the ground. The voluntary spilling of semen outside of intercourse between man and woman is a monstrous thing. Deliberately to withdraw from coitus in order that semen may fall on the ground is doubly monstrous."

5. For an overview of Christian readings of Onan, especially ones that read the story to describe a contraceptive method, see Feldman, *Birth Control in Jewish Law*, 145–48.

6. Tissot, *Thoughts on the Sin of Onan*. The treatise is a summary of a longer work by Tissot, which is simply titled "L'Onanisme."

7. See, for example, Westermann, *Genesis 37–50*, 52; Rad, *Genesis*, 362; Niditch, "Wronged Woman Righted."

about it. This leaves us with four possible answers to the question of why Onan dies:

1. Coitus interruptus

2. Masturbation

3. Failure to perform the duty of brother-in-law

4. Failure to obey and be truthful to his father

For what it is worth, I believe the story describes coitus interruptus, not masturbation, but that modern exegetes are right: the problem is Onan's refusal to do the duty of the brother-in-law. This means that the text does not condemn a particularly sexual practice, be that masturbation, non-procreative sex, or the use of contraceptives. These are the means by which Onan skirts his obligation, but the means themselves are not the point. Had Onan point-blank refused to do as his father said, that too may have raised God's ire, though it would have been less deceptive and would have spared Tamar a sexual relationship unlikely to produce children.

In defense of this interpretation is the latter part of the story, in which Tamar pretends to be a prostitute, has sex with her father-in-law, Judah, becomes pregnant by him, and is almost burned at the stake before presenting proof to Judah that he is the father of her child. Rather than being horrified, Judah exclaims, "She is more righteous than I, since I did not give her to my son Shelah" (Genesis 38:26, NASB). Sleeping with your father-in-law would not have been considered an appropriate sexual practice (see Leviticus 18:15 and 20:12[8]), but that concern seems to be trumped by Tamar's pursuit of providing herself and Er with offspring. She does what Onan will not and what Judah, by withholding Shelah, has been reluctant to do. This interpretation also fits with the larger context in Genesis. One of its themes is the continuation of what will eventually be the line of David: the many obstacles that threaten the line, the ways in which God steps in, the cleverness and trickery practiced by humans to ensure babies are born. Tamar works to promote David's line; Onan

8. Leviticus prohibits having sex with your daughter-in-law. As is the case with many biblical texts, the imagined audience is adult men, not women. The law therefore prohibits forms of sex men might have. The mirror prohibition (don't sleep with your father-in-law) is not stated explicitly. Note that having sex with your sister-in-law is also prohibited, though this is presumably only valid during the lifetime of your brother.

obstructs it. Their actions and the evaluations of those actions within the text fit within a larger pattern in the book of Genesis and within the larger concerns of the book.

GENESIS 38: GETTING FROM THE DETAILS OF THE TEXT TO ITS ETHICS

The conclusion that Genesis 38 concerns a failure to honor the obligations of the brother-in-law may make it seem like Tamar and Onan have little to teach us about ethics. If the problem was a specific sexual practice, we could avoid it (more on that later), but if the problem is abiding by the obligations of the brother-in-law, this does not transfer well to modern conditions. We no longer practice levirate marriages. If my husband were to die, and a relative of my husband offered to marry me (he has no brothers; it would have to be a cousin), I'd be offended and shocked, not grateful.

So how do you think about ethics in relation to a text that seems so removed from life in the twenty-first century? I would suggest, instead of trying to find ethical precepts you can lift from the text, you think of the text as a conversation partner. Rather than a rule book, think of it as a critical and sometimes difficult friend that asks questions about your life, the "you" here being communal as much as individual. Here are some questions Genesis 38 raises for me.

1. The practice of having a brother-in-law marry the widow of his brother is about family obligation, about taking care of both the dead brother and his widow, about continuing the family line. In what ways do we care for our families? What happens when someone is suddenly in a vulnerable position, after job loss, divorce, long-term illness, or aging? How do our family practices keep people safe, provide for them, and facilitate their active community participation? Do we need better practices?

2. Levirate marriage is a way of addressing interruptions of lines of decent and the vulnerabilities of widowed women without children. How do we provide for people when they are in vulnerable situations? What responsibilities fall to families, to the state, or to other institutions, like churches? Is this distribution how we want to do things, or should it change? Which of our cultural practices are about ensuring that

vulnerable people have a viable place in our communities? How might we strengthen these practices?

3. The story of Genesis 38 is driven by a cultural emphasis on offspring. Children are essential for continuing a man's line and for keeping his inheritance in that line, and they are also a social safety net for women, taking care of them in their old age. Children do not play an identical role in our society, but they are still important. How do we talk about childlessness, including unwanted childlessness, and what are our responsibilities to people who want children but don't have them? What about people who choose childlessness? Are some of the ways we talk about the importance of children unhealthy or unhelpful?

4. Onan circumvents his responsibility towards Tamar by deceit. He does not tell his father that he refuses to provide Er with offspring. Instead, he has sex with Tamar, but does what he can to ensure that that sex is nonprocreative. How do we manage disagreements over individual responsibilities to the community? How do we voice such disagreements? What do people do when they feel unable to voice disagreement, and what are practices that can help us be self-reflective about our own motives for avoiding a particular responsibility?

5. Onan's actions place Tamar in a sexual relationship whose parameters differ from those she has agreed to. What are ways in which we fudge consent? How might we talk about and practice consent so that it goes beyond the legalese of consent forms and instead considers and is responsible to the dignity and well-being of other people?

SUGGESTIONS FOR QUESTION TO GUIDE YOU WHEN LOOKING TO SCRIPTURE FOR ETHICAL GUIDANCE

The questions above may seem like they have taken us quite far from the text. How is this sticking with the ticket? At least discussions that try to derive from this story guidelines for sex are concerned with the details of the text. They seem like an effort to figure out what that ¾ means, more so than the list of open questions I have provided.

I don't mean to say that the details of the text are unimportant. I do think it matters what sexual practice Onan engages in, but I don't think figuring out the answer to that question automatically tells us what to do. In getting from one to the other, from details to ethics, I consider questions along these lines:

* How do the details of the text relate to each other?

* Are some details emphasized more than others? Why do I think some details are emphasized?

* Do aspects of the text repeat themes emphasized elsewhere in the book or in the Bible? Why are these repeated?

* What analogues can I draw between the situations and details in the biblical text and my own context?

* Which analogues best address the emphases of the story? Which analogues are more superficial?

* What problems, conflicts, or shortcomings does the text illuminate? Or, what virtues or models does it present us with?

* Who is benefited by my reading? Who is harmed?

* What biases and preferences does my reading betray? Am I trying to avoid anything in the text?

* What about my reading makes me hopeful? Angry? Worried? Comforted? What might someone else feel about my reading?

* Does my reading help me see anything new about the world?

* How might someone from a different time or culture read this story? Why would their interpretation differ from mine?

This is not a prescriptive list of questions (I wouldn't suggest you go through them one by one every time you read a text), but only suggestions for how to develop an intimate, reflective, and self-critical relationship with the Bible. For the sake of illustration, let's consider Onan and Tamar again, and assume that you have convinced me that the reason God kills Onan is that he uses a contraceptive method. How do we apply these kinds of questions to the text now? Can we simply assume that God forbids us to use contraceptives?

No. It is not just that following every direction in the Bible literally is impossible, or that the Bible contains contradictory directions (one example: profane slaughter, that is, slaughter divorced from sacrifice: permitted or not permitted?), but that the Bible is not a list of rules that imprisons us with a "just do what I say because I say so" approach to ethics. It trains us in living. That requires our active participation, our questioning of ourselves and of the text. If I were to become convinced that Onan dies due to his use of a contraceptive method, I would still need to ask questions. Is our context the same as the context of the story in Genesis 38, or similar enough that the rules that apply to Onan apply to us? Why is it evil in God's eyes that Onan uses a contraceptive method? Would it be equally evil if we did? Why is nonprocreative sex discouraged in this story? Does nonprocreative sex carry the same problems in our time? What costs would avoiding contraceptives entail, and who would carry those costs?

These questions are not efforts to escape the text or to find a loophole to avoid doing what it asks of us. While I do not want to live in a world without contraceptives, being committed to the Bible means being committed to having my way of life questioned by it, however uncomfortable and inconvenient that is. Admittedly, I feel some relief that I don't think this story is about contraceptives as such; we all come to the text with preferences, needs, and commitments. But looking to the Bible for ethics is always about seeing new worlds through it, about being willing to let go of old viewpoints. What kind of life does it allow us to imagine and pursue? How might it raise our standards for what justice is, for what we owe one another, for what kindness and faithfulness look like in our communities? Another way to put this is that being obedient to the Bible is harder than obeying a set of rules. The Bible asks us to struggle with obedience again and again, to read the text another time, to take another look at our world, to wonder again what God demands of us. Obedience always takes the form of a conversation, one that we are never done with. We "work out" our obedience "with fear and trembling" (Philippians 2:12). We don't just show up and do as we're told.

CONCLUSION: THERE'S NEVER JUST ONE ANSWER

We won't ever arrive at one final answer to the questions the Bible asks of us. For example, take Onan's family responsibilities. Family responsibilities differ between cultures. What my parents expect of me is shaped by the fact that my parents are Norwegian, and by the specifics of their own lives. If my family were Pakistani, or Portuguese, or American, we would have different expectations of each other. My parents did not pay for my undergraduate degree, and I did not expect them to, but my American husband's parents paid for his. Had they not, that would have been a different action than my parents not paying for my degree. When interacting with the text and allowing it to critique how we fulfill our family obligations, the specifics of our cultures matter. The point is not to figure out what ancient Israelite family obligations looked like and to try to mimic them as closely as possible. It is to let justice, kindness, and faithfulness guide our own family obligations, to be open to the text showing us how to be better family members.

This means that different people will arrive at different ethical guidelines, each of which may be faithful and obedient to the text. Knowing that can be scary. How do we know if our reading and our ethical conclusions are good, if more than one reading can be good? And of course, sometimes our readings aren't good. Part of sticking with the ticket is living with that possibility and going back to the text again and again. Does the reading you did a year ago still seem valid to you today? Have you discovered something in yourself or in the text that makes you doubt your reading, or have you learned from someone else something that makes you think it needs revision? Does someone else's reading seem better and truer than your own? Unlike Harry's train ticket, which can be thrown out once he's on the train, sticking with the Bible means going back to it again and again. It means that our ethics are always provisional, always open to new revelation, new interpretation, and to God calling us in new directions.

Another way to put this is to say that the purpose of theological education is not to give you the answer sheet to the Bible. No such answer sheet exists, and if it did, I think we'd be worse off. Instead, theological education will hopefully aid you in your commitment to the Bible and in asking of it and of yourself good questions, and give you the tools to deepen your connection with the text. It is like a relationship course for you and the Bible, helping you be closer, more intimate friends. And theological education should give you confidence. When faced with a tricky ticket, with 9 ¾, or Ezekiel lying on his side for a year (Ezekiel 4:4–5), or God trying to kill Moses (Exodus 4:24–26), you have tools and a relationship with the text that can stand a little difficulty and struggle. You are able to stick to the ticket, to try different things, to ask new and interesting questions, to relate consciously and conscientiously to all the ambiguity that exegesis involves. And, if you should ever find yourself at King's Cross Station, lost and carrying an owl, you too would be able to find your way to Hogwarts, or at least to somewhere equally interesting, equally surprising, and equally beautiful.

10

There Might Not Be Christian Ethics, but We Do Have Neighbors

On Listening for Human Life and Becoming Shaped by Jesus Christ

ASHLEY JOHN MOYSE

As THE STORY GOES, George Florovsky began his lectures on Christian ethics provocatively, saying, "For Orthodox Christians there is no such thing as Christian Ethics."[1] Such a claim might strike us as odd. Yet Florovsky is not alone in making such a statement. D. Steven Long, for example, reminds his reader, "neither 'Christian' nor 'ethics' identifies a single, coherent subject matter upon which all could agree."[2] So to put the terms together simply adds little clarification at all, while also rendering the couplet general, i.e., void of any particular, meaningful content.

Moreover, Rémi Brague has offered argument opposing the adjectival nature of "Christian" as a reference to moral behaviors: "there are no such things as morals with an epithet."[3] One could say, therefore, as

1. As Thomas Hopko has previous recounted in his "Orthodox Christianity and Ethics" reflections for the Orthodox Education Day book (October 7, 1995).

2. Long, *Christian Ethics*, 3.

3. Brague, *Curing Mad Truths*, 85.

142

Brague suggests, there is no such thing as pagan or Jewish or Buddhist moral behaviors either. Brague even suggests the ethics that emerge from both Athens (Greeks) and Jerusalem (Christians), for example, seem to agree fully on what is right and wrong. To make his point, Brague posits that few would argue, concretely, "there are not that many ways to help an old [person] across a street . . . ."[4] To give aid to this person attempting to cross the road is not uniquely [fill in with an epithet]. Whether you or I, or our secular humanist neighbors, give aid to this person, the right thing is done.

Add to these negative claims regarding Christian ethics (i.e., what Christian ethics is not) yet another. Karl Barth writes, quoting Dietrich Bonhoeffer, that Christian ethics "cannot be a book in which there is set out how everything in the world actually ought to be but unfortunately is not, and an ethicist cannot be a man who always knows better than others what is to be done and how it is to be done."[5] After all, as Georgia Harkness comments, "the complexities of living are such that 'circumstances alter cases'. Jesus did not undertake to provide his followers with any such manual of rules [with which an ethicist might wield expertise], and it would be presumptuous for a modern Christian to attempt what our Lord apparently was too wise to do."[6] But what is it then? Surely we might say something positive at the outset?

Surely, we will! Maybe?

Rowan Williams's essay "Making Moral Decisions," for example, begins by introducing his reader to both Rush Rhees and Herbert McCabe. The former raises ethics as a kind of problematic exercise; discerning between what one must do verses what one might want (at a particular moment) is not an easy task. And the latter is seemingly realistic about this exercise, suggesting that ethics is about what one wants, and nothing else. Yet humanity is fallen and deceived most readily concerning such desires. But Williams explains further what Rhees and McCabe are ultimately attempting to tease out: "[ethics] is a difficult discovering of something about yourself, a discovering of what has already shaped the person you are and is moulding you in this or that direction."[7] Ethics, after all, as Paulinus Ikechukwu Odozor demonstrates, is concerned with

---

4. Brague, *Curing Mad Truths*, 85.

5. Barth, *Church* Dogmatics, III/4, 10. See also Bonhoeffer, *Ethics*, 369–70.

6. Harkness, "What Is Christian Ethics?," para. 3.

7. Williams, "Making Moral Decisions," 3.

"the human person as a being and as a moral actor."[8] Odozor thus affirms, citing also Klaus Demmer's *Shaping Moral Life*, "The moral life of the Christian flows directly from his or her being; the imperative dimension, what one *ought* to do, is grounded in the indicative—what one *is*."[9] Positively, this imagery of shaping is important. But it no less difficult to discern, at times, given the ways the discipline of ethics, or theological ethics for that matter, are often understood and practiced.

So, with these theologians introducing Christian or theological ethics as they have done, questions remain: Where and with what does one begin the study if there is *no such thing* as Christian ethics? Where and with what does one begin to study if Christian ethics does not include a rule book to set out or to follow? Where and with what does one begin the study Christian ethics if the discipline suffers from a lack of integrity or delimited epistemic content? How might we discover anything about ourselves? To where or to whom does one turn?

For us here, and in a book that aims to introduce readers to preliminary *content* one might need to know when considering theological education and for those on the way toward *becoming* thoughtful, engaged, and generous scholars and clergy, where does one begin to understand the moral tradition of Christians?

One begins somewhere. Yet the answer does not come by *our* turning toward something or someone on our own. Such turning must be accompanied by rebuke, as you will see. Nevertheless, the following will point toward, rather bear witness to, the shape of the human being in the world, the shape of human being made known by Jesus Christ. It will point also to a corresponding posture that the Christian is invited to practice as she is conformed by and in Christ, and thereby formed to be a human being.

So, while there might not be such a thing as Christian ethics, the Christian can bear witness to two realities that not only inform an understanding but also determine the moral life of Christians: that God dwells among us, and turns toward us, inviting us to follow the Way. Here we might be introduced to a pedagogical reality, which shapes us, opposing the Pelagian heresy that we have everything we need within us and "can achieve the good through our own resources."[10] And that we might

---

8. Odozor, *Morality Truly Christian, Truly African*, 206.

9. Odozor, *Morality Truly Christian, Truly African*, 206; quoting from Demmer, *Shaping the Moral Life*, 4.

10. Long, *Christian Ethics*, 2.

learn to see (and therefore accompany) others struggling between human being and nothingness, as Sergei Bulgakov might suggest;[11] to see these others are struggling amidst the ambiguities of a present moment. And to see that so too are we. Here we might be introduced to a principal posture, which must be practiced, habituating a way of being in the world that is *human*.

I will bear witness to these realities as I introduce you to a principal question that I will repeat two times with different emphases, for the Christian attempting to live her life in the world: *Who* is my neighbor? Who is *my* neighbor?[12]

WHO IS MY NEIGHBOR?
CHRIST AND THE HUMAN CONDITION

Michael Banner's Bampton Lectures, "Imagining Life: Christ and the Human Condition," captures the principal thrust of Banner's ethics, which he expounds in his book *Ethics of Everyday Life*. He argues that those interested in studying theology and ethics should labor well to examine the lived life of human beings, and *the* human being, Christ. Only then might one be able to "narrate the good as a form of life with its own logic and sense."[13] Gabriel Marcel suggests something similar. His dialectical process of reflection moves between life and reflection, teaching that we will work "up from life to thought and then down from thought to life again, so that [we] may try to throw more light upon life."[14] To do such work, Marcel argues that one must first map out human life as it is lived in a concrete sense (he calls this secondary reflection), rather than outlining its shape in abstraction—or worse, coercing a lived experience determined by such abstractions. What is at stake, then, is not the adjudication of right and wrong but rather what is at stake in understanding what it is to be human—or as Rowan Williams noted above, what it is that is shaping us in this or that direction, toward being or toward nothingness, humanity or inhumanity.

11. To learn more about the ontological struggle between being and nothingness, see Bulgakov, "Lamb of God."

12. Barth, *Ethics*, 351.

13. Banner, *Ethics of Everyday Life*, 17.

14. Marcel, *Mystery of Being*, 41.

To locate such understanding, however, we cannot turn toward ourselves. We cannot turn toward ourselves, as such a turn would risk our
own deceptions and would only repeat the Pelagian heresy noted above.
I'll say nothing more on that here. Yet I will say this: we cannot turn
ourselves toward Christ, either. Rather, the *good* is known as Jesus turns
toward us.

Origen's commentary on Matthew 16 might offer sufficient rationale
while examining the significance of both turning and following. As Jesus
turns, he reproaches Peter, "Get behind me, Satan." Origen compares
this scene with an earlier story in the desert, where Jesus is promised
the world. In Matthew 4, however, Jesus does not direct the devil to get
behind. There is no addition to the rebuke. Returning to Matthew 16,
Jesus does give to Peter instruction, which accompanies the admonition.
And such instruction is a good thing: "as a general principle observe the
expression 'behind'; because it is a good thing when any one goes behind
the Lord God and is behind the Christ; . . . And Jesus says this to Peter
when He 'turned,' and He does so by way of conferring a favor. . . . For
observe that, when He "turned," it is for the advantage of those to whom
He turned."[15]

Such an understanding might be found as we learn the answer to the
question, "*Who* is my neighbor?" The answer to the question begins as we
are seen by Christ—the one from whom the invitation to "follow me" is
given. Following disciplines the moral life of those wayfarers behind their
pedagogue—the place where they have been gathered, and the place from
which they might be attentive to the words and actions of their teachers
and learn to understand themselves and their neighbors rightly—as human beings struggling together in the present toward a reconciled future.

"Follow me." Gathered by Christ, we are invited to get behind, sur-
rendering our experiences and education to the Way. The Way, therefore,
is a *paideutic* discipline.[16] Paideia situates persons under the tutelage of
Christ, who creates and sustains the moral space of the church (gathered
in and for the world). Such discipline illuminates how theological stories,
known by Scripture and tradition, known principally because of God's

---

15. Origen, *Commentary of the Gospel of Matthew* 12.22.

16. To learn more about *paideia*, begin with Jaeger, *Early Christianity and Greek
Paideia*. Drawing from Jaeger, and others, I trace the importance of *paideia* for forming persons readied to live in the world, while looking at the ways the modern technological imaginary has functioned as a kind of *dys-paideia*, malforming human being;
see Moyse, *Art of Living for the Technological Age*.

own self-disclosure in Christ (because of his turning toward us), invite a particular performance. The performance trains the way not only to say but also to see the world as creation moving towards its eschatological future and confronted by the apocalyptic, or *inbreaking*, actualities of Christ who has *already* transformed the world.

And so, as I have come to understand, the moral life of Christians must be grounded christologically and pedagogically in this way. This means that we must allow Jesus Christ to orient us within the moral space, which he also creates by his encounter with humanity. That which the good *is*, accordingly, is the very moral reality perfected by the presence and activity of Christ, a presence and activity we are not simply shown but also invited to participate and to perform, both quietly and cheerfully in the world.

This community gathered in the moral space (created and sustained by Christ) might learn what it means to live within and for a community as they engage in events of conversation, listening for and discerning the command of God. That is, the fundamental mark of the moral life of Christ is an engaged and thoughtful, wholly conversational, gathering within a community of moral neighbors (neither strangers nor enemies, no matter how different one might be). Thus, we must not withdraw toward those ethics that demand allegiance to abstract principles applied *ab extra* (from outside ourselves), giving answers to moral dilemmas before a crisis. We must not withdraw toward those ethics of interiority, which abide universal maxims as expressions of self-will, either. We must, however, demand personal human action to, with, and for those gathered. We must demand individual responsibility conditioned by concrete actualities of the human, viz. community, life that is made known by way of Christ's being in and for the world. In this way, Christians must demand a public exercise of hearing and receiving, of proclamation and confession, such that life is lived together with and for the other.[17] The Way, in essence (and in part), is a performance of solidarity, of love— where the witness of those gathered (whether living or dead[18]) might be

17. Such a public exercise is also important, for theology, the Way, is not simply for the Christian. Rather, theology offers an "outlook on life as a whole, with ramifications, therefore, not simply for a narrowly conceived religious sphere, but for all dimensions of life" (Tanner, "Public Theology," 79).

18. On the "living and dead," see my discussion about the way that bodies might speak, claiming others for responsibility, in Moyse, "Responsibility for the Broken Body."

heard, and the life of oneself and that of the other may be respected and ultimately transformed.

One might look to the early history of Christians in the Graeco-Roman world a kind of conversational community, wresting to live in the world rather than aiming to construct a rigid moral dogma or ethics program that closes down conversation. In this time, one might observe paiduetic practices that shaped the moral life of both Greeks and Christians. Christians in this time continued to introduce their children to the classical schools of education, which exposed the young pupils not only to the literature but also to the gods of the Greeks. They did not, as Jennifer Herdt reminds her reader, "displace the usual classical education" for a safe sanctuary of Christian schooling; instead, children were "routinely required to grapple with deep ambiguity, with rival exemplary models sanctioned by competing authorities."[19] That is to say, it would prove true that the experience and education of the virtues tradition would discipline the students to be transformed by the icons of the good while also introducing poisonous doctrine that was attractive. Yet closing down rather than opening up encounter with rival schools was not considered as an answer for these early Christians. After all, under such classical schooling, Christians discovered ar[macron over e]ēte, the good enfleshed, both encountered and practiced. As I have written elsewhere, these early Christian understood "*paideia* as formative, and the classical material for learning [as] beneficial."[20]

Yet not all material was positive. Thus, discrimination was also beneficial. That is to say, education in the Way was essential—the dual schooling in religious training outside of the classical schools served as an antidote to poisonous doctrine.[21] Basil of Caesarea used the imagery of a bee, which flies a great distance encountering many different flowers, learning to discern between petals and thorns.[22] If a bee is to flourish as a bee (while also giving of its livelihood for the well-being others), it must bring back that which it can use to make honey and wax. Likewise, his brother, Gregory of Nyssa, reflected on his classical schooling and introduced the religious schooling under his sister Macrina as that which

---

19. Herdt, *Putting on Virtue*, 64.

20. Moyse, *Art of Living for the Technological Age*, 136.

21. Herdt, *Putting on* Virtue, 64.

22. Basil, *On Greek Literature*, 377–435.

disciplined a prudence to discern poisonous doctrine that must be opposed, for such teachings are sterile and do not bear life.[23]

But one thing was certain: the aim was not to erect duplicate exemplary models of excellence. This schooling was not to be a manufacturing of such sterile images. The culture of *paideia*, both Greek and Christian, handed down from teacher to pupil the habits of excellence, or virtue. The culture handed down the invitation to imitate the pedagogue but did not intend to "result in strict uniformity."[24] Rather, such training was to open up the person to the world and to the experience(s) of human being, of flourishing, in a community of others, each one and all confronting the ambiguities and crises that persist.

Situated, therefore, as we are by and in Christ, the Christian moral life is not sterile. It bears life. The moral space inaugurated and preserved by Christ is to be that space where we might learn to listen for and to hear again and again the command of God, which is to be heard as a permission, granting liberty to "learn to live with others . . . in the midst of the abundance of the concrete tasks and processes of life . . . [permitting] human beings to live *as* human beings before God."[25] And concern for being a *human being* and the everyday life where humanity emerges or disappears requires us, as Banner suggests, to engage in a ranging conversation that remains open to the possibility of listening to the voices and taking into account the experiences of people in their concrete everyday lives. Understanding what we do, what we can do, and what we ought to do is to be discerned in the company of the other—where ethics is realized as a social task (and not as a project).[26]

In an open social exchange, we learn to attend to the particularities of the other, rather than to the order of a determinative moral construct to be followed as a kind of disincarnated reason demands. In this way, ethics becomes a response to the concrete demands of mutually responsible human lives. There is, thus, an *unavoidable* casuistry that demands critical reflection on particular events and experiences confronted by the community of (particular) persons that have gathered. To this extent, such casuistry precludes moral mastery. It bristles at abstracted universals,

---

23. Gregory of Nyssa, *Life of Moses*, 1.18, 2.13, 2.11; 34, 57–58.

24. Herdt, *Putting on* Virtue, 64.

25. Bonhoeffer, *Ethics*, 370, 383.

26. A project is conditioned by *our* desires. It is something that "we decide to undertake, whereas a task is entrusted to us by some higher power: nature in pagan style, or God in biblical style" (Brague, *Curing Mad Truths*, 4).

which remain disincarnated, obscure, and unspecified. Finally—and I am repeating myself in order to emphasize the point—such casuistry must not be thought of as a form of *free* choice or selection, which is but a form of constraint (the sin of determining the good for ourselves) shrouded by the illusion of freedom. Instead, the encounter with our neighbor(s), both near and far (both similar and dissimilar to ourselves), nurtures a practice of ethics around radical sociality—rather, after the freedom, which is a permission, to be one with and for the other. In such an exchange, humanity might collectively struggle against dehumanizing powers and toward human flourishing.

As we exchange moral speech with our neighbors and labor to learn from the range of voices and cultural imaginaries offered, we must set ourselves to the task: discerning the command of God, which presents itself to us as the permission to live, and to live as a human being! Perhaps Dietrich Bonhoeffer's words will serve us well here as well: "God did not become an idea, a principle, a program, a universally valid belief, or a law. God became human. That means ... Christ does not abolish human reality in favor of an idea that demands to be realized against all that is real. Christ empowers reality, affirming it as the real human being and thus the ground of all human reality."[27] And since human reality is enfleshed, the very bodily existence of ourselves and our neighbors, including the preeminent neighbor, Christ, constitutes a particular kind of union. It is, after all, the body that affords the relation humanity has with Christ and its fellows. But not only Christ and fellows; importantly also, the body affords the relation a human being has with the earth as well. Our bodily existence, our reality as human beings, is affirmed as the ground from which one will "find their brothers and sisters and find the earth"[28]—each one a neighbor with whom and for whom we are made responsible.

Thus, as I am trying to make clear above, we must engage in the long labor of exchanging moral speech, with each other, with our neighbors (including the earth, groaning for her *telos*), and with the very human Christ, who too is the very divine God. Let us labor diligently as we learn to see the world *rightly*[29] such that we might become truly human, and therefore oriented in concern and communion with and for our fellows.

27. Bonhoeffer, *Ethics*, 99.

28. Bonhoeffer, *Creation and Fall*, 79.

29. "Only because God became human it is possible to know and not despise real human beings. Real human beings may live before God, and we may let these real people live beside us and before God without either despising or idolizing them. This

WHO IS *MY* NEIGHBOR? ON OPENNESS WITH
AND FOR THE OTHER

To engage in such a labor, as outlined above, one must be(come) open to encounter the other—not only in their similarities, but also in their differences; a kind of nonecumenical openness that fosters conversation rather than monologue. But to learn openness requires attention toward postures of human being that must be practiced—practices that nurture resolve against excesses of deficiency and abuse.

Being open to the other, after all, is not always an easy thing to do. In fact, as Ernest Becker has suggested, confronting those persons who are different from us often results in great distress and is a cause of much degradation and destruction toward such others.[30] This is exemplary of the sort of excessive deficiency, or vice, that a failure to practice such a posture might cultivate. A symptom of such vice can also be seen in attempts toward programmatic secularism, where "any and every public manifestation of any particular religious allegiance is to be ironed out,"[31] coercing moral strangers to let their special insights remain a private concern while public speech is disciplined to form, so everyone talks like everybody else (where genuine encounter, and surprise, is rendered an impossibility).

Being open to exchange moral speech with neighbors, whether near or distant (similar or dissimilar), is a hallmark of the rightly formed Christian—formed to see in the face of another the Face of all faces, as Nicholas of Cusa might commend.[32] We thus clothe, and feed, and shelter (and guide across the street) these others who turn toward us, as though Christ claiming us for such responsibility (Matthew 25:31–46). We do these things in response to, with, and *for* others. So, rather than seeing in the other's eyes a stranger or enemy to be ignored or overcome, visions of the other one might learn to see in and to practice through two familiar

---

is not because of the real human being's inherent value, but because God has loved and taken on the real human being. The reason for God's love for human being does not reside in them, but only in God. Our living as real human beings, and loving the real people next to us is, again, grounded only in God's becoming human, in the unfathomable love of God for us human beings" (Bonhoeffer, *Ethics*, 87).

30. See Becker, *Denial of Death*. One might also explore Terror Management Theory (TMT), the social and evolutionary experimental psychological theory that has examined Becker's proposals.

31. Williams, *Faith in the Public Square*, 2–3.

32. Nicholas of Cusa, *De Visione Dei* 6.22.

modern theories exposited by Adam Smith and Karl Marx, respectively, Christ invites us to practice a kind of availability and fidelity that nurtures human being, in both our neighbors and ourselves.

It is for this reason that Banner argues, "to be human is to be with and for the other, thus taking exception to those anthropologies [as above] which reckon that to be human is to be without or against the other."[33] That is to say, the disposition of openness is one that is available and ready to hear, and therefore respond to accordingly, the call and claim of God—the call and claim we might hear through the confession and proclamation of the church, but also through the speech of our near and distant neighbors. Barth thus declares: "Accordingly, the Church must be open to hearing God's Word issuing forth from the lips of the apparently indifferent and godless; for 'it may be that the Lord has bidden those outside the Church to say something important to the Church. The Church therefore has every reason not to ignore the questions and warnings of the outside world."[34]

It is such an event of conversation, of listening and hearing and exchanging moral speech, that motivates Barth (and Bonhoeffer) to suggest that ethics for the Christian cannot be thought of as a book or a stereotyped system closed down to such discussion. Neither is it a discrete justificatory procedure to be executed by a haughty expert, positioned at distance from both the crisis and the community of persons gathered around it. Ethics so delimited are, as William Stringfellow argues, "dehumanizing."[35] The moral life of the Christian requires an attentive listening to others gathered into a peculiar community and around the particularity of a crisis. Such attentive listening, however, for the Christian, is a listening for that which God wills of our will—that we might be(come) who we are, human.

Continuing on with our discussion about listening, Barth, perhaps hyperbolically, invites his reader to consider that "God might even speak to us through Russian communism, through a flute concerto, through a blossoming shrub or through a dead dog."[36] He goes on to explain, "God may speak to us through a pagan or an atheist, and in that way give us to understand that the boundary between the Church and the profane

33. Banner, "Doctrine of Human Being," 139.

34. Barth, Against the Stream, 228–29.

35. Stringfellow, Conscience and Obedience, 27.

36. Barth, Church Dogmatics, I/1, 60.

world still and repeatedly takes a course quite different from that which we hitherto thought we saw."[37] The Christian must insist, therefore, that moral discourse encourage individuals to listen carefully to *all* the voices gathered around a particular crisis. There is much to learn from others.

Christian moral guidance, as such, "is not an authority which we are in a position to quote against others . . . [I]t is the basis for the mutual conversation between them and us."[38] Rather, the faithfulness of Christ serves to narrate and ground the moral space where we are enabled to do more than eavesdrop. It is the space where authentic encounter, relationship, and responsibility might be nurtured. It is a public space, which is the space where authentic life is lived, and where *the practice and attitude of openness* (solidarity, fellowship, and love for others)[39] must be basic.

Thus, the Christian must be disciplined, meaning shaped through experiences of learning and by education across time, to become one who is able not only to listen patiently but also to respond in haste to the claims placed upon her, while seeking freedom for the other. However, openness, what ought to be a hallmark posture of the Christian moral life, is not simply about responding uncritically to the needs or demands of the other. It is also about listening to the other—waiting to hear the good command or will of God, which is to be received as a liberating permission shared person to person. Rather, the command of God heard and received in a community of persons is an ethics of permission, granting liberty to live a human life, to live as an icon of *the* human life, before God. Or, to put it differently, in every state of life, and for all persons, the law of Christ is plain: love what is good for the other person, and seek the other person's advantage.

But as Bonhoeffer noted above, human persons are not only united to Christ and other persons. The body affords a union with the earth as well. And it is on this matter that I recall conversations with Sallie McFague, who had completed a manuscript exploring kenosis and climate change—a book on Christology for our time—before her death. In our conversations about the concluding chapter of the manuscript,

---

37. Barth, *Church Dogmatics*, I/1, 60.

38. Barth, *Protestant Theology in the Nineteenth Century*, 14.

39. Speaking of Barth's ethics and a reason why we must listen to the other whom we encounter within the public space, Nigel Biggar has written, "When Barth speaks of 'solidarity' or 'fellowship' with others, or when he speaks of 'love' for others, what he has in mind above all else is the practise and attitude of 'openness'" (Biggar, *Hastening That Waits*, 148).

she would remind me, critical of a kind of modern hubris, we cannot conquer nature. Nature is not ours to control. But we may, and therefore must, through our participation in God's life, practice a kind of kenotic (self-dispossessing) friendship, or openness, so that God's love for his creation might work through us while seeking its advantage. As the earth, and the creatures in it, groan, expressing their needs, longing for their *telos*, Sallie taught me the law of Christ remains plain.

That is to say, what Sallie taught me might be a surprise to some: Barth might not be exaggerating, after all. Blossoming flora and dead fauna do speak! So, if I am to be(come) a friend to the earth, and all of its inhabitants, I must learn to listen, to hear, and to exchange moral speech with her, and her inhabitants, too.[40]

Such openness, such solidarity, fellowship, or the excellence (virtue) of love, is to be the basic posture that the moral life of the Christian, of the church, is to model.[41] A critical and careful, but wholly conversational, engagement within a community of gathered neighbors is the primary mark of an ethics, which demands responsibility conditioned by *the* human life. In this way, the individual is known in multiple relationships with others, and the relevant moral goods are correlated. The moral life of the Christian, therefore, must demand a *public* and not parochial exercise of hearing, receiving, and exchanging moral speech such that life is lived together with and for the other.

CONCLUSION

At this point, a question might be sitting with us now: Why have I presented an essay that is to be on Christian ethics as I have? For those who might have some familiarity with ethics, as it is often presented, you might have anticipated a discussion about natural law, or deontology (duty), or (I write while shuddering) values, or the like. You might have wanted that. You might have wanted to see a theological ethics that mirrors the kinds of moral schema introduced since the late 1960s, which offer applied models indebted to consequentialist reasoning and/or conditional obligations for adjudicating dilemmas and resolving tensions that arise in

---

40. Sallie McFague's unpublished manuscript is now in preparation for posthumous publication with Fortress under the title *A New Climate for Christology: Kenosis, Climate Change, and Befriending Nature.*

41. Barth, *Church Dogmatics*, I/2, 588–90.

particular contexts. But theology is not a program or framework; neither is Christ—and that might be where I should start in answering this first question.

While it is not made explicit above, the reason I have presented the essay as I have relates to the ways in which *technological rationalities* have disciplined a way of seeing things, including ethics, as a human activity and as a constellation of means to accomplish practical aims and desires.[42] I have also remained deeply critical on the methods and modalities introduced in contemporary ethics classrooms that offer justificatory models that take advantage of "common moralities" that remain unsituated, unclarified, and evacuated of any content. The assumption being that a discrete selection of shared, albeit general, values or principles are sufficient to guarantee dialogue amidst difference and to guide moral actions by one's own reason.[43] That these values or principles, or models of ethics, are typically focused around difficult quandary cases also does little to address the ways in which we might labor to live everyday human lives.[44] Such a way of approaching ethics is opposed by Greek and early Christian *paideia* traditions—not to forget about *philanthrôpía* (loving what makes us human)—which consider the world and the human being in the world as a mystery to journey toward and into, pursuing the *telos* as a kind of inexhaustible flourishing rather than a circumscribed terminus. The mystery is not, therefore, a path toward interiority. It is a path toward the Other—toward both God and neighbor.

Of course, the goal of all Christian *paideia* is communion with God. The limitlessness of human flourishing is bound up in the eternal love of God for his creation. However, Andrew Louth suggests that such love is not a lifeless proposition, but reveals "the very lineaments of the mystery of Christ—a mystery which draws the student into itself; a mystery that invites a response."[45] Louth continues: "This mystery becomes the fact that transforms the whole of history: the summit of history, the fact of Christ presupposed history, and its radiance transfigured history." And so, we learn, by the very being and act, the contours and context, of the mystery of Christ, that communion with God, perhaps paradoxically, is expressed as with learn to commune with others.

42. See Moyse, *Art of Living*, 3–95.

43. Moyse, *Reading Karl Barth*.

44. See Banner, *Ethics of Everyday Life*, 1–34.

45. Louth, *Discerning the Mystery*, 120.

That there is another, always an other, demands a kind of participation in the world that trains us to move out from our selves. The Way offers such training (and freedom). The mysteries of God and of human being, the mystery of ethics, if you will, unfold as we learn not only to participate with Christ but also to express the transfigured life, human being remade into Christ's likeness: "The whole Law is fulfilled in one word . . . 'You shall love your neighbor as yourself'" (Galatians 5:14, NASB).

The second reason relates to the contemporary polis, where neither the commonweal nor the commons is cultivated as a space where one might exchange moral speech with her neighbor and find in her neighbor someone not only to see but also to be given toward[46]—as someone worthy of both attention and fidelity.[47] Instead, as seems to be evident in many a political theater, political life is reduced to that place where persons neither listen to nor learn from one another but take opportunity to demean and to dismiss, to disparage and to disfigure—affirming, in part, some of Becker's hypotheses about one's reactions to the other, as noted briefly above. The aim, so often, is not to seek the advantage of the other, but to thwart it as though the stranger or enemy is a problem to resolve (which of course, takes us back to the first reason for this essay).

A second question might be this: What ought we to take away from such an essay while examining those essentials that might benefit our thinking about and preparation for theological education? While there might be several ways to respond to this question, I will close with the following:

First, while there might not be such a thing as Christian ethics, there are many neighbors around, with and for whom we must give our attention, our fidelity, and our charity. Second, I have offered, implicitly, the endorsement that all of theology is *ethics*. Rather, explicitly, the study of God *in se* (within Godself) and God *ad extra* (in the world) orients us toward the moral life. Moreover, the surrender of each one to the invitation "follow me," and the material and social performances disciplined by the life of the church (in liturgy and in sacrament), serve as the basis for an education in the Way. The *corpus mysticum* (the mystical body of Christ), the church, gathered and sustained by Christ, is therefore churched in this way. And the repetition afforded by the Christian calendar (which is

46. Dart, *North American High Tory Tradition*.

47. For explorations of both availability and fidelity, which ground a kind of community of hope, see Marcel, *Being and Having*.

not simply linear, but circular as though a wheel traveling along a road allowing us to revisit the call and claim of Christ upon humanity apocalyptically, in a present moment, while moving toward the eschatological future), offers us a vision of time that is not disciplined by clocks or by capital.[48] Taking all of this together, such theology *is* an ethics, bearing witness to the One who interrupts and transforms us, teaching us not only to say but also to see the world, and all of humanity, including ourselves, in it according to the Way. Such theology trains us to see our life, with our neighbors (including creatures of all kinds), as a struggling *together* toward the reconciled future in the unclarities of the present. Such an ethics, therefore, is a listening for (which includes the permission given toward, and the invitation to participate in) human life becoming shaped by Jesus Christ.

A POSTSCRIPT: WHEN WE NO LONGER HEAR OF HUMAN LIFE. DISSENT.

As in previous days, ours are troubling. Ours are a time of unrest. Ours are a time when hope is needed. But hope will not come without humanity. In many ways, the preceding is a call to human being, which we must learn and practice. Being is a becoming. But, as I alluded to above, so is nothingness:

I have watched with grief and lament as children and families at border sites become fodder for politicized inhumanity and instrumentalized dehumanization, whether or not persons are caged or lost to unforgiving waters. The persons attempting entry to new lands, whether by clandestine or legitimate means, are denounced and disparaged. They are othered and demeaned. And for those suffering abuses at the hands of persons in positions of authority, the depredations incurred will be lasting and at times (too many times) prove fatal.

I have watched with woe as 725 kilometers of blacktop British Columbian highway weeps for Indigenous women and girls, missing or murdered. And I have watched with anguish as reports feature the role of calloused law enforcement personnel and judicial complicity in the harm directed toward Indigenous persons across Canada—Indigenous persons who disproportionately fill incarceration ledgers and prison cells and the back seats of police vehicles taking young Indigenous men on

48. Williams, *Being Human*, 77–79.

"starlight tours" to be abandoned to their death in rural Saskatchewan winterscapes.

I have watched with disgust as the lives of unarmed persons are snuffed out by police, whether shot in the back, killed while in the refuge of their home, suffocated on the ground, and suffocated again, while repeating that now familiar cry for help, "I can't breathe!" I have watched with sorrow as the lives of young black men are lynched by so-called community watchmen-come-executioners.

Toward such border sites, blacktop, and body bags, and toward those persons complicit in the dehumanization, maltreatment, and murder of neighbors, I must practice dissent. I must call others, much closer than I to the physical borders and bodies, closer than I to these neighbors with names and faces, to practice dissent too.

I must confess, however: I have watched at a distance.

Yet I cannot *watch* anymore! I must dissent. I must call others to dissent because in these times it is difficult to hear for human life!

Toward those politicians in office, and those bureaucrats peddling policy and principle, and those in armchairs trained by the hyperbole and deceit of state-sanctioned propaganda, and those in pews coerced by ravenous wolves (Matthew 7:15), I must summons you to open your eyes to the Babylon that has blinded you: do not participate in her sins (Revelation 18:4)!

Toward those of us malformed by systemic racism, which sits in our consciousness and, as M, Shawn Copeland laments, "shapes our ideas, attitudes, and dispositions; directs our cultural norms, rules, and expectations; guides our linguistic, literary, artistic, media representations and practices,"[49] I likewise offer a summons: see the profane doctrines that have, whether wittingly or unwittingly, shaped us. The social practices, theological heterodoxies, and political performances have made many of us into icons of inhumanity. I must dissent such inhumanity, trusting that such protest will not be in vain.

Toward those who stand dispassionately adjacent to these borders and body bags, who stand in positions of power over these persons who have become objectified for political inscriptions, corporate profit-making, and grotesque moralizing by the familiar calculus of costs and benefits coupled with rhetoric of safety and sovereignty, law and order; toward those persons who wield the Scriptures like Satan tempting Christ, and

---

49. Copeland, "Overcoming Christianity's Lingering Complicity," para. 3.

others who manufacture photo ops that instrumentalize the church while blaspheming Christ: get away from me and my fellows (Matthew 4:10; 16:24)—and listen for Christ's rejoinder, "Follow me."

Such call for dissent, however, must not be misunderstood as call to contempt and belligerence. It is not a call to match power for power, as though the tactics of dehumanization are justifiable. They are not!

Rather, this is a call to protest the inhumanity heaped upon our neighbors, both near and distant, by exercising one's humanity. It is a call to learn that our endurance in these difficult times, our humanity, will be strengthened when it reflects the way of Christ, whose faithfulness trains us toward a hope that interrogates and admonishes "the principalities about their vocation as creatures to serve the social needs of human beings."[50] It is an active, embodied hope that clothes the naked, feeds the hungry, comforts the distressed, shelters the destitute, cares for the infirmed and imprisoned, and embraces the neighbor (both enemy and friend) with love and in haste (Matthew 25). By such an active, embodied performance, we all might be humanized. Even if it risks sacrifice.

By such dissent, as the American lawyer and lay theologian William Stringfellow reminded his readers, we might learn to "live most humanly."[51]

So, let this be a call to become discerning of the poisonous doctrines, political schema, and social practices that coerce and constrain our being, and the being of others, and where inhumanity is fostered, contempt is flaunted, and despair flourishes.

Let this be a call to dissent, which is a call to become human again so that a human society might emerge and hope might become real, viz. enfleshed, as we learn to participate in those opportunities to follow Christ on his way, where neighborliness is practiced and life might be risked, in prayer and passion, for the sake of others.

Only then might our neighbors, both near and distant, discover a kind of strength that resources a patience to hasten justice that invigorates humanity.

Dissent when we no longer hear of human life! Be(come) human in these troubling times.

---

50. Stringfellow, *Ethic for Christians and Other Aliens*, 57.
51. Stringfellow, *Ethic of Christians and Other Aliens*, 156.

11

Embracing Indigenous Values
for Theological Education

RAY ALDRED

I AM THE Indigenous element. A purveyor of exotic raw data sent here to illuminate and beguile, to be faithful yet a bit treacherous, a singer of songs, a teller of stories, a hunter and a traveler.

Indigenous people in Canada and the United States have all experienced trauma[1] and it has been our companion and told us tales in the dark that shaped us and made us see some things clearer and at other times distorted our vision. In the Indigenous Studies Program we are attempting to see and work on our distortions. The eschaton reminds us that we see only partially, and we need a community to see a bit clearer. So, listening to the voices of Indigenous people, Vancouver School of Theology, through the Indigenous Studies Program, gives back space to try and hold these two stories beside each other: Indigenous identity and Christian faith, until they can be told together.[2] Our hope at the Vancouver School of Theology is that by the end of their program a student would be familiar with at least two Indigenous spiritualities so that graduates are equipped to by an ally with Indigenous people.

---

1. Brokenleg, "Spirituality of Self-Determination".
2. Wesley, "Traditional Aboriginal Spirituality.".

As I write this piece, and the Indigenous Studies Program operates at the Vancouver School of Theology, we are mindful that we are all on the unceded territory of the Musqueam people. They have welcomed us here and we are living as guests, according to their way of understanding things. We respect one another, so we will not fight about our different religions and will make room for one another to be who we were created to be.

Vancouver School of Theology has adopted this Indigenous value of making room for people to be who Creator made us to be and this forms part of the rational for an Indigenous Studies Program at a seminary. Vancouver School of Theology is changing because of its relationship with Indigenous people and Indigenous people are changing and growing because of the relationship with Vancouver School of Theology. The creation and nurture of this reciprocal relationship is the goal of reconciliation.[3]

You will notice that the first page of this essay has been taken up in the preliminary comments; this is protocol. Protocol is how we approach one another and hold and care for one another in a respectful manner. For the Indigenous world, the preliminaries or the protocol is always important. Put another way by my friend Adrian Jacobs, for Indigenous people the preamble is as important as the rest of the proceedings. The preamble includes giving introductions and reminding ourselves of all our relatives and the land. Relationships are what is most important for Indigenous people and for Indigenous studies. Now that we have done the work of protocol or preamble, we can move on to the question of: how do we talk about Indigenous studies?

The late Vine Deloria asks, "how do we talk about [Indigenous Identity] intelligently?" In light of the colonial legacy, how do you have a conversation about Indigenous theology and identity and its relationship with Christian faith without quickly becoming polarized and politized in thinking about Indigenous life and identity? What is needed is a respectful dialogue with Indigenous thought and people. Deloria suggest that there are at least three things necessary to begin to understand and form an Indigenous philosophy. I am suggesting that Deloria's ideas could help those not familiar with North American Indigenous people begin to indigenize their own thinking. Deloria first emphasized that in order to embrace an Indigenous thought and life there is a need for mutual respect

3. Truth and Reconciliation Commission of Canada, *Honouring the Truth*, iv.

by acknowledging that an Indigenous approach to life and ultimately theology is different from modern Western thought, but equal (and better at some points).[4] Indigenous studies helps people to develop a way of looking at the world in new and different ways that are innovative.

For example, Leslie Newbigin points out that the West has lost the ability to see its own scientific worldview through the lens of the gospel. As a result, the call of the gospel, according to Newbigin, is reduced to maintaining the status quo. He suggests, and I agree, that in order for the West to hear the call to conversion it must hear the gospel told back to it from another culture. The Indigenous church is one such voice in North America. Of course, this is extending Deloria's idea from philosophy into the realm of theology and mission, but this would not be the first time that philosophy was pressed into service by theology. Indigenous theology and Western theology are different but they are equal.

Second, in order to enter into an Indigenous way of proceeding in theology, newcomers must adopt or respect Indigenous boundaries in specific places.[5] For example, Indigenous scholars, because of their focus on relationship, relate stories from relatives and elders, which means the research paper is often in the form of a first-person narrative. This has rubbed some Enlightenment thinkers the wrong way, particularly researchers who claim objectivity rules supreme. Part of the hegonomy of the West has been that it claims to be the arbitrator of what counts for a scientific worldview and that all other peoples must speak as they speak. This kind of thinking has spilt over into popular thought, which has produced scholars who believe their task is to collect and refine "exotic raw data" for their project.[6] Therefore at VST we have sought to create a space that respects Indigenous boundaries. For example, you cannot reduce Indigenous peoples to one group; therefore, we engage in culture-specific examples in our teaching. There is, as well, a greater attention given to the oral nature of Indigenous wisdom, which requires a narrative approach that honors the community's approach to keeping wisdom.[7] This has included research projects that took on alternative forms from written papers. Honoring Indigenous boundaries also means that some things are out of bounds to speak about. The researcher must respect

---

4. Deloria, "Philosophy and the Tribal Peoples," 5–9.

5. Deloria, "Philosophy and the Tribal Peoples," 9.

6. Tienou, "Indigenous Theologizing: From the Margins to the Center," 10.

7. Eigenbrod and Hulan, *Aboriginal Oral Traditions*, 140–45.

communities' rules about recording information and guard against cultural appropriation.

Finally, Deloria suggests that one must embrace an Indigenous communal identity to understand Indigenous philosophy.[8] For example, acknowledging whose traditional territory we are standing in is a beginning of this process. We must understand that we are responsible to all our relationships, to live in a respective way toward all our relatives. I have found that Indigenous people can teach the enlightened autonomous individual about communal relationship. The modern world is consumed with individual rights, but in Indigenous country we want to make choices that honor our relatives, which includes those who have passed on and those who will arrive in the future. It requires that newcomers listen more than talk. For other newcomer individuals, entering an Indigenous learning space will mean they must give up their perceived right to verbalize their thoughts. Communal identity means learning to see the web of relationships all around and acting responsibly in that context.

The ongoing work of seeking a just society means that Indigenous studies requires an ethical attitude that moves us to seek restorative justice.[9] In the process of research many newcomers, still in the fog of institutional amnesia, will not only come face to face with the injustice of the past but also discover they are implicated and share the shame and guilt. This will require them to move away from the comfort of academic apathy, sometimes called objectivity, and examine their own motivation for studying with Indigenous people. An ethical attitude means that the research must work toward righting wrongs. An ethical attitude means that Indigenous studies is not primarily the examination of a people for observation from a distance; it is studying with Indigenous people and allowing yourself to be led by Indigenous people. Thus, in the face of historic injustice, the newcomer is asked to respond to Indigenous people's call for reconciliation. Vancouver School of Theology, through the Indigenous Studies Program, for example, is always responding to the voice of Indigenous people, not seeking to lead Indigenous people, but seeking to ethically respond to the historic trauma of colonization and work to heal and be healed with Indigenous people.

8. Deloria, "Philosophy and the Tribal Peoples," 10.
9. Kulchyski, "What Is Native Studies?," 14.

Seeking to understand and enter an Indigenous learning space means that newcomers must understand protocol. As mentioned above, protocol could be considered the ceremony necessary to enter into a sacred space. The space between us is respect and honor; protocol ensures that we can collaborate to achieve together what is impossible if we were to stay in our own group. For example, newcomers are given the opportunity to enter into Indigenous story. Sophie McCall writes that Indigenous story provides a place for collaboration, but the story must be listened to in a respectful fashion. This listening is part of protocol and insures we are pursuing harmony.[10] Harmony or proper relatedness is the understanding that undergirds Indigenous shared space. This is an ethical way of relating to one another in the Indigenous Studies Program, but also at the Vancouver School of Theology as a whole.

As Taiaiake Alfred points out, crucial to a place for development of Indigenous leadership is a noncoercive, egalitarian space that respects the individual and communal autonomy of Indigenous people and communities. Vancouver School of Theology has sought to build this into its governance structure by having an Indigenous advisory board that advises the director of the Indigenous Studies Program. In this way, Indigenous thought and voice guides the development of the Indigenous Studies Program. This respect for Indigenous voices is built into the governance of the school but also requires that newcomer learners to learn to study according to Indigenous boundaries to begin to enter into a communal identity with Indigenous people.

Indigenous people have suffered and continue to suffer from systemic racism in Canadian institutions, including churches and seminaries. The residential schools in Canada and the United States prove this point. An ethical attitude for the Vancouver School of Theology has meant that we work hard to ensure that we have a safe learning environment. Maintaining this safe place for Indigenous studies requires that newcomers practice the following before offering their advice. First, listen so that you understand people's contexts. Second, research to see if your prior understanding about Indigenous people is in fact the case. There are a set of myths (the myth of Columbus discovering America; the myth of *terra nullias* or empty land) about Indigenous people that circulate in society that maintain paternalism and racism. Third, make sure you are not leading the conversation to your desired outcome, but

10. McCall, "What the Map Cuts Up," 309." <style face="italic">Essays on Canadian Writing</style>, no. 80 (Fall 2003)

seeking to learn. Finally, these steps may help you realize and confront your own assumptions about Indigenous people.

Peter Kulchyski writes that Indigenous studies involves the recognition, creation, and legitimization of knowledge.[11] For example, Indigenous scholar Steve Charleston writes that there is a native Old Testament and suggests this needs to be explored to enlarge the understanding of the church.[12] This and other aspects of Indigenous thought and research help break open the Enlightenment theological magisterium,[13] which has held shut its canon from innovation by Indigenous method. This does not mean an outright rejection of modern theological or academic thought; it does mean that we attempt to hold these two approaches, as stated above, as different but equal, comparing and contrasting as we all seek to develop better ways of relating to one another. This means, however, that Indigenous thought must take prominence because Western Enlightenment thought is the default for the academy.

The implication for newcomers is a shift away from a predominately utilitarian approach to other groups.[14] Indigenous thought must be appreciated in its own right, not reduced to information or given value based only on what it produces. Newcomers need to be in relationship with Indigenous people to develop a new national and world narrative, a narrative that affirms the intention of the Creator to return all things to harmony.[15] The Indigenous nations in Canada and the United States have a history of seeking ways to live in harmony with one another. If you listen, you can hear the voice of Indigenous people speaking, as it has for many centuries.

There is always a decolonizing aspect to Indigenous studies. After all, we are questioning Western theology and the West's way of doing education and research. Many newcomers who enter into an Indigenous learning space encounter resistance within themselves as they learn to see things in a different way. Ethnocentrism is present within most people, and at times in Canada and the United States this ethnocentrism rhas resulted in seeing Indigenous studies as exotic or peculiar. This ends up

11. Kulchyski, "What Is Native Studies?," 13–14.

12. Charleston, " Old Testament of Native America," 71.

13. Paul Ricoeur explores moving past the ruling catagories of the magisterium. See Ricoeur, "Toward a Hermeneutic," 2.

14. James McClendon explores the tendancy among North American churches to operate primarily out of a utilitarian ethic. See McClendon, *Biography as Theology.*

15. Ricoeur, *Political and Social Essays,* 148.

being pejorative since Indigenous studies is seen as optional or contingent for the theology and life of the average non-Indigenous researcher. Indigenous studies was not, however, considered fundamental to understanding the world or the academy or theology. VST is attempting to change the perception of Indigenous studies as contingent to a recognition that Indigenous studies is essential to theology in North America.

According to Indigenous scholar Shawn Wilson, the academy has moved through different periods of decolonization.[16] 1940 to 1970 was the assimilation stage. There were little or no decolonizing efforts happening, and Indigenous people were studied for the needs of outsiders. From 1970 to 1990, however, there was a shift toward Indigenous people doing Indigenous research, but it was still driven by a Western method and was considered exotic. This was followed by a period roughly from 1990 to 2000 in which decolonization took root and Indigenous studies began to question all Western methods and claims of objectivity. Since 2000 Indigenous people have set the agenda for Indigenous studies. VST was ahead of the curve on this, having begun the Indigenous Studies Program in 1984 with mostly Indigenous instructors populating the courses since at least 1990. In fact, VST has taken the lead for Indigenous studies in offering an MDiv by extension as well as offering a competency-based program. The Indigenous Studies Program is the base or foundation on which VST operates. Indigenous studies is not contingent but central to the training of thoughtful, engaged, and generous leaders.

I want to reiterate the necessity of understanding that Indigenous studies is not merely a field of research; it involves entering into relationship with Indigenous people. Indigenous life in Canada is not the study of extinct culture but engagement with a living, dynamic, traditional way of life. This means that a learner from the outside must guard against assuming that Western academic research methods ensure objectivity. Because you are entering into relationship with Indigenous people, you are by definition in a subjective relationship and need to be. Indigenous studies is not about fitting Indigenous thought and understanding into Western forms; it is about seeing in new ways what before was overlooked. It is about seeing the spirituality of Indigenous people, which includes a historical relationship with Jesus Christ and the church. Secularized approaches to Indigenous studies often disregard the indigenization of the church and faith by Indigenous elders. We encourage learners to consider

16. Wilson, *Research Is Ceremony*, 45–59.

a breadth of Indigenous voices and not merely rely on self-proclaimed experts.

For example, Susan Neylan, writing about the Tsimshian people embracing Christianity, does not attribute their receiving Christ solely to unscrupulous missionary pressure. She notes that Indigenous people embraced Christian faith and began to indigenize Christian faith to further their own goals for their society, despite missionary pressure and tactics.[17] Neylan's work highlights the complexity of holding together Indigenous identity and a Christian faith that has been dominated by the Euro-Western church. The Indigenous Studies Program at the VST seeks to embrace that complexity and be shaped in the midst of it.

To do Indigenous studies involves working through historical trauma. We take great care in how we talk about trauma. As mentioned above, we acknowledge that the Vancouver School of Theology is located on the traditional ancestral unceded territory of the Musqueam people. This simple statement exposes the historical trauma of stolen land. Indigenous studies involves delving into the depths of the reality of this trauma through qualitative research, not merely talking about the number of people displaced by colonial policy, but hearing from the survivors of residential schools and from Indigenous leaders working on self-determination, and understanding how to form an alliance with Indigenous peoples. This is a challenge to newcomers because they become aware of how they have benefitted from the oppression of Indigenous people. We work hard, however, to also offer guidance and instruction on how to begin to take responsibility and work to be an agent of healing and reconciliation.

Indigenous studies involves learning the story of Indigenous people from Indigenous people. It is then learning to the tell your own story in light of this new relationship with Indigenous people. As the Indigenous Studies Program takes back space by focusing upon the development Indigenous leaders for the Indigenous church, we invite the newcomer to our traditional territories to enter into a relationship with us. Enter our story, the Indigenous story. You will be changed, and we will change because of this relationship, but we will not become something we were never meant to be.

---

17. Neylan, *Heavens Are Changing*, 6, 245.

12

Approaching Interreligious Studies

WHY STUDY INTERRELIGIOUS STUDIES?

TRIBALIST. UNCHANGING. DIVINE CHOICE. Gospel. Heavenly Hybrid. Sea Goddess. Love Temple. Zen Rose. What is this list?

Could it be a poetic description of increasing interreligious openness? It could be. But it is actually a list of lipstick colors. You can find them at the Mac cosmetics department in The Bay, Canada's largest department store.

Take a moment to wonder at the work of Mac's marketing professionals. "How," they asked themselves, "can we associate our products with beauty?" And they answered, "People associate religion and spirituality with beauty. Let's give our lipsticks religious and spiritual names! We will use beautiful images from Indigenous, Jewish, Christian, Buddhist, Hindu, pagan, and hybrid traditions." One could take offense at this superficial hijacking of religions into the world of commerce. But I prefer to find it delightful. Religious traditions are a beautiful part of the cultural landscape.

Some years ago, North Americans spoke of the "secular" and "religious" spheres of public life. But the secular sphere, as many new immigrants noted, was actually Christian. Shopping hours, legal holidays, and ceremonial prayers at public events expressed primarily Christian traditions. New Canadians of other religious traditions found this challenging. If you celebrate your Sabbath on Saturday, stores are closed on Sunday, and your employer only gives you weekends off, when do you shop for your household? If the only legal religious holiday is Christmas, but Diwali is your biggest festival, how do you fulfill your family obligations? If police officers wear a regulation hat, but your religious tradition mandates a turban, what do you wear to work? One possible response to this multicultural critique might be to push religion more strongly out of the public sphere. Canada, however, has moved in the opposite direction. Here, we are experimenting with a new legal understanding of secularism. An "open" secular public square would not be devoid of religious expression. Instead, it would be welcoming to all religious traditions. Of course, dissonances would arise; but these would be solved through respectful debate, policy, litigation, and legislation.[1]

So, if we wish to be culturally literate religious leaders, scholars, and chaplains, we need to know about multiple religious traditions.[2] We will be called to work with interfaith families. On matters of civic engagement, such as food security, income inequality, and environmental protection, we will need to work with leaders of other traditions. When political issues of interreligious violence make headline news, we will be asked to respond. These are common professional challenges in today's world. They call us to be a bit like *multifaith* leaders, who can reach out to people with different beliefs; *interfaith* leaders, who can find common beliefs despite differences; *interspiritual* leaders, who can build community through shared experience of the divine; *interreligious* leaders, who can work within and across religious institutions; or *multicultural* leaders, who respect historical and cultural differences between traditions. These five terms overlap, naming interwoven dimensions of our culture's religious landscape. To rise to the challenges they describe, we need knowledge, spiritual openness, listening skills, and an understanding of interreligious activity.

1. Bouchard and Taylor, *Building the Future.*
2. Kujawa-Holbrook, *God Beyond Borders.*

DEEP ECUMENISM: A NEED FOR KNOWLEDGE

Return with me for a moment to the cosmetics counter, as I tell a story. Spoiler alert: this is a story about falsely imagining we know other religious traditions. One evening, my adult daughter and I took a field trip to The Bay. My daughter loves theatre. She has been an actor, director, film producer, stage manager, festival curator, costume designer, and theatre manager. Staying up to date with seasonal fashion is important for her art. So, we visited the cosmetics counter to see this season's features. Fortunately for her, but unfortunately for me, *a lot* of new colors were on display. Soon, I realized she was going to sample every one of them.

Bored, I looked around, hoping for some interesting people to watch. Over by the checkout counter, I saw a customer passionately negotiating with a store clerk. Impolitely, I walked over so I could eavesdrop. The customer turned to me. "I have a store gift card," she said. "Someone gave it to me as a present. But I just finished my PhD and I've got so many student loans. I need household cash, not luxury gifts. The store won't buy back the card. Would you buy it?"

"Congratulations on your PhD!" I said. "What was your dissertation topic?"

"I'm a musicologist," she said. "I studied the spirituality of music. Specifically, I looked at the different musical tones and vibrations used in different denominations and traditions."

"Wow!" I said. "I'm also interested in different religious traditions. I'm a rabbi, and I teach interreligious studies at an ecumenical Christian seminary."

"Ah!" she said. "You and I are both hoping for the same thing. Have you heard about Rabbi S.?" she asked. "He's in Jerusalem, giving great talks, bringing all kinds of people into the fold."

Gradually, I realized that Rabbi S. is a Messianic rabbi. He practices Jewish traditions while preaching the Christian gospel. Most Jews and Christians today find Messianic Judaism an odd hybrid. But this musicologist did not. Instead, she saw it as a fusion highlighting what all spiritual traditions have in common. She truly believed that all religious traditions have the same ultimate goal. We all wish to live in a spiritual kingdom on earth, headed by God's anointed messenger.

Of course, I said nothing to correct her. Our meeting was so serendipitous. She was so friendly. By chance we had discovered a common interest. We were not ready for a debate. So, I said I'd look up her teacher.

I wished her well. And, being very familiar with graduate school debt, though I had paid mine off years ago, I bought her gift certificate.

But, privately, I wondered, "How could she be so fundamentally wrong about what religious traditions actually share? Why would she think every tradition is like Christianity, fusing the idea of God and Messiah? Doesn't she know that the Divine is infinite spiritual energy, that all religious ideas point to this one God, and that all religious people want only to feel God's presence everywhere?" Then, suddenly, an insight blew into my mind. The musicologist thinks her Christianity expresses the essence of all religion. In the same way, I think my Judaism expresses the essence of all religion. From childhood, I had been taught that God is One.[3] And on one day, all traditions will wake to a shared realization: we all call that same God by many different names. These two points are key themes in Jewish liturgy. In fact, I had chanted them so many times that they had become basic building blocks of my religious thinking. But now I saw they were blocks of a different kind: blocks that prevented me from understanding religious traditions on their own terms. As a Jew in Canada, I am a member of a religious minority. Still, I now understand, I had subtly seen all religious traditions as variations on my own. In fact, I had subtly believed all were immature versions of my tradition. Thus, I needed a new way to think about the coexistence of multiple traditions.

Without knowing academic theory, I had tried to live into Christian writer Matthew Fox's concept of "deep ecumenism." Fox begins with the idea of ecumenism, i.e., unity of purpose between different churches. Then, he posits a unity of purpose across all religious traditions. Divine spirit underlies all everyday reality, he says, like an underground river of life-giving water. Religious traditions help people access that river. Thus, each tradition is like a differently formed well, drawing water from the one river of Divine Spirit.[4] The Christian concept of Christ, for example, is a well. When you draw down into the river, you connect with the "Cosmic Christ," the infinite divine presence animating all religious traditions.[5]

Deep ecumenism is a generous concept, inviting us to see humanity as a single spiritual family. A first glimpse into that unity is a powerful experience of God's infinity. But the concept of deep ecumenism is

3. Hammer, *Entering Jewish Prayer*.

4. Fox, *One River, Many Wells*.

5. Fox, *Coming of the Cosmic Christ*.

only one possible first step. On the one hand, it directs our attention to a picture bigger than the ritual or doctrinal details of a particular tradition. But it glosses over the social, psychological, and spiritual power of those details. On the other hand, deep ecumenism uses language and imagery from one tradition to talk about universality. This language can block us from attending to the actual elements of other traditions. It can lead us to claim, as both the musicologist and I did, that "your religion is *really* a version of ours."

The first and simplest way to avoid this superficial glossing is to learn more about different traditions. How do they articulate the most important themes of their traditions? Sacred texts and stories offer one accessible starting point. For example, the opening lines of the Jewish Torah, Christian New Testament, and Islamic Qur'an each summarize their tradition's worldview. Through the creation story, Torah teaches that God, who exists beyond time, was-is-will be. Heaven and earth, which exist in time, are infused with Divine Presence.[6] With a genealogy of Jesus, the New Testament teaches that God fulfills promises in history, through the life of a chosen Messiah.[7] With a poetic hymn of praise, the Qur'an explains that God, with justice, has set out for us a strict ethical path. With compassion, God has showed us how to follow it.[8] Had the musicologist learned about these themes, she would not have assumed we shared messianic expectations. Had I known about them earlier, I would not have reached adulthood believing that all traditions focus on divine infinity.

COMPARATIVE THEOLOGY: SPIRITUAL OPENNESS

There are, of course, other ways to enter interreligious appreciation, though they do all involve learning. Francis Clooney, a Jesuit priest and scholar of Hinduism, calls his approach "comparative theology." We do not have to choose, he says, between appreciating religious particularity and experiencing God's infinity. Instead, Clooney says, we can allow the divine to speak to us through the symbols of other traditions. Through this, we can deepen our understanding of our own traditions.[9]

---

6. Schneersohn, *True Existence.*

7. Ehrman, *New Testament.*

8. Mir, *Understanding the Islamic Scripture.*

9. Clooney, *Comparative Theology.*

Clooney discovered comparative theology on a research trip. He was traveling in India. He stopped in a tiny town. He entered the town's tiny temple. He stood before the devotional statues of gods and goddesses dressed in glittery clothing. It was a research stop like any other—until, suddenly, he felt addressed by the maternal goddess Lakshmi. In that moment, his inner dialogue was something like this. "Oh my, I feel the goddess. She is speaking to me. But I can't listen. I'm a Christian; we don't worship goddesses. I had better shut down. But I'm doing ethnographic research. I'm supposed to open my mind to new meanings. So, I should open. But if I do, I might convert. I should close!" Finally, he surrendered to the moment, feeling that he and the goddess Lakshmi saw one another.

For months, he tried to process his mystical experience. He looked for analogies in Christian tradition. His first find was the Catholic tradition of revering Mary, mother of Jesus. He studied the medieval hymn *Stabat Mater*, literally "the mother stands," sorrowfully at the scene of her son's crucifixion. As Jesus dies, Mary becomes the "font of hope for those who wish to live."[10] She, a maternal figure, becomes the gateway to an experience of the divine. Thus, Clooney understood, the poet's experience of Mary was like his experience of Lakshmi. He could now appreciate the hymn, and the reverence for Mary, more deeply. So, he wondered, who else reveres Mary? He discovered that Mary is an important character in the Qur'an. Many Islamic women see Mary, the birthing mother, as a spiritual inspiration. Clooney continued to wonder. Is Mary the only example of a motherly spiritual facilitator in Christian tradition? His research led him to read about the mystical visions of Sojourner Truth (1797–1883), American anti-slavery and women's rights activist. Truth was the mother of five, a former slave, and a Methodist preacher. At her lowest point, she said, Jesus the liberator appeared to her to encourage her work for human rights. Through this work, Truth became a spiritual mother to many.

In India, Clooney had encountered a portal to the divine through unfamiliar symbols. The experience awakened new spiritual keys within his psyche. When he turned towards Christianity with those keys, he unlocked deeper dimensions of familiar Christian ideas. Interreligious study had deepened his understanding of his own tradition. My own experience resonates with Clooney's. Some years ago, I came to VST as a Jewish student. My rabbinic studies had included clinical pastoral

10. Clooney, *Comparative Theology*, 93.

education, counseling, and psychology. Still, I felt something lacking in my congregational work as a pastoral caregiver. In my interactions, I did not feel I was drawing on the Divine. So, I entered VST's spiritual direction program. Of course, I worried about opening this spiritual door. What if Jesus appeared and taught me to be a Christian? How would I explain it to my Jewish parents? But I walked through the door anyway to learn Christian spiritual concepts and practices: the dark night of the soul, the interior castle of St. Theresa of Avila, centering prayer, praying with icons. Each new concept and experience deepened my understanding of spirituality. With my deeper understanding, I saw additional dimensions in my Jewish tradition. In my worship leadership, I lived more fully into the meaning of famous hymns. As a pastoral counselor, I quietly brought spiritual energy into a room. When needed, I could pray spontaneously for healing, or teach a reflective spiritual practice with the help of Jewish concepts. Over time, I became a better rabbi.

Crossing boundaries into this kind of comparative theology is not easy. We all belong to complex religious cultures, with multiple sects and denominations. Thus, we learn to define and advocate for our own sects. Denominational protection and self-defense become default habits. It can be a challenge to switch hats and say, "We are here to be open to something different."

ETHICAL ENGAGEMENT: OPENING TO LISTEN

But sometimes the only way to move forward is to be open to something different. Indigenous Canadian reconciliation places us in such a time. The modern nation of Canada was settled by British and French colonialists. In order to turn an economic profit, early settlers took over land and resources belonging to Indigenous peoples. At times, Canadian colonialists used violence, oppression, suppression, and reeducation to achieve their goals. Multiple Christian denominations participated actively in reeducating Indigenous youth in the abusive residential school system.[11] Their participation had many motives, including racism, political power, and the religious belief that Christianity is the one correct expression of spirituality for all humanity. The last residential school closed in 1990, and the Canadian government formally apologized in 2008. But Canadians are just beginning to learn what it means to decolonize. Churches, in

11. Eshet, *Stolen Lives*.

particular, have the opportunity to decolonize religion. Decolonization can *only* happen when Christians open to understanding of Indigenous traditions. To understand, we must listen with an open mind. To open our minds, we must disengage from some of the concepts that normally frame our thoughts.

Canadian Indigenous legal scholar Willie Ermine speaks of this open-mindedness as "ethical engagement." Often, he says, groups come into dialogue to solve community problems. And usually one group has designed the format. Subtly, the format will express the worldview and goals of the designers. Such a space can block genuine encounter and, thus, genuine change. So, the first step towards a productive community dialogue is collaborative preplanning. Representative participants learn about one another's cultures, share ideas about dialogue, and design a meeting space that can hold different perspectives. For example, he says, imagine representatives planning a discussion of the right to land ownership. Productive discussion is only possible when participants understand that Indigenous concepts of a tribe holding land in common differ from Euro-Canadian concepts of private ownership.[12] Even when such understandings are established, Ermine says, people often enter discussion suspicious of one another. Certain that their own preconceptions are correct, they fail to listen to one another. Thus, he recommends ritual gestures that disrupt hierarchy and division. Such gestures could be as simple as, for example, asking everyone to remove their shoes and sit together on the floor.[13]

Here, Ermine has in mind Indigenous Canadian and Euro-Canadian encounters. But his idea of ethical engagement helps us think more carefully about practical issues in interreligious learning. What are effective structures for learning together? We could study texts from multiple traditions, but that leaves no room for traditions that transmit stories orally. We could share rituals in a collaborative prayer service. In that case, which tradition's definition of "prayer" and "service" would we use? We could discuss the basic tenets of our faith traditions. But some traditions define themselves through practice, not faith. Before we begin to learn together, it seems, we need to learn a lot. The Interfaith Amigos have much to say about the journey.

---

12. Ermine, "Ethical Space of Engagement," 193-203.

13. Ermine, "Ethical Space in Action," YouTube video, 5:28, https://www.youtube.com/watch?v=ZUfXu3gfVJ8.

A SHARED JOURNEY TO UNDERSTANDING

The Interfaith Amigos are Imam Jamal Rahman, Pastor Don MacKenzie, and Rabbi Ted Falcon. Through decades of team teaching, they have learned a great deal about interreligious study. It does not make sense, they teach, to think through a theology of interfaith activity before you start. Actually, before you start, you do not know where the activity will take you. All you can commit to is a shared journey. The Interfaith Amigos do not recommend creating a step-by-step process. They do say, however, that, in their experience the journey unfolds in five stages: (1) moving beyond separation and suspicion, (2) inquiring more deeply, (3) sharing both the easy and the difficult parts, (4) moving beyond safe territory, and (5) exploring spiritual practices from other traditions.[14]

Moving beyond separation and suspicion might simply be a decision to reach out. Groups might plan a social event where people ask one another, "How are you? Where are you from? Who is in your family? Do you like cats or dogs, neither or both?" Or, groups might get together for a simple community action project, where conversation flows easily around the task at hand. Inquiring more deeply happens when people begin to talk about their practices, theologies, and cultures. When people become comfortable, they sometimes share their own challenges, e.g., prayers they never understood, rituals they always avoided, ideas they disagree with. Increased ease opens the door to difficult questions. What is the role of women in your tradition? How have you welcomed LGBTQ individuals and groups? What is your attitude towards violence in the history of your tradition?[15] Through honest discussion of these questions, people begin to trust one another. They invite one another to share rituals and practices, and accept invitations with an open heart. Mutually, they expect to be moved spiritually, without fear of losing their own religious identity.

For me, it has been comforting to hear this account of five stages. Often, religious communities schedule interfaith events as a one-time-only special event. Afterwards they may wonder, "Why was the exchange so superficial? What did we do wrong?" In fact, they did nothing wrong. Instead, they graciously began to move beyond suspicion and separation with a polite, welcoming outreach event. No one can say in advance how many hours, days, or years it will take to deepen the exchange. Only that if

14. Mackenzie, Falcon, and Rahman, *Getting to the Heart of Interfaith*.

15. Mackenzie, Falcon, and Rahman, *Religion Gone Astray*.

you stay with the relationship, it will deepen. And if you journey together long enough, you will share spiritual experiences. You will not merely observe one another as guests, but will be moved in ways that awaken new spiritual perspectives. And, as Clooney teaches, through these new perspectives you will deepen your relationship with your own tradition.

CONCLUSION

At the Vancouver School of Theology, every student engages in interreligious learning. We study Scripture and story, are introduced to spiritual practices, develop listening skills, and approach Indigenous spirituality as a major world tradition. Through classes, programs, and field trips, we meet teachers of non-Christian traditions. These teachers become professional contacts and, in some cases, friends. Through friendship, as philosopher Maria Lugones says, we have a unique opportunity to enter each other's worlds.[16] Friendships between leaders from different faith traditions can have profound effects on communities. A single friendship may not bring about world peace, but it can certainly help bring about communal peace. As the anthropologist Margaret Mead reportedly said, "Never doubt that a small group of thoughtful, committed citizens can change the world. Indeed, it is the only thing that ever has."

16. Lugones, "Playfulness, 'World'-Traveling."

13

Things They Do Teach
Reflections on Theological Field Education

BRENDA FAWKES

WHEN I FIRST BEGAN as Director of Theological Field Education at VST I came across a social media site called: *Things They Didn't Teach Us in Seminary.* I immediately began following the group, convinced that it would become a valuable source of insight for me, and other faculty, as we attempted a responsive and relevant curriculum. My hope had been to hear from the field on what was useful and adaptive given the current context for ministry leadership. What I soon discovered were prolific posts suggesting that they were inadequately prepared for all kinds of ministry and leadership situations. Given their self-identified deficiencies, I quickly concluded that there was no possible way to cover everything they were missing. It would be impossible to cover all ground and check off a laundry list of skills in one degree—especially with pressure to decrease credit hours and shorten degrees. I don't begrudge the existence of the TTDTUIS group. What it seems to accomplish is to provide collegial support for those in ministry, a place to share resources, to find compassion in the difficult moments, to express gratitude and pray. However, it does not inform curriculum or assure us that if followed, we will adequately form competent leaders.

The temptation in the church and theological formation is to come up with lists of skills and characteristics to answer the question: How do we prepare leadership for the exercise of ministry? This question is especially acute in the area of field education and ministry practice. For it is in field education where one is tested on one's ability to turn thought into action—to bridge the gap between academy and field.

PROFESSIONAL LEADERSHIP

All Association of Theological School–accredited theological schools have to include field-based learning in their degrees that prepare people for professional pastoral and ministerial leadership. This has not always been the case.[1] Traditionally field education was not part of the curriculum or a component of a degree. In early years, students gained experience through an apprenticeship model, sometimes living with a minister for a period of time. Later, in the early to mid twentieth century, a student would look for, or the church would provide, a summer paid position in a church. This provided students with experience, an income to return to the college in the following term, and coverage for clergy who took vacation. Often these positions were rural and isolated—perhaps a contributor to the term "field work" and a narrative of survival in the earliest experiences of ministry.

By the mid to later twentieth century, faculty in theological schools began to notice that students who had been in the field for the summer came back to academic study with a lot of important questions. They had more of a sense of what they needed to learn and their questions started to form the basis for combining theory and practice.[2] Soon having students in ministerial practice became part of the education and formation instead of summer work (field education vs. field work). As early as 1934 the Conference of Theological Seminaries in the US and Canada published a report promoting supervised field work as being in tune with newer and more progressive theories of education.[3]

My experience of students over the years is that some look forward to field education as part of their theological school formation. Others dread it. This makes sense. If we were keeping the dichotomy perpetuated and

---

1. Flooding, "What Is Theological Field Education?," 1.
2. Flooding, "What Is Theological Field Education?," 2.
3. Klassen, *Theological Field Education in Canada*, 3.

separating systematic or academic learning from practice, it would make sense for a student to feel more comfortable on one side of the divide. Field educators and other faculty have been intentional to acknowledge that one isn't subordinate to the other in professional formation. Like it was for the early summer students in the field, without practice one does not know what they don't know. Without tradition, history, analysis, knowledge, and a reflective classroom community a student in practice is impoverished and cannot apprentice well.

WHAT MAKES IT PRACTICAL?

Field education is part of the branch of theological study known as practical or pastoral theology. That said, I have had colleagues who teach systematics quip, "Isn't all theology practical?" I agree. Theology is our conversation, thinking, doing, in relation to the divine. As people of faith, it helps us meaning-make, live faithful lives, discern our particular response both to God's incarnation in Christ (for Christian belief) and how we practice our vocations of loving, serving, and mending God's world. Dorothy Bass and Craig Dykstra emphasize that Christian practices are human practices that have theological and normative content because they are interpreted through the gospel: "Christian practices are patterns of cooperative human activity in and through which life together takes shape over time in response to and in the light of God . . . ."[4]

In its simplest form field education or ministry practice can be defined as providing skill development, ministerial reflection, discernment of vocation (testing or affirming one's call), forming of mentor relationships, and allowing one to live into the transformation of self and leader.

A more careful analysis would describe field education as the constant art of dialogue between theory and practice. Or, as Janet Gear has suggested, the bidirectional tug between the *inward* to the heart of what is life about and *outward* toward how it is lived.[5]

Back to the laundry list. Most theological schools and denominational judicatories have lists of competencies or outcomes they require a student to have before they accredit them for leadership (usually ordination). These resemble checklists that I disclaimed at the outset. There is a critical difference. Lists of skills tend to require checkboxes. They assume

4. Bass and Dykstra, "Theological Understanding of Christian Practices," 3.
5. See chapter 5.

a skill is attainable and once learned it is complete. Competencies require deeper learning. A competency is "the development, through substantial experience in the field, of the habits or arts of ministry that leads to effective ministry leadership."[6] There may be a minimum demonstration of competence needed, but because of the extreme diversity in context it would be impossible to be expertly competent in all things and to require no further learning—even after graduation. This is the habit of adult learning and ministry reflection. As Abigail Johnson, former director of field education at Emmanuel College, Toronto, has taught and has learned, education does not cease. Rather education is a process, even for adults. Such education is transformative. But it requires that persons remain open to a kind of learning that leads toward transformation— a transformation that is outward facing and communal and, ultimately, hopeful.[7]

This means we never stop working toward competency. That is a fundamental assumption of VST's graduate professional degrees and of the denominations affiliated with the school. A professional degree like the Master of Divinity or Master of Arts in Pastoral and Public Leadership has to involve field education or practice.

In an examination of graduate-level professional education and related pedagogy it was found that "professionals train people in what William Sullivan calls the three apprentices: the cognitive apprenticeship which focuses on developing knowledge and cultivating habits of mind; the practical apprenticeship which focuses on habits of practice and the moral apprenticeship, which focuses on learning the values, ethical commitments and personal responsibilities of the profession."[8] In theological field education these same foci are often described as knowing, doing, being. In my work with students I use the three components of formation: knowledge, skill, and identity.

It is not hard to imagine what kind of deficiencies and strengths one would embody if one of these components were more developed than the others. Students have often heard me say that I am interested in what your eschatology is. However, if you can't demonstrate how that eschatology lives out at the bedside of someone's beloved mother, there is more work to be done.

6. Office of Vocation of the United Church of Canada, "Candidacy Pathway Policy Office," 9.

7. Johnson, *Shaping Spiritual Leaders*.

8. Cahalan, *Introducing the Practice of Ministry*, 118.

In fact, when instructing students and supervisors on how to write learning goals, I suggest at least one goal in each of the areas of knowledge, skill, and identity.

CONTEXTUAL

Most theological schools, as part of their faculty, include a position that is devoted to field education. Some call it "ministry practice," others "contextual education," and many retain it as "field education." I have always described the work as that of being a bridge—bridging the work of academic pursuits and transformation with that of church leadership. It may sound like a cliché, but "we learn by practice" is the field education director's mantra!

> A minister becomes a minister in and through the practice of ministry. They receive a tradition of practice, they study the meaning of the practice, but it is neither in repeating what others have done nor memorizing theories of practice that they become a minister. It is in the practice combined with knowledge of the received tradition and contemporary insights and critiques, repeated over time in which the practice become integrated in the life and vocation.[9]

It is important that, although they benefit from the demonstration of competence from their supervisors or mentors, students integrate their own knowledge, charisms, call, and skills into their work, not becoming clones to mentors or reaching toward a cookie cutter approach.

The academic journal that resources theological field education is called *Reflective Practice*. It summarizes the pedagogy of practice. Practice without reflection is loss. Reflection without practice is just theory.

Field education utilizes the circle or spiral of transformational and adult learning, which is repetitive and constant integration and deepening. Whether we start learning as observers or experimenters, we need to complete the circle so that we augment our conceptualization and direct our next steps as leaders, educators, and meaning-makers (See Figure 13.1).

9. Cahalan, *Introducing the Practice of Ministry*, 107

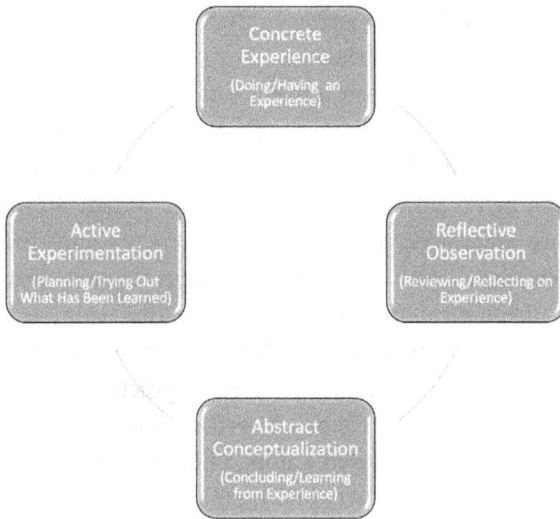

Figure 13.1. Phases of the Learning Cycle. Kolb Learning Style Inventory.[10]

I mentioned that the early field workers cued faculty to the importance of field-based learning when they returned to seminary or theological schools with good questions or mindfulness of what they didn't know and wanted to develop more.

In intentional field work students are guided to pay attention to the places where there is dissonance or where they felt underresourced or, on the opposite side, where they felt celebration or affirmation of vocational call. These are the places of fertile ground for deeper and advanced learning. Affirmation and dissonance recreate one's map or legend for one's leadership perspective. It calls forth an openness and generosity in learning.

THEOLOGICAL REFLECTION

The reflective practice of field education is further deepened in that it is not simply analysis but rather theological reflection. Barbara Blodgett and Matthew Flooding trace the roots of this methodology back to an

10. Adapted from Kolb and Kolb, "Kolb Learning Style Inventory 4.0 Guide," https://learningfromexperience.com/research-library/the-kolb-learning-style-inventory-4-0/.

example from Scripture. In the story of Pentecost, when those gathered bear witness to God's deeds of power in their respective languages, they ask the question, "What does this mean?" (Acts 2:12).[11] Theological reflection is meaning-making and informs our faith, leadership, spiritual lives, and ministry. Like the Pentecost reflectors, it is intentional in drawing out meaning. Some field educators suggest that theological reflection in ministry can be boiled down to the questions: What? So what? Now what? Here we are paying attention to experiencing and determining what that then means and what action or impact comes next?[12] What distinguishes theological field education reflection from others who theorize the link between belief and action is the return after that last question (now what?) to a differently informed practice, leadership, and openness to more experience. Neither does the learning always go in that same direction. James and Evelyn Eaton Whitehead describe reflection as a continuum between ministry and theology. It ranges from starting with the questions out of practice and seeking meaning from the faith tradition to starting with Scripture, doctrine, and history and seeking out ways that shows up in experience.[13] Nevertheless, it is fair to say that theological field education leans heavily in the direction of ministry as the starting point. It is "the messy particularity of everyday lives examined with excruciating care and brought into conversation with the great doctrines of the Christian tradition."[14]

GRACE OF LEARNING

Another core value of field education involves what I call the grace of learning. While attending an Association of Theological Field Education gathering, I heard an inspiring preacher talk about learning, shortcomings, failure, and inspiration in the field. He talked about our human need for perfection and our tendency (common for many in ministry) to see ourselves as imposters. The preacher challenged us to embrace our shortcomings—both theological and in the business of learning. Theologically, it was to embrace our humanity. In our learning, it was to

11. Blodgett and Flooding, "Role of Theological Reflection," 269.

12. Blodgett and Flooding, eds., *Brimming with God*, 13.

13. Whitehead and Whitehead. *Method in Ministry*, ix.

14. Miller-McLemore and Gill-Austern, eds., *Feminist and Womanist Pastoral Theology*, 86.

recognize that our failures teach us as much, or more, than our successes. He compared failings—when we don't hit the mark—as similar to the agitators in washing machines. This was, of course, prior to front-loading energy-efficient machines. The agitator moves things around and creates the right reaction for the achieved outcome. It is not comfortable but can be transformative. I guess this is parallel to our current embrace of disruptors who act as modern prophets—mirroring our shortcomings, hopefully inspiring new and deeper transformation. While the preacher's conviction was persuasive, I respectfully disagree with his example. I believe in, and construct the field education program on, the opportunity to learn from best practices. Any good field education is only possible with the presence, in the field, of supervisors and mentors who can inspire learning and offer a crucible where students can mix their knowledge, identity, and skills.

I was fortunate to do my ministry practice and formation at a time in the United Church of Canada when there was opportunity to do overseas internships. One of my learning goals was to understand the nature of Christianity in dominant culture. So I asked to learn in a country where other religions formed a tighter relationship with the state. I landed the opportunity to spend five months in various places in North India working with the Church of North India. Seven weeks of that time was spent in Calcutta at a seminary. Daily I traveled with students who were on field placements in various churches and agencies in the city. This led to a great diversity of experiences at orphanages, brothels, schools, and slums. One day I followed a female student who worked in a local church. She essentially was not permitted to do anything except observe male supervisors and teachers undertake ministries of education, preaching, and pastoral care. I inquired why she didn't get to do anything. Was it a lack of basic-level education or confidence? She explained that in the tradition of the denomination she was part of she was not permitted to lead as a woman.

When we returned to the college I spoke with the director of field placement on faculty. He had already taken me under his wing and provided this foreigner with hospitality and care. He explained that he had sent this young woman to that particular placement so that she could learn that women were subordinate in her tradition and she would not be welcomed easily into leadership. I challenged him. I suggested that perhaps she did not need to learn her oppression—she already had that competency. What she needed was an environment that could fan the flames of her call and increase her sense of competency and hope to exercise leadership in response to the call of discipleship. To my surprise, the director returned to me a few days later and presented me with a gift of a tapestry of women working in the field to show me that he had learned from my challenge. It still hangs in my home as a sign of our mutual transformation. We often don't learn best from failure and discrimination but rather from encouragement, hope, imagination, and support.

STUDIO: THE ART OF LEADERSHIP[15]

The definitive course relating to field education at VST is known as the Leadership Studio. The name of the course is always a puzzling one—what is a studio class at theological school? The answer serves the question of how we can adequately prepare leadership for current pastoral and public context. The studio is precisely positioned to respond to the adaptive challenges of today. Ron Hefeitz, founding director of the Center for Public Leadership at the John F. Kennedy School of Government, says that "if the global commons where those who offer leadership must contend with a myriad of significant challenges is complex, diverse and fraught with ambiguity, then the space devoted to learning effective leadership for such a world might be usefully similar . . . " [16] In other words, the classroom can't set up a false container of easy answers for leadership. Reconstruction of the learner into leader involves a sturdy holding environment so that upon leaving seminary or school they don't have all the answers but have an attentive response and presence to the art of ongoing leadership. The studio is set up as a combination of theory and familiar classroom parameters as well as experience and reflection to hone one's adaptive abilities. The raw material students work with is a combination of knowledge and theory plus both positive and confounding experiences from real-time leadership situations. These materials draw the learner out at the edge of their identity, and require continual analysis and interpretation of their context as well as acute theological reflection. The studio or lab is messy and yet a crucible for transformation. It is a place for practice, trial, reshaping, imagination, and continual feedback.

15. The original vision and imagination for the course, The Studio for Strategic Leadership, belongs to the Rev. Dr. Keith Howard. The leadership matrix involving the intersection of four stories and a curriculum using adaptive leadership methodology was inherited from his teaching in the first years of the course.

16. Daloz-Parks, *Leadership Can Be Taught*, 48.

A present iteration of the Leadership Studio facilitated by VST faculty introduces the course description this way:

> Theologically trained professionals serving congregational or social ministries, agencies, organizations and other institutions are continually presented with a changing context and the need for their organizations to respond. A key critical leadership challenge is to identify opportunities which are truly strategic and then to assist the organization to embrace the occasion.
>
> The Studio is designed to be a crucible into which we bring ourselves—our gifts, hopes, vulnerabilities, strengths, weaknesses, uncertainties, experience—so that we may become transformed, effective leaders. . . .
>
> Here there will be an opportunity for those preparing for pastoral and public leadership to combine instruction in leadership theory and theology with on-the-ground experience of discerning and developing leadership challenges and ministry opportunities. Alongside The Studio, students will be located in a ministry/leadership site, with a mentor/supervisor, where they will engage in a collaborative, creative, experiential and educational environment. A broad range of partners in church and society may become involved in the project, thus presenting learning opportunities for interdisciplinary collaboration. In all cases, we will understand the leadership opportunity to be one of serving the community in a specific context. The Studio mentors and instructors will assist the students to research, prepare, exercise and evaluate their leadership in the context in which they are situated.[17]

The core work of integration continues around the conversation at the intersection of four stories: story of self (identity); story of God (*Missio Dei*) encountered and revealed; story of place (the particular context that a student has covenanted to learn within), and story of context (social and global commons) (See Figure 13.2).

17. See the 2020 course outline for PT652, "Studio for Strategic Leadership: Part 2," available at https://vst.edu/courses/leadership-studio-pt2/.

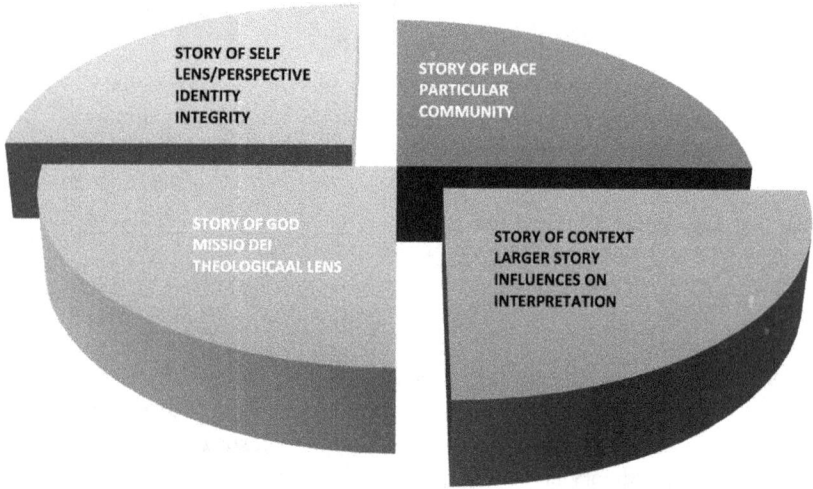

STORY OF SELF
LENS/PERSPECTIVE
IDENTITY
INTEGRITY

STORY OF PLACE
PARTICULAR
COMMUNITY

STORY OF GOD
MISSIO DEI
THEOLOGICAAL LENS

STORY OF CONTEXT
LARGER STORY
INFLUENCES ON
INTERPRETATION

Figure 13.2 Learning at the Intersection: A Leadership Matrix

Early on in my time as director of field education, and as students found themselves over the years at the threshold of integrating theory and practice, I remain convinced that no degree, list of competencies, or intention could satisfy the deficiencies named in the *Things They Didn't Teach Us in Seminary* group. In her book on *Shaping Spiritual Leaders*, Abigail Johnson describes ministerial and pastoral leadership as comparable to white-water canoeing. We don't just develop skills to implement but we need to learn to navigate in the rapid waters of social, technological, and demographic change.[18] The list of skills and tools required would change as quickly as the time it would take to identify them. Instead, we need a healthy balance of skill (paddling), knowledge of the river (context), and the ability to discern correct leadership in certain situations. Do you go with the current or challenge it?

At the Vancouver School of Theology our currency is not one of checklists. It is, rather, equipping students to feel competent in whatever waters they will paddle.

It is what is learned in seminary.

18. Johnson, *Shaping Spiritual Leaders*, 15.

14

To the Ends of the Earth (and Around the Corner)

Missional Leadership in an Age of Secularity

ROSS LOCKHART

IT WAS MAUNDY THURSDAY and I was nestled into a pew as my five-year-old daughter drove her Transformer toy all over the hymnbooks and caused general mayhem before the program started. I was in church during Holy Week but not for worship. I sat in St. Anselm's Anglican Church on the University of British Columbia (UBC) campus waiting for the performance of my thirteen-year-old daughter and others who had participated all week in a UBC drama camp. Now, the camp simply rented space at the local Anglican church—nothing more, nothing less. And as I waited for the performance to begin, I did what I usually do in public spaces: I eavesdropped shamelessly.

The family in the pew behind me, eager to see their own daughter/granddaughter perform, shared this little gem of a conversation with me:

> Boomer Grandfather (roughly late sixties): "Wow, I can't believe I didn't get hit by lightning coming into this place. (His wife cackles loudly.) Who knows, maybe I'll still burst into flames at some point . . . "

Adult Gen X Daughter (mid fourties), in a more reflective tone: "Dad, didn't we used to go to church like at Christmas and Easter and stuff? I seem to remember being in a church like this when I was little—is that right?"

Boomer Grandfather: "Well, yeah, that was a long time ago and I can't remember the last time I was in a church. Most of us figured out that you don't need to come to a place like this to be a good person."

Adult Gen X Daughter: "Well, Dad, do you know what your granddaughter said when I dropped her off here at camp on the first day? She said, 'Mummy, what is this place? I've never been inside a place like this before. What do they do here?' (She paused and continued in a quieter voice.) It was weird—I didn't know what to say. And I felt ashamed."

This fascinating cross-generational witness of the end of Christendom was interrupted by the millennial-aged drama camp instructor, who welcomed us to the performance and noted (in usual West Coast fashion) that we were meeting on the traditional ancestral and unceded territory of the Musqueam peoples. No word was given, of course, that we were also meeting in a sacred space of Christian worship.

I left that lovely drama performance during Holy Week thinking about another dramatic event that we reenact every Sunday, proclaiming God's victory over sin and death through the empty cross and empty tomb. How are we equipping missionary disciples to witness to the wonder of our Easter faith in a world caught in Holy Week and doesn't even know it? What might mission and evangelism look like to:

Boomers: so many of whom walked away from the church and retain only a disfigured Sunday school memory of the Christian faith.

Gen Xers: the first generation "raised without religion: according to Vancouver author Douglas Copeland, and yet many of us in this generation retain some structural memory of Christendom through school and society.

Millennials: raised with more secular/civic religion beliefs like environmentalism and respect for ancient cultures (Indigenous, etc.)—all good of course, but tricky to witness to with no Christian memory.

> Generation Z/iGen: even further along the secularity path, now open to hearing about Christianity without the baggage that their boomer grandparents often attach to the faith.

How might those of us whose lives have been marked, blessed, and changed for good by the gospel of Jesus Christ speak and act in order to bear witness to the One whose selfless death and spectacular resurrection adopted us into the inner life of God: Father, Son, and Spirit?

Within this curious cultural/social space, the Vancouver School of Theology understands its calling to educate and form thoughtful, engaged, and generous Christian leaders. The church is hungry for effective and passionate leaders to lead God's people in praise and service for the world Christ died to save. Missional leaders discern, articulate, and build enthusiasm alongside fellow church members to participate in what the triune God is actively doing in the places where they live, work, and play. Aubrey Malphurs defines this kind of visionary missional leader that the church needs in the post-Christendom West as a "godly servant (character) who knows and sees where he or she is going (mission and vision) and has followers (influence)."[1]

One of the visionary missional leaders that students at the Vancouver School of Theology encounter is Lesslie Newbigin, who once declared, "The Church . . . is not so much an institution as an expedition sent to the ends of the earth in Christ's name." Lesslie Newbigin made this bold declaration in his 1960s work *Trinitarian Doctrine for Today's Mission*. The English-born, Church of Scotland–sent, Church of South India–consecrated bishop became the first director of the World Council of Church's Division of World Mission and Evangelism in Geneva before returning home to a secularized United Kingdom. Once repatriated, he learned to apply his missionary skill set from abroad to the very country that once sent him out to the mission field. Newbigin is a fascinating example of a missionary sent out (in a classic sense for "foreign mission") only to return from the mission field to find an equally (if not more) pressing need for mission and evangelism—not at the ends of the earth but just around the corner. Newbigin's story reflects the changing nature of gospel and culture in the late twentieth and early twenty-first centuries as the West transitioned out of the 1,500-year experiment of church privilege with state power known as Christendom. Since the early fourth Century and Roman Emperor Constantine's embrace, or domestication,

---

1. Malphurs, *Developing a Vision for Ministry*, 23.

of the Christian movement, the institution of the church has been a solid partner of the culture in moral, spiritual, political, and economic power. The great unraveling of that privileged status in the West in general, and Canada in particular, has left many Christians here today feeling a bit bewildered and overwhelmed by the pace of change. Now, the church has moved from central to peripheral, from the courts of power to the margins. Recent research by Presbyterian and United Church scholars Stuart Macdonald and Brian Clarke has narrated the steps of mainline Christian denominational decline in the final decades of the last century. In *Leaving Christianity* Macdonald and Clarke describe the contemporary context this way:

> Decline in Christian affiliation, membership, and participation started in the 1960s and has picked up pace rapidly since then. This trend is likely to continue and, indeed, accelerate as an increasing portion of the country's population—among youth especially—have never been exposed to Christianity . . . . In short, Canadian society is entering into a new era, a post-Christian era. The end of Christendom, we will argue, occurred in the closing decades of the twentieth century, as churches lost their social power and their place in the nation's cultural fabric.[2]

Noting the loss of the baby boomer generation, *Leaving Christianity* acknowledges that now we have an increasing number of Canadians who have left the church for whom the gospel is a strange and foreign message. Macdonald and Clarke call this the distinction between being "de-churched and non-church." They suggest, "The de-churched are those who at some point in their lives attended church but now no longer do so. The non-church have never attended except perhaps for a funeral or wedding of a friend or relation." To them Christianity is, in the words of the "Church of England's report *Mission Shaped Church*, 'an utterly foreign culture.'"[3] Many in the mainline church remain uncomfortable with the language of "mission" and find "evangelism" even more unseemly in light of devastating colonial-era mission projects that mixed Western culture, power, and values with the sharing of the gospel. A particular sensitivity to the language of mission and evangelism exists in Canada in light of the residential schools legacy, which had mainline churches operate boarding schools on behalf of the state for Indigenous children (forcibly

---

2. Clarke and Macdonald, *Leaving Christianity*, 11.

3. Clarke and Macdonald, *Leaving Christianity*, 171.

removed from their homes) for the expressed purpose of "westernizing" the children. In addition to a degradation of Indigenous culture and the breaking up of family units, many children suffered psychological, physical, and sexual abuse, most recently brought to light in the *Commission on Residential Schools*. Mindful of this mission heritage, there is the pressing issue of the converting power of the market and secularity upon a new generation of Canadians for whom religions faith is an unknown experience. As Macdonald and Clarke conclude, "First, people are not only leaving churches; they are leaving Christianity. And many of them have no interest in returning. Second, an increasing and significant proportion of the population has never had any first-hand experience of organized religion."[4]

For such a time as this, God continues to call leaders for the church to help God's people in praise and proclamation, discipleship and devotion, service and sanctification. But congregations and denominational offices look to seminaries and ask, "What kind of leader do we need right now?" What kind of leadership is required when the mission field is no longer overseas or in the urban core of our cities but in the rural and suburban contexts where once people were born nominally Christian? Newbigin's call to join an expedition to the ends of the earth reorientates us to the kind of leadership that is both at home in a minority status and witnesses boldly with the confidence of John Knox, who once declared that with God a person is "always in the majority."

Students preparing for ministry today at the Vancouver School of Theology engage head on this shift from a Christendom to a post-Christendom reality, with millennial (and younger) students having no working memory of that privileged status of the church in Canadian society. Instead, students must grapple with how to lead Christian witnessing communities that are either church plants or church revitalization projects, that take seriously the need to have a culture and process of helping secular people take steps towards faith in Jesus. To that end, near the end of the last century a group of missiologists worked on a project entitled *Missional Church: A Vision for the Sending of the Church in North America*. Published in 1998, the book was edited by Darrell Guder, now Professor Emeritus at Princeton Theological Seminary and Senior Fellow in Residence at the Centre for Missional Leadership, St. Andrew's Hall, Vancouver. *Missional Church* launched a new conversation on the

---

4. Clarke and Macdonald, *Leaving Christianity*, 210.

theology and practice of mission in the West. Having coined the term "missional," scholars on the project and subsequent missiologists further developed the "missional theology conversation" that placed an emphasis upon the *Missio Dei*—the Trinitarian mission of God and invitation for humankind to participate in the redeeming and reconciling love of Father, Son, and Spirit on the journey from creation, covenant, Christ, church, and, one day, consummation. Mission no longer would be seen as a department or mission of the church, but rather *the very nature* of the triune God as revealed in Scripture.

Missional theology is often summarized as the reality that the church does not have a mission, but rather *God's mission has a church*. The triune God invites us as sinful and fallible creatures to come alongside and participate in the Creator's redemptive mission of empty cross and empty tomb with that simple Spirit-breathed invitation, "Come and follow me." The church is the instrument of God's mission in the world. But too often mission and evangelism have been synonymous in the church and there *is* value in making a distinction between the two concepts. "Mission," according to David Bosch, is the wider of the two concepts and involves the

> Total task that God has set the church for the salvation of the world. In its missionary involvement, the church steps out of itself, into the wider world. It crosses all kinds of frontiers and barriers: geographical, social, political, ethnic, cultural, religious, ideological. Into all these areas the church-in-mission carries the message of God's salvation. Ultimately, then, mission means being involved in the redemption of the universe and the glorification of God.[5]

Again, by using the language of "missional" we are leaning into the understanding that the essential vocation of the church is to be God's called and sent people in the world, trusting that God's mission has a church.[6] Recognizing that a hard-and-fast definition of "missional church" is elusive, it is possible to say missional leaders seek an alternative imagination for being the church in the world where God's Spirit is at work, transforming us as a community through mystery, memory, and mission.[7] With a deep trust to the witness of the triune God, missional

5. Bosch, "Evangelism," 9.

6. Guder, ed., *Missional Church*, 11. Rooted in a deep witness to the Triune God, Guder defines missional ecclesiology as biblical, historical, contextual, eschatological and possible for all disciples to practice.

7. Roxburgh and Boren, *Introducing the Missional Church*, 45.

leadership recognizes that God's being and doing are one, and since God's actions always flow from who God is as Father, Son, and Holy Spirit, so too should the church seek to unify its being and doing.[8]

If we understand mission to be the very nature of the triune God and the church participates in that mission by making disciples for Christ who participate in the redemption of the whole world and the healing of the nations, then we need to be clear as well about the narrower definition of evangelism.

In making a distinction between mission and evangelism, David Bosch contends that evangelism is that dimension and activity of the church's mission which seeks to offer every person, everywhere, a valid opportunity to be directly challenged by the gospel of explicit faith in Jesus Christ, with a view to embracing him as Savior, becoming a living member of his community, and being enlisted in his service of reconciliation, peace, and justice on earth.[9] To help us better understand what this ministry of evangelism looks like, Robert Webber suggests three key marks of evangelism: "Evangelism is a process. Evangelism takes place over a period of time. Evangelism brings new believers to spiritual maturity."[10] Perhaps to Webber's good work we could add a fourth mark—the role of the Christian community. It is primarily within the work and witness of local congregations that people are nurtured through evangelism into a lasting relationship with, and discipleship to, Jesus Christ. As Lesslie Newbigin said so beautifully, "The congregation is the hermeneutic of the gospel." It is the local congregation that provides opportunities for people to, in time, become evangelists themselves on behalf of the community of faith.

While we live and minister in a post-Christendom context today, too often we echo our Reformed ancestors' assumptions that when it comes to the gifts Christ offers his church in Ephesians 4 we too often value prophets, pastors, and teachers in mainline congregations over apostles and evangelists.[11] By locating our evangelism in the heart of congregational ministry, we seek to claim back the gifts of evangelism that Christ has bestowed upon the church, his body in the world, so we

8. Sparks, Soerens and Friesen, eds., *New Parish*, 81. As the Parish Collective argue, "Mission cannot be conceived as a project of the church, rather, the church exists within God's reconciling mission."

9. Bosch, "Evangelism," 17.

10. Webber, *Ancient-Future Evangelism*, 13.

11. Ephesians 4:11–14.

may reach "the full stature of Christ." Therefore, my working definition of evangelism is: *a congregational process that helps people place their trust in Jesus, and by the Spirit's power transforms them within community into disciples of Christ who participate in God's saving mission for the world.*

This calls for the formation of Christian witnesses who are living examples of the opposite of that stereotype so readily provided by Western media and Hollywood movies—brash, intolerant, arrogant, and rude. Surely God calls us by our baptism to ministry, but may that witness be a gentle one in a world torn asunder by violence and greed. In reflecting on this dilemma, I shared recently with students in my evangelism class at the Vancouver School of Theology a story of growing up in Manitoba where the driver's education program put fifteen-and-a-half-year-olds behind the wheel with an instructor—a rather bold move now that I think of it. I had a lovely teacher who had a penchant for McDonald's drive-thru cuisine and a frequent craving (every single driving session in fact) for a hot fudge sundae with extra peanuts. While I was dubious about this weekly ritual, she assured us that navigating a drive thru was a normal part of any driver's education and, in fact, we could possibly be tested on it one day!

To be fair, driving around the pot-holed streets of Winnipeg daily with teenagers struggling to learn how to operate an automobile must have been extremely stressful. This poor woman was entitled to whatever increased her patience—hot fudge sundae with extra peanuts, or perhaps something stronger when she got home. What I remember her for the most, however, was the lesson she taught us on gentleness. One day a high school buddy was driving especially hard, slamming on the brakes, honking the horn and so forth. The instructor ordered him to the side of the road as the extra peanuts tumbled on the floor mats of the car. To this cram-packed car of gangly teenage boys she offered a moral lecture, as she ate her ice cream sundae, on the importance of being a gentle driver. "Boys," she said with a chirp-like tone to her voice, sounding something like the Chicken Lady from *Kids in the Hall,* "why are people weary of buying rental cars when they come up for sale?" Silence. "Um, because they're not cool enough," said the boy in backseat beside me after an eternity. "No," she replied sternly, "because people are never gentle with rental cars; they treat them too roughly. Now, I will teach you how to be a gentle driver. No more slamming on breaks, cutting people off, honking horns. *You will be gentle and the world will be better off for it.*"

"You will be gentle and the world will be better off for it." Her words landed somewhere between testimony and prophecy. Gentleness, something that is available to all of us, as a gift from God, a fruit of the Spirit. Gentleness in our mission and evangelism is not something you hear much of in the church these days and yet Paul the evangelist and missionary-apostle echoes the driving instructor's advice in Philippians 4, "let your gentleness be evident to all." "Gentleness" in the biblical Greek has a close association with "meekness," a word that has lost most, if not all, of its appeal in our society. When you stand behind the hockey bench or on the sidelines of the soccer pitch coaching your kids, do you shout, "Blessed are the meek, for they shall inherit the earth"? No, you shout . . . well, I won't say what you shout. That's because meekness is often unfairly associated with weakness. Is that also true with gentleness?

In 1 Peter 3:15, we hear a call for testimony, a missional enactment through an evangelistic lens: "But in your hearts revere Christ as Lord. Always be prepared to give an answer to everyone who asks for the hope that you is within you." It's like the Galilean fisherman-turned-apostle is encouraging us to prepare our elevator speech for Jesus, right? When someone wants to know what makes you you, what would you say about your faith? This is particularly challenging for mainline Christians, who excel at swinging a hammer or signing a petition or taking a meal to a neighbor but get a little tongue-tied when it comes to talking about our faith in Jesus.

First Peter 3 says that we need to be ready with an answer, our elevator speech for Jesus, when our life as followers of the risen Christ demands a testimony. It's an invitation to practice articulating why we do what we do and love what we love about Jesus, the church, and world. But note that little piece at the end of the passage from 1 Peter 3:15, "but do this with gentleness and respect." I love that part. It feels ideally suited for Christian witness in the post-Christendom West. We are to bear witness to the confession of our faith that Jesus is Lord, and not Caesar, our mortgage, our reputation, or whatever else you'd like to add in place of Christ's lordship. But how we do so should be with gentleness and respect for others. In other words, knowing whom we love and what we believe has to be combined with how we live, with gentleness and reverence. That's how we live; that's how we share our testimony about Jesus. It's as if Peter is saying, "I will teach you how to be gentle and the whole world will be better off for it."

Every now and then you get a chance to witness this gentle testimony and love in action. I recall a flight from Los Angeles to Seattle where I watched with interest as a large, rough-looking biker dude settled into the row in front of me by the window while a neatly dressed businessman in a suit took his seat beside the guy. I assumed the business guy would plug into electronics and keep a safe distance from the rough-looking fellow next to him. In fact, the opposite happened. I heard the businessman ask a few polite questions like, "Were you down here on business or pleasure." The biker dude responded, "My mom is really sick, and I was spending time with her and my stupid sister." They sat in silence for a moment. "That must be really hard caring for your mom," replied the business guy. I eavesdropped on this evolving conversation as our airplane took off and climbed to thirty-thousand feet. The rough-looking man in the window seat no longer gave short, clipped answers but now was fully engaged in conversation with the businessman. After fifteen minutes came a new question. "What do you think about spirituality? Would you consider yourself a spiritual person?" asked the businessman. "I guess I believe in God," replied the man in the window seat, "but I haven't been in a church in years." "I wonder if that might help right now," replied the man as their conversation took a turn towards Jesus. After a few minutes the businessman said, "Well, I've got to get a little work done here," reaching for his laptop, "but if it's okay I'll pray for you and I actually have a little book with me that might be helpful, something written by the pastor of my home church named Rick Warren." As he handed a spare copy of *The Purpose Driven Life* to the man beside me, I thought, "I've just been witness to one of the most beautiful, gentle evangelistic moments I can remember."

Now, I know the typical mainline thing to do here is for eye rolls to happen at the mention of a megachurch pastor from the United States. Instead, I sat there and wondered, "What kind of community helps shape a disciple to so beautifully, respectfully, and gently engage relationally with another hurting human being and offer them the hope of the gospel?" Before we judge or dismiss that encounter, I wonder how our own local churches are equipping people for their witness in the community in the midst of one's everyday, ordinary routines? Watching this businessman reach out in such a gentle and loving way to a stranger made me think that maybe my driver's education instructor was more of a theologian than I realized. "You will be gentle and the whole world will be better for it."

From megachurch to the Vatican, Pope Francis reminds us in *Evangelii Gaudium* that local churches are full of missionary disciples acting as evangelizers and therefore should never look like "someone who has just come back from a funeral," but rather Christian communities must recover and deepen that

> delightful and comforting joy of evangelizing, even when it is in tears that we must sow... And may the world of our time, which is searching, sometimes with anguish, sometimes with hope, be enabled to receive the good news not from evangelizers who are dejected, discouraged, impatient or anxious, but from ministers of the Gospel whose lives glow with fervor, who have first received the joy of Christ"[12]

Pope Francis's challenge of our witness in the broader community invites our conversation on evangelism and mission deeper into the area of missional leadership. Missional leadership takes seriously the triune God's active present in the world playing out in God's story of redemption between Christ and consummation. Missional leaders are trained to exegete both the Scriptures and the communities God calls them to serve. This dual focus on text and context, gospel and culture, is important given the shifting sands of ministry within our North American landscape and especially here on the West Coast and throughout Cascadia.

Today, many within church and academy take for granted the dramatic impact of post-Enlightenment secularity in the West.[13] Secularism, that philosophical and political ideology that strives to remove religious symbols, beliefs, and influence from public life, has indeed permeated North American culture, seeing that all the world religions have an equal place—at the back of the bus.[14] Charles Taylor notes that in the West "the shift to secularity . . . consists . . . of a move from a society where belief in God is unchallenged and indeed, unproblematic, to one in which it is

---

12. Francis I, *Evangelii Gaudium*, 10.

13. In his masterful work *A Secular Age*, Canadian philosopher Charles Taylor works through the impact of secularity, comparing Western life in 1500 to 2000. Taylor explores secularity's impact in public spaces, decline in religious belief and practice, and the conditions of belief.

14. In his excellent work *Faith and the Public Square*, Rowan Williams makes the helpful distinction between procedural and programmatic secularism. Procedural secularism, the kind that I refer to above, is secularism that gives equal voices to all manner of religious and political thought. Programmatic secularism attempts to eliminate religious voices from the public realm, and for that Williams charges liberal modernity with being a fixed concept that approaches a new "pseudo-religion."

understood to be one option among others, and frequently not the easiest to embrace."[15]

Ministerial leadership in this new culture of "the Secular Age" must pay close attention to the intersection of life and faith, gospel and culture, as we move from older generations with Christian memory to those who now know little or nothing of the faith tradition once dominant in the West. Missional leaders do not see the world as the enemy, but rather as the space that the triune God is actively at work redeeming, reconciling, and making new. As Stefan Paas notes in his excellent work *Church Planting in the Secular West*, "We may consider to what extent Christians need the world—and especially the powerful world of the secular West—to remain humble, dependent on grace, and continually surprised by the extent of God's grace and love. The world is not just a dark background of our evangelistic mission; it is God's world. The church can only be the church if there remains a world outside of her, challenging her, threatening her, and sometimes welcoming her."[16]

Christopher James offers a helpful caution to those who would throw themselves in too quickly with the "joining God in the neighborhood" approach to missional leadership. James writes, "Missional ecclesiologies have tended to root ecclesiality exclusively in the church's participation in the Trinitarian mission, without sufficiently considering what it might mean for the church to participate in and mirror the Trinitarian community."[17] Holding in tension the economic and the imminent Trinity is not something that surfaces often in missional circles and is an important contribution to the discussion. As one who has lived his whole life in the Reformed tradition, that opening line of the Westminster Shorter Catechism about "glorifying God and enjoying Him forever" is a helpful corrective to the usual "sending" language within the missional world. After all, in Luke 10, after Jesus sends the disciples out with training wheels on, he gathers them again unto himself. This classic pattern that Barth highlighted in *Church Dogmatics* of the people of God gathered, up-built, and sent needs to undergird our missional practice.

To say it differently, our local Christian witnessing communities need to be places of evidence to the transforming grace and mercy of God. How many people within our churches could articulate what Jesus

---

15. Taylor, *Secular Age*, 3.

16. Paas, *Church Planting and the Secular West*, 119.

17. James, *Church Planting in Post-Christian Soil*, 223.

has saved them from and has saved them for? Mark Labberton tells the delightful story in his book *Called* of shaking hands on a Sunday morning and meeting a newcomer who said that they were trying to figure out faith and were a little confused. The newcomer had visited a number of churches where they talked a lot about Jesus but not so much about the world. Then the newcomer noted that he worshipped in other churches that talked on and on about the world and what was wrong with it but rarely mentioned Jesus. He told Mark Labberton that at "his church" he was pleased to find a place that talked about both Jesus and the world. Mark was pleased as well to hear that! But then the newcomer asked a question that Mark found unsettling. "Pastor, if I keep coming back to this church, will I meet people like Jesus?" Ouch. Mark did what many of us as pastors would do: he looked over the guy's shoulder and hoped that this newcomer wouldn't meet this person or that person who was known to be unkind and mean-spirited in the church. Imagine—church as a place where we met people *like* Jesus. Christopher James's work is a helpful reminder that participating in the Trinitarian mission in the world also involves us in deep and authentic/accountable relationships of mutual self-giving love in the local church. As James argues, "The church in a post-Christian context cannot rely on predominate culture to nurture people even halfway toward a way of life constant with the Reign of God. The church in such an environment must be, and is, a conversion community."[18]

This conversion community is a community on the move as Christendom institutions crumble and Christians gather in new and innovative ways for worship and witness. As the expedition of the church, under the guidance of the Holy Spirit, continues towards the consummation of God's mission, the "ends of the earth" are closer than we could ever have imagined; in fact, it's just around the corner from where you sit right now. Indeed, as we minister to and receive ministry from a global and diverse Christian family that is engaged in Christian witness around the world and in our local neighborhood, together we are becoming the sign, foretaste, and instrument of the kingdom of God that Lesslie Newbigin once prophetically imagined, and now we live into by grace.

18. James, *Church Planting in Post-Christian Soil*, 222–23.

Afterword

JANET MARTIN SOSKICE

WHAT A GREAT IDEA for a volume and what a treasure trove of essays! Richard R Topping sounds the keynote and it is growth—the sort of growth that does not mean discarding past wisdom but building on it. Most trees grow, after all, because they stand on roots. We need to proclaim the gospel without embarrassment in an age that scarcely thinks it needs the Christian faith—an age in which, as Richard Topping points out, "six of the seven deadly sins are medical conditions—and pride is a virtue."

Speaking out without embarrassment does not mean shooting your mouth off without listening. We need to be open to the new, as Richard says, charitable in our reading, and porous to new needs and visions—engaging with care for the created order, working for social justice, repentance, renewal, forming a just society, looking after the poor, imprisoned, and suffering. Loving God with all your heart, soul, strength, and mind does not mean discounting everything else because *everything else* is God's good, if wounded, creation.

Theological college education is not a matter of getting filled up with all the answers you need for a subsequent lifetime's ministry but of acquiring the tools—as Jason Byassee says, it is a matter "of learning how to learn." That is why the teachers at a theological college are always themselves learners.

Sometimes learning defies preconceived expectations of what we need. I recall a Catholic priest who came as a mature student to the Anglican seminary where I then taught. He was taking Anglican orders to marry the women with whom he'd fallen in love. To a rapt audience of his young fellow students (and myself, then a quite young lecturer) he explained that that his own priestly formation had been done several decades earlier entirely in Latin. They had had a year-long course—again, entirely in Latin—on the medieval philosopher Duns Scotus. His subsequent ministry was entirely in a desperately poor parish in central Birmingham. We were shocked. "How on earth did that course help you in your ministry?" he was asked. "It was vital," he replied, "because I knew in all those years that there was something else."

I would not wish to advocate a return to a year of Duns Scotus in Latin, but if seminarians aren't at some stage challenged beyond what they came in with, then something is lacking. Christian formation for ministry means learning about Scripture, tradition, translation, preaching, history, the Christian success stories and sad failures—and learning how to keep learning.

Saint Augustine's wonderful classic *On Christian Teaching* has the same ambiguity in the English title as it does in the Latin, *De Doctrina Christiana*. "Teaching" here is both that which is taught and the very enterprise of teaching itself. What better example for a set of theological educators to set their pupils than to show how informed faith is always still growing—permeable and open to the challenges that face Christ's church in each new time and in each local space. A new generation of pastors and priests will be facing tasks and challenges their predecessors could scarcely dream of—and who needs to be told this in a time of COVID?

This takes formation—in prayer, in learning, in shared common life, and in what Grant Rodgers calls "pastoral imagination." A good pastor is always learning simply because a good Christian is always learning. We are the growth points of Christ's body; even as we grow old we can be, with God's grace, its green shoots.

Contributors

Joas Adiprasetya is Dean of Public Relations of Jakarta Theological Seminary, where he also teaches constructive theology and theology of religions. He holds a ThD from Boston University School of Theology and was a Fulbright Senior Research Fellow at Pittsburgh Theological Seminary. He is a member of the World Council of Churches Reference Group for Interreligious Dialogue and World Communion of Reformed Churches Reference Group for Mission and Ecumenical Engagement.

Ray Aldred is status Cree from Swan River Band, Treaty 8. He is the director of the Indigenous Studies Program at the Vancouver School of Theology, whose mission is to partner with the Indigenous church around theological education. He served as the former chairperson and board member for Indigenous Pathways. He is former Director for the First Nations Alliance Churches of Canada, and is now a committee member, where he works to encourage Indigenous churches.

Jason Byassee teaches preaching at the Vancouver School of Theology, where he is the inaugural holder of the Butler Chair in Homiletics and Biblical Hermeneutics. He is the author or coauthor of thirteen books, including, most recently, *Surprised by Jesus Again* (Eerdmans, 2019)

Laura Duhan-Kaplan is Director of Inter-Religious Studies and Professor of Jewish Studies at Vancouver School of Theology. Laura is also Professor Emerita of Philosophy at University of North Carolina at Charlotte, Rabbi Emerita of Or Shalom Synagogue, and a U.S. Professor of the Year. She lives in Vancouver, Canada, on the traditional territories of the Coast Salish peoples, with her husband (and musical partner), Charles, their young adult children, and a changing array of companion animals.

Patricia Dutcher-Walls retired as Professor of Hebrew Bible at the Vancouver School of Theology. She holds a ThD in Old Testament/Biblical Studies from the Graduate Theological Union and a MDiv from Harvard Divinity School. She has published several books and a number of articles in scholarly and religious journals, including *Reading the Historical Books: A Student's Guide to Engaging the Biblical Text* (Baker Academic, 2104). A minister in the Presbyterian Church in Canada, she regularly appears as a guest preacher and leader for adult education courses, retreats, and continuing education courses.

Brenda Fawkes served as Director of Theological Field Education at VST and instructor in the Leadership Studio from 2011 until 2019. She is an ordained minister of The United Church of Canada serving in the Lower Mainland of British Columbia. Currently she is the Office of Vocation Minister for Pacific Mountain and Chinook Winds Regions (BC, Yukon and Southern Ontario) of the United Church supporting ministry personnel and the formation of candidates for ordination.

Janet Gear was Assistant Professor of Public and Pastoral Leadership and Director of United Church Formation at the Vancouver School of Theology from 2006 to 2019. She is the recipient of both the United Church Foundation's Davidson Trust Award for Teaching (2015) and the McGeachy Senior Scholarship (2018). Janet is an ordained minister in the United Church of Canada and has supported the life and work of the United Church and ecumenical partners primarily in the areas of education for ministry and leadership, spirituality and social justice, and theology and faith.

Mari Joerstad is a biblical scholar whose research focuses on ecology, land, migration, and belonging in the Hebrew Bible. She will join the the Vancouver School of Theology faculty in 2021 as Associate Professor of Hebrew Scripture and Academic Dean. Mari grew up in Norway but moved to Canada as a teenager. For the last ten years, she's been in North Carolina, where she has studied and worked at Duke University.

Ross Lockhart is Dean of St. Andrew's Hall and Professor of Mission Studies at the Vancouver School of Theology. An ordained minister in the Presbyterian Church in Canada, Ross is author of *Lessons from Laodicea: Missional Leadership in a Culture of Affluence* and *Beyond Snakes and*

Shamrocks: St. Patrick's Missional Leadership Lessons for Today. Ross is the Founding Director of the Centre for Missional Leadership at St. Andrew's Hall and lives in North Vancouver with his family.

Harry O. Maier is Professor of New Testament and Early Christian Studies at the Vancouver School of Theology and a fellow of the Max Weber Center for Advanced and Cultural Studies at the University of Erfurt. He is the author of several books including *New Testament Christianity in the Roman World* (2019) and *Picturing Paul in Empire: Imperial, Image, Text and Persuasion in Colossians, Ephesians and the Pastoral Epistles* (2013). He has coedited several volumes including *Encountering the Other: Christian and Multifaith Perspectives* (2020) and *Desiring Martyrs: Locating Martyrs in Space and Time* (2021).

Ashley John Moyse is the McDonald Postdoctoral Fellow in Christian Ethics and Public Life in the Faculty of Theology and Religion, University of Oxford. He is also a research associate and sessional lecturer in Christian Ethics at the Vancouver School of Theology. He is the author of *The Art of Living for the Technological Age* (Fortress, 2021) and *Reading Karl Barth, Interrupting Moral Technique, Transforming Biomedical Ethics* (Palgrave, 2015), and the coeditor of several books including *Treating the Body in Medicine and Religion* (Routledge, 2019).

Robert Paul served as Dean of St. Andrew's Hall and Professor of Mission Theology at the Vancouver School of Theology. Prior to coming to Canada, he served as a Presbyterian pastor in Washington, Oregon, and California, and as president of two international mission organizations. In his retirement, he continues to teach mission theology and leadership, and works with churches to recognize opportunities for creative mission in contemporary culture.

Grant Rodgers retired as Director of Anglican Formation at the Vancouver School of Theology. Grant has served as a priest of the Anglican Church of Canada for over thirty-five years, in three dioceses, as archdeacon, regional dean, university chaplain, and chair of numerous diocesan committees (e.g., Examining Chaplains, Evangelism, Ecumenical and Inter-Faith). He has extensive experience supervising and mentoring curates, the newly ordained, and student interns. Grant's role at VST includes teaching, mentoring, liturgical leadership, serving as liaison with students' dioceses, and serving as part of the faculty team on a variety of committees

Melissa M. Skelton is an Assisting Bishop for the Diocese of Olympia in the Episcopal Church and the Episcopal Visitor to the Society of Catholic Priests. Prior to this, she served as the Archbishop of the Diocese of New Westminster in the Anglican Church of Canada and Metropolitan of the Ecclesiastical Province of British Columbia and Yukon. Before moving to Canada, she was Canon for Congregational Development and Leadership in the Diocese of Olympia and Rector of St. Paul's, Seattle. While in the Diocese of Olympia she founded the College for Congregational Development. Besides her MDiv, Melissa holds an MA in English, an MBA, and a certificate in Organization Development from National Training Labs.

Janet Soskice is Professor Emerita of Philosophical Theology at the University Cambridge, where she is also an Emeritus Fellow at Jesus College. She is also William K. Warren Distinguished Research Professor of Catholic Theology at the Divinity School of Duke University.

Richard Topping is President and Professor of Studies in the Reformed Tradition at the Vancouver School of Theology. He is published in the areas of dogmatic theology, homiletics, and philosophical and Reformed theology. He is the author of *Revelation, Scripture and Church* (Ashgate, 2007) and editor and contributor to *Calvin@500* (Wipf and Stock, 2011).

Bibliography

Alter, Robert. *The World of Biblical Literature*. New York: Basic Books, 1992.

Anger, Bob. "Historical Vignettes: Snapshots from Our History." Exhibit at the website of the Presbyterian Church in Canada Archives, June 9, 2014. https://presbyterianarchives.ca/2014/06/09/historical-vignettes-snapshots-from-our-history/.

Anglican Church of Canada. *The Book of Alternative Services*. Toronto: Anglican Book Centre, n.d.

———. "Competencies for Ordination to the Priesthood." https://www.anglican.ca/wp-content/uploads/2012/04/Competencies_web.pdf.

———. "Our Beliefs." https://www.anglican.ca/about/beliefs.

Asad, Talal, Wendy Brown, Judith Butler, and Saba Mahmood. *Is Critique Secular?: Blasphemy, Injury, and Free Speech*. Oxford: Oxford University Press, 2013.

Association of Theological Schools. "Educational Models and Practices in Theological Education: Duration. Reduced Credit (MDiv) Peer Group Final Report." July 2018. https://www.ats.edu/uploads/resources/current-initiatives/educational-models/publications-and-presentations/peer-group-final-reports/peer-group-final-report-book.pdf.

Augustine. *Confessions*. Translated by R. S. Pine-Coffin. Harmondsworth: Penguin, 1985.

———. *On Christian Doctrine*. Translated by J. F. Shaw. Mineola, NY: Dover, 2009.

———. "On Music." In *The Immortality of the Soul; The Magnitude of the Soul; On Music; The Advantage of Believing; On Faith in Things Unseen*, 151–380. Translated by Robert Catesby Taliaferro. The Fathers of the Church 4. Washington, DC: Catholic University of America Press, 2002.

———. "Sermon 117." In *Sermons: The Works of Saint Augustine: A Translation for the 21st Century*. Translated by Edmund Hill. Edited by John Rotelle, pt. 3, vol. 4, *Sermons 94A–147A on the New Testament*, 209–23. Brooklyn: New City, 1992.

———. "Sermon 339.4." In *Sermons: The Works of Saint Augustine: A Translation for the 21st Century*. Translated by Edmund Hill. Edited by John Rotelle, pt. 3, vol. 9, *Sermons 306–340A on the Saints*, 279–91. Brooklyn: New City, 1994.

———. *Treatises on Marriage and Other Subjects*. Translated by Charles T. Wilcox. Edited by Roy J. Deferrari. The Fathers of the Church 27. Washington, DC: Catholic University of America Press, 1999.

Balthasar, Hans Urs von. *Explorations in Theology*. Vol. 1, *The Word Made Flesh*. San Francisco: Ignatius, 1989.

Banner, Michael. "A Doctrine of Human Being." In *The Doctrine of God and Theological Ethics*. Edited by Alan Torrance and Michael Banner, 151–59. London: T. & T. Clark, 2006.

————. *The Ethics of Everyday Life: Moral Theology, Social Anthropology, and the Imagination of the Human*. Oxford: Oxford University Press, 2014.

Barks, Coleman. *The Essential Rumi*. New York: HarperCollins, 1995.

Barth, Karl. *Against the Stream: Shorter Post-War Writings*. London: SCM, 1954.

————. *Barth in Conversation*. Vol. 2, 1963. Edited by Eberhard Busch. Translated by Karlfried Froehlich, Darrell L. Guder, Matthias Gockel, and David C. Chao. Louisville: Westminster John Knox, 2018.

————. *Church Dogmatics*. Translated by Geoffrey W. Bromiley and T. F. Torrance. 14 vols. Edinburgh: T. & T. Clark, 2004.

————. *Ethics*. Edited by Dietrich Braun. Translated by Geoffrey W. Bromiley. New York: Seabury, 1981.

————. *The Foundation of the Christian Life. Church Dogmatics IV/4, Lecture Fragments*. Translated by Geoffrey Bromiley. Grand Rapids: Eerdmans, 1981.

————. *From Rousseau to Ritschl: Protestant Theology in the 19th Century*. Translated by Brian Cozens. London: SCM, 1959.

————. *Protestant Theology in the Nineteenth Century: Its Background and History*. Translated by Brian Cozens and John Bowden. London: SCM, 2001.

————. *The Theology of the Reformed Confessions* 1923. Edited by Darrell and Judith Guder. Louisville: Westminster John Knox, 2005.

————. *The Word of God and the Word of Man*. Translated by Douglas Horton. New York: Harper Torchbooks, 1957.

Barthes, Roland. "The Death of the Author." In *Image, Music, Text: Essays on Semiology*. Translated by Stephen Heath, 142–49. New York: Hill and Wang, 1977.

Barton, John. *The Bible: The Story of the World's Most Influential Book*. London: Penguin Randomhouse, 2019.

————. *The Nature of Biblical Criticism*. Louisville: John Knox, 2007.

Barton, John, and Michael Wolter Morgan, eds. *Die Einheit der Schrift und die Vielfalt des Kanons* (*The Unity of Scripture and the Diversity of the Canon*). Berlin: De Gruyter, 2003.

Basil. *Hexaemeron*, Homily 1 ("In the Beginning God Made the Heaven and the Earth"). Translated by Blomfield Jackson. In *Nicene and Post-Nicene Fathers*, 2nd ser., vol. 8. Edited by Philip Schaff and Henry Wace. Buffalo, NY: Christian Literature, 1895. Revised and edited for New Advent by Kevin Knight. http://www.newadvent.org/fathers/32011.htm.

————. *On Greek Literature*. Translated by Roy J. Deferrari and Martin R. P. McGuire. Loeb Classical Library 270. Cambridge, MA: Harvard University Press, 1934.

Bass, Dorothy, and Craig Dykstra. "A Theological Understanding of Christian Practices." In *Practicing Theology: Beliefs and Practices in Christian Life*. Edited by Miroslav Volf and Dorothy C. Bass, 13–32. Grand Rapids: Eerdmans, 2002.

Becker, Ernest. *The Denial of Death*. New York: Free Press, 1973.

Biggar, Nigel. *The Hastening That Waits: Karl Barth's Ethics*. Oxford: Oxford University Press, 1993.

Blodgett, Barbara J., and Mathew Flooding, eds. *Brimming with God: Reflecting Theologically on Cases in Ministry*. Eugene, OR: Wipf & Stock, 2015.

————. "The Role of Theological Reflection Within Field Education." *Journal of Reflective Practice* 34 (2014) 268–83.

Blythe, Stuart. "The Research Supervisor as Friend," *Practical Theology* 11:5 (October 20, 2018) 401–11.

Bolsinger, Tod. *Leadership for a Time of Pandemic*. Downers Grove, IL: InterVarsity, 2020.

Bonhoeffer, Dietrich. *Creation and Fall: A Theological Exposition of Genesis 1–3*. Edited by John W de Gruchy. Translated by Douglas Stephen Bax. Dietrich Bonhoeffer Works 3. Minneapolis: Fortress, 1997.

————. *Ethics*. Edited by Clifford J Green. Translated by Reinhard Krauss, Charles C. West, and Douglas W. Stott. Dietrich Bonhoeffer Works 6. Minneapolis: Fortress, 2005.

Bosch, David J. "Evangelism: Theological Currents and Cross-Currents Today." In *The Study of Evangelism: Exploring a Missional Practice of the Church*. Edited by Paul W Chilcote and Laceye C. Warner, 4–17. Grand Rapids: Eerdmans, 2008.

————. *Transforming Mission: Paradigm Shifts in Theology of Mission*. Maryknoll, NY: Orbis, 1991.

Botta, Alejandro F., and Pablo R. Andiñach, eds. *The Bible and the Hermeneutics of Liberation*. Atlanta: Society of Biblical Literature, 2009.

Bouchard, Gerard, and Charles Taylor. *Building the Future: A Time for Reconciliation*. Quebec City: Government of Quebec, 2008.

Brague, Rémi. *Curing Mad Truths: Medieval Wisdom for the Modern Age*. Notre Dame, IN: Notre Dame University Press, 2019.

Breu, Clarissa, ed. *Biblical Exegesis without Authorial Intention?: Interdisciplinary Approaches to Authorship and Meaning*. Biblical Interpretation Series 172. Leiden: Brill, 2019.

Brokenleg, Martin. "The Spirituality of Self-Determination." Anglican Indigenous Sacred Circle, Prince George, BC, August 7, 2018.

Brown, Dan. *The Da Vinci Code*. New York: Doubleday, 2003.

Brown, Peter. *The Rise of Western Christendom*. Oxford: Blackwell, 1996.

Bude, Heinz. *The Mood of the World*. Translated by Simon Garnett. Cambridge, MA: Polity, 2018.

Bulgakov, Sergii. "Lamb of God: On the Divine Humanity. 1933. " In *Sergii Bulgakov: Toward a Russian Political Theology*. Edited by Rowan Williams, 163–228. Edinburgh: T. & T. Clark, 1999.

Burke, Daniel. "The Evangelical Lutheran Church in America Just Became the Country's First 'Sanctuary Church Body.'" *CNN*, August 8, 2019. https://www.cnn.com/2019/08/08/us/lutheran-sanctuary-church/index.html.

Burke, Tony. *Introduction to the Christian Apocrypha*. Grand Rapids: Eerdmans, 2013.

Busch, Eberhard. *The Barmen Theses Then and Now*. Translated by Darrell and Judith Guder. Grand Rapids: Eerdmans, 2010.

Byassee, Jason. *Surprised by Jesus Again: Reading the Bible in Communion with the Saints*. Grand Rapids: Eerdmans, 2019.

Cahalan, Kathleen A. *Introducing the Practice of Ministry*. Collegeville, MN: Liturgical, 2010.

Calvin, John. *Calvin's Commentaries*, vol. 8, *Psalms, Part I*. Translated by John King. http://www.sacred-texts.com/chr/calvin/cc08/cc08005.htm.

————. *Commentaries on the First Book of Moses, Called Genesis, Part II.* Vol. 2 of *Calvin's Commentaries,* Translated by John King. https://www.sacred-texts.com/chr/calvin/cc02/index.htm.

————. *Institutes of the Christian Religion.* Edited by John T. McNeill. 2 vols. Philadelphia: Westminster, 1960.

Campbell-Reed, Eileen R., and Christian A. B. Scharen. "Are Your Graduates Ready?: Six Key Findings from the Learning Pastoral Imagination Project." *Colloquy Online,* April 2017. https://www.ats.edu/uploads/resources/publications-presentations/colloquy-online/are-your-graduates-ready.pdf.

Canada's Residential Schools: The History, Part 1, Origins to 1939. The Final Report of the Truth and Reconciliation Commission of Canada. Montreal: McGill-Queens University Press, 2015.

Carter, Charles E., and Carol L. Meyers, eds. *Community, Identity, and Ideology: Social Science Approaches to the Hebrew Bible.* Sources for Biblical and Theological Studies 6. Winona Lake, IN: Eisenbrauns, 1996.

Ceulemens, Reinhart. "The Septuagint and Other Translations." In *The Oxford Handbook of Early Christian Biblical Interpretation.* Edited by Paul M. Blowers and Peter W. Marten, 33–55. Oxford: Oxford University Press, 2019.

Chalcraft, David J., ed. *Social-Scientific Old Testament Criticism: A Sheffield Reader.* Sheffield, UK: Sheffield Academic, 1997.

Chardin, Teilhard de. *The Divine Milieu.* New York: Harper & Row, 1968.

Charleston, Steve. "The Old Testament of Native America." In *Native and Christian: Indigenous Voices on Religious Identity in the United States and Canada.* Edited by James Treat, 69–80. New York: Routledge, 1996.

Chesterton, G. K. *Orthodoxy.* New York: Barnes & Noble, 2007.

Clarke, Brian, and Stuart Macdonald. *Leaving Christianity: Changing Allegiances in Canada since 1945.* Montreal: McGill-Queens University Press, 2017.

Clooney, Francis X. *Comparative Theology: Deep Learning across Religious Borders.* Malden, MA: Wiley Blackwell, 2010.

Coakley, Sarah. *God, Sexuality, and the Self: An Essay 'On the Trinity'.* Cambridge: Cambridge University Press, 2013.

————. "The Spirit in the Trinity: Mystical Theology." Special lecture, Vancouver School of Theology, October 5, 2018. Recording available at https://youtu.be/8O9SdjezVvY.

Collini, Stefan. *What Are Universities For?* London: Penguin, 2012.

Comaroff, Jean, and John L. Comaroff. *Of Revelation and Revolution,* vol. 1, *Christianity, Colonialism, and Consciousness in South Africa.* Chicago: University of Chicago Press, 1991.

Copeland, M. Shawn. "Overcoming Christianity's Lingering Complicity." *In the Shadow of Charleston.* A Syndicate Network Symposium. July 20, 2015. https://syndicate.network/symposia/theology/in-the-shadow-of-charleston/.

D'Agoulême, Margaret, Queen of Navarre. *L'Heptameron des nouuelles de tresillustre et tresexcellente Princessse Marguerite de Valois, Royne de Nauarre:/ remis en son vray ordre, confus au parauant en sa premiere impression: & dedie a tresillustre & tresvertueuse Princesse Ianne, Royne de Nauarre, par Claude Gruget Parisien.* Paris: Par Benoist Preuost, 1560.

Daloz-Parks, Sharon. *Leadership Can Be Taught: A Bold Approach for a Complex World.* Boston: Harvard Business School Press, 2005.

Dart, Ron. *The North American High Tory Tradition*. New York: American Anglican, 2016.

David, Ellen F. "Losing a Friend: The Loss of the Old Testament to the Church." *Pro Ecclesia* 9:1 (December 2000) 73–84.

Davis, Ellen F., and Richard B. Hays, eds. *The Art of Reading Scripture*. Grand Rapids: Eerdmans, 2003.

De Waal, Esther. *Seeking God: The Way of St. Benedict*. Collegeville, MN: Liturgical, 2001.

Deloria Jr, Vine. "Philosophy and the Tribal Peoples." In *American Indian Thought*. Edited by Anne Waters, 5–9. Maldan, MA: Blackwell, 2004.

Demmer, Klaus. *Shaping the Moral Life: An Approach to Moral Theology*. Translated by Roberto Dell'Oro. Washington, DC: Georgetown University Press, 2000.

Dilley, Andrea Palpant. "The Surprising Discovery about Those Colonialist, Proselytizing Missionaries." *Christianity Today*, January 8, 2014, 34.

Diocese of New Westminster. "Discernment Process for Holy Orders." June 1, 2018. https://www.vancouver.anglican.ca/diocesan-resources/ordination.

Dutcher-Walls, Patricia. *Reading the Historical Books: A Student's Guide to Engaging the Biblical Text*. Grand Rapids: Baker Academic, 2014.

Ehrman, Bart. *The New Testament*, 4th ed. New York: Oxford University Press, 2007.

Eigenbrod, Renate, and Renée Hulan, *Aboriginal Oral Traditions: Theory, Practice, Ethics*. Black Point, NS: Fernwood, 2008.

Ekblad, Bob. *Guerila Gospel: Reading the Bible for Liberation in the Power of the Spirit*. Burlington, VT: People's Seminary Press, 2018.

Enns, Fernando, and Susan Durber, eds. *Walking Together: Theological Reflections on the Ecumenical Pilgrimage of Justice and Peace*. Geneva: World Council of Churches, 2018.

Ermine, Willie. "The Ethical Space of Engagement." *Indigenous Law Journal* 6:1 (2007) 193–203.

———. "The Ethical Space in Action." Video. Filmed October 2010, posted to YouTube September 2011. https://www.youtube.com/watch?v=ZUfXu3gfVJ8.

Eshet, Dan. *Stolen Lives: The Indigenous Peoples of Canada and the Indian Residentials Schools*. Toronto: Facing History and Ourselves, 2015.

Feldman, David M. *Birth Control in Jewish Law: Marital Relations, Contraception, and Abortion as Set Forth in the Classic Texts of Jewish Law*. New York: New York University Press, 1968.

Felski, Rita. *The Limits of Critique*. Chicago: University of Chicago Press, 2015.

———. *The Uses of Literature*. Oxford: Blackwell, 2008.

Flooding, Matthew. "What Is Theological Field Education." In *Welcome to Theological Field Education!*. Edited by Matthew Flooding, 1–16. Herndon, VA: Alban Institute, 2011.

Ford, David, and Rachel Muers, eds. *The Modern Theologians: An Introduction to Christian Theology Since 1918*. Oxford: Wiley-Blackwell, 2005.

Fox, Matthew. *The Coming of the Cosmic Christ: The Healing of Mother Earth and the Birth of a Global Renaissance*. New York: Harper & Row, 1988.

———. *One River, Many Wells: Wisdom Springing from Global Faiths*. New York: Tarcher/Penguin, 2000.

Francis I. *Evangelii Gaudium: On the Proclamation of the Gospel in Today's World*. Apostolic exhortation. Vatican, November 24, 2013.

Frankfort, Henri. *Kingship and the Gods: A Study of Ancient Near Eastern Religion as the Integration of Society and Nature.* Chicago: University of Chicago Press, 1948.

Franks, Christopher. *He Became Poor: The Poverty of Christ and Aquinas's Economic Teachings.* Grand Rapids: Eerdmans, 2009.

Fritz, Volkmar. *The City in Ancient Israel.* Sheffield: Sheffield Academic, 1995.

Frye, Northrope. *The Great Code: The Bible and Literature.* Toronto: Penguin, 2014.

Gadamer, Hans-Georg. *Truth and Method.* New York: Seabury, 1975.

Gamble, Harry Y. *The New Testament Canon: Its Making and Meaning.* Eugene, OR: Wipf & Stock, 2002.

————. "The New Testament Canon: Recent Research and the Status Quaestionis." In *The Canon Debate.* Edited by Lee Martin McDonald and James A. Sander, 267–94. Grand Rapids: Baker Academic, 2002.

General Synod of the Anglican Church of Canada. "Competencies for Ordination to the Priesthood in the Anglican Church of Canada." The Primate's Commission on Theological Education and Formation for Presbyteral Ministry, 2013. https://www.anglican.ca/faith/ministry/education/competencies-priesthood/.

Gin, Deborah H. C., and Stacy Williams-Duncan. "Faculty Development: perk or priority." *In Trust*, Summer 2018, 20–22.

Greenwood, Robin. *Transforming Priesthood: A New Theology of Mission and Ministry.* London: SPCK, 1994.

Gregory of Nyssa. *The Life of Moses.* Translated by Abraham J. Malherbe and Everett Ferguson. New York: Paulist, 1973.

Griffiths, Paul. *Intellectual Appetite: A Theological Grammar.* Washington, DC: Catholic University Press, 2009.

————. *Religious Reading.* New York: Oxford, 1999.

Gross, Robert, and Mona West, eds. *Take Back the Word: A Queer Reading of the Bible.* Cleveland: Pilgrim, 2000.

Guder, Darrell, ed. *Missional Church: A Vision for the Sending of the Church in North America.* Grand Rapids: Eerdmans, 1998.

Hammer, Reuven. *Entering Jewish Prayer: A Guide to Personal Devotion and the Worship Service.* New York: Schocken. 1994.

Harkness, Georgia. "What Is Christian Ethics?" Ch. 1 in *Christian Ethics.* New York: Abingdon, 1957. Republished by *Religion Online.* https://www.religion-online.org/book/the-gospel-and-our-world/.

Harmless, William. *Augustine in His Own Words.* Washington, DC: Catholic University Press, 2010.

Heft, James. "It Is Time to Get Past the Snobbery against Pastoral Theologians." *America: The Jesuit Review*, July 13, 2017. https://www.americamagazine.org/faith/2017/07/13/it-time-get-past-snobbery-against-pastoral-theologians.

Herdt, Jennifer A. *Putting on Virtue: Legacy of the Splendid Vices.* Chicago: University of Chicago Press, 2008.

Hilary of Poitiers. *On the Trinity.* In *Nicene and Post-Nicene Fathers*, 2nd ser., vol. 9. Translated by E. W. Watson and L. Pullan. Edited by Philip Schaff and Henry Wace, 40–1357. Peabody, MA: Hendrickson, 1994.

Horrell, David G. *The Bible and the Environment: Towards a Critical Ecological Biblical Theology.* London: Routledge, 2015.

Hurowitz, Victor Avigdor. *I Have Built You an Exalted House: Temple Building in the Bible in the Light of Mesopotamian and North-West Semitic Writings*. Journal for the Study of the Old Testament Supplement Series 115. Sheffield: JSOT, 1992.

Irvin, Dale T., and Scott W. Sunquist. *The History of the World Christian Movement*. Vol. 1, *Earliest Christianity to 1453*. Maryknoll, NY: Orbis, 2011.

Jaeger, Werner. *Early Christianity and Greek Paideia*. Cambridge: Belknap, 1961.

James, Christopher. *Church Planting in Post-Christian Soil*. Oxford: Oxford University Press, 2018.

Jenkins, Philip. *The Next Christendom: The Coming of Global Christianity*. Oxford: University Press, 2002.

Jenson, Robert. *A Theology in Outline: Can These Bones Live*. New York: Oxford, 2016.

John Hall, Douglas. "The Future of the Church: Critical Remembrance as Entrée to Hope." The Kenneth Cousland Lecture, delivered at Emmanuel College, University of Toronto, October 16, 2013.

Johnson, Abigail. *Shaping Spiritual Leaders: Supervision and Formation in Congregations*. Herndon, VA: Alban Institute, 2007.

Johnston, William, ed. *The Cloud of Unknowing*. New York: Random House, 1973.

Kaiser, Walter C. "The Meaning of Meaning." In *An Introduction to Biblical Hermeneutics: The Search for Meaning*. Edited by Walter C Kaiser and Moisés Silva, 27–46. Grand Rapids: Zondervan, 1994.

Kavanaugh, Aidan. *Elements of Rite: A Handbook of Liturgical Style*. New York: Pueblo, 1982.

King, Philip J,. and Lawrence E. Stager. *Life in Biblical Israel*. Library of Ancient Israel. Louisville: Westminster John Knox, 2001.

Klassen, John. "Theological Field Education in Canada." Unpublished DMin paper, 1998.

Kolb, Alice, and Kolb, David A. "The Kolb Learning Style Inventory 4.0 Guide." Experience Based Learning Systems, 2013. https://learningfromexperience.com/research-library/the-kolb-learning-style-inventory-4-0/.

Kort, Wesley. *Take; Read: Scripture, Contextuality and Cultural Practice*. University Park: Pennsylvania State University Press, 1996.

Kujawa-Holbrook, Sheryl A. *God Beyond Borders: Interreligious Learning Among Faith Communities*. Horizons in Religious Education. Eugene, OR: Pickwick, 2014.

Kulchyski, Peter. "What Is Native Studies?" In *Expressions in Canadian Native Studies*. Edited by Ron F. Laliberte, Priscilla Settee, James B. Waldram, Rob Innes, Brenda Macdougall, Lesley McBain, and F. Faurie Barron, 13–26. Saskatoon: Saskatchewan University of Saskatchewan Extension Press, 2000.

Leddy, Mary Jo. *Radical Gratitude*. New York: Orbis, 2014.

Lewis-Anthony, Justin. *If You Meet George Herbert on the Road, Kill Him*. London: Bloomsbury, 2013.

Long, D Stephen. *Christian Ethics: A Very Short Introduction*. Oxford: Oxford University Press, 2010.

Louth, Andrew. *Discerning the Mystery: An Essay on the Nature of Theology*. Rev. ed. Oxford: Clarendon, 1999.

Lowry, Eugene. *The Sermon: Dancing on the Edge of Mystery*. Nashville: Abingdon, 1997.

Lugones, Maria. "Playfulness, 'World'-Traveling, and Loving Perception." *Hypatia* 2:2 (1987) 3–19.

Luther, Martin. *Luther's Works*, vol. 33, *Career of the Reformer III*. Edited by Philip Watson. Philadelphia: Fortress, 1972.

———. *Luther's Works*, vol. 35, *Word and Sacrament I*. Edited by E. Theodore Bachman. Philadelphia: Fortress, 1960.

MacIntyre, Alasdair. *Whose Justice? Which Rationality?* South Bend, IN: University of Notre Dame Press, 1988.

Mackenzie, Don, Ted Falcon, and Jamal Rahman. *Getting to the Heart of Interfaith: The Eye-Opening, Hope-Filled Friendship of a Pastor, a Rabbi & an Imam*. Woodstock: Skylight Paths. 2009.

———. *Religion Gone Astray: What We Found at the Heart of Interfaith*. Woodstock, VT: Skylight Paths. 2011.

Malphurs, Aubrey. *Developing a Vision for Ministry*. Grand Rapids: Baker, 2015.

Marcel, Gabriel. *Being and Having*. Translated by Katherine Farrer. Westminster: Dacre, 1949.

———. *The Mystery of Being*, vol. 1, *Reflection and Mystery*. Translated by G. S. Fraser. London: Harvill, 1950. Reprint, South Bend, IN: St. Augustine's.

McCall, Sophie "'What the Map Cuts Up, the Story Cuts Across': Translating Oral Traditions and Aboriginal Land Title." *Essays on Canadian Writing* 80 (Fall 2003) 309." <style face="italic">Essays on Canadian Writing</style>, no. 80 (Fall 2003 2003

McClendon, James William. *Biography as Theology: How Life Stories Can Remake Today's Theology*. Philadelphia: Trinity, 1990.

McDonald, Lee Martin. *The Formation of the Bible: The Story of the Church's Canon*. Peabody, MA: Hendrickson, 2012.

———. *The Formation of the Biblical Canon*, vol. 2, *The New Testament: Its Authority and Canonicity*. London: Bloomsbury, 2017.

McFague, Sallie. *Blessed Are the Consumers: Climate Change and the Practice of Restraint*. Minneapolis: Fortress, 2013.

———. *A New Climate for Christology: Kenosis, Climate Change, and Befriending Nature*. Minneapolis: Fortress, forthcoming.

McIntosh, Mark. *Divine Teaching: An Introduction to Christian Theology*. Oxford: Blackwell, 2008.

McNutt, Paula. *Reconstructing the Society of Ancient Israel*. Library of Ancient Israel. Louisville: Westminster John Knox, 1999.

Meyer, Marvin W., ed. *The Nag Hammadi Scriptures*. San Francisco: HarperOne, 2007.

Meyers, Carol. *Discovering Eve: Ancient Israelite Women in Context*. New York: Oxford University Press, 1988.

Miller-McLemore, Bonnie, and Brita L. Gill-Austern, eds. *Feminist and Womanist Pastoral Theology*. Nashville: Abingdon, 1999.

Miller, Patrick D. *The Religion of Ancient Israel*. Louisville: Westminster John Knox, 2000.

Mir, Mustansir. *Understanding the Islamic Scripture: A Study of Selected Passages from the Qur'an*. New York: Pearson Longman, 2008.

Moltmann, Jürgen. *Experiences in Theology: Ways and Forms of Christian Theology*. London: SCM, 2000.

Moore, Stephen D., and Yvonne Sherwood. *The Invention of the Biblical Scholar: A Critical Manifesto*. Minneapolis: Fortress, 2011.

Morton, Nelle. *The Journey Is Home*. Boston: Beacon, 1985.

Mott, John R. *The Evangelization of the World in This Generation*. New York: Student Volunteer Movement for Foreign Missions, 1900.

Moyse, Ashley John. *The Art of Living for the Technological Age: Toward a Humanizing Performance*. Minneapolis: Fortress, 2021.

———. *Reading Karl Barth, Interrupting Moral Technique, Transforming Biomedical Ethics*. New York: Palgrave, 2015.

———. "Responsibility for the Broken Body." In *Treating the Body in Medicine and Religion: Jewish, Christian and Islamic Perspectives*. Edited by John J. Fitzgerald and Ashley John Moyse, 17–28. London: Routledge, 2019.

Murrin, John M. "Religion and Politics in America from the First Settlements to the Civil War." In *Religion & American Politics: From the Colonial Period to the 1980s*. Edited by Mark A. Noll, 19–43. New York: Oxford University Press, 1990.

Newbigin, Lesslie. *Unfinished Agenda: An Updated Autobiography*. London: SPCK, 1993.

Neylan, Susan. *The Heavens are Changing: Nineteenth-Century Protestant Missions and Tsimshian Christianity*. Montreal: McGill-Queen's University Press, 2003.

Nicholas of Cusa. *Nicholas of Cusa's Dialectical Mysticism: Text, Translation, and Interpretive Study of De Visione Dei*. Edited and translated by Jasper Hopkins. 3rd ed. Minneapolis: Arthur J. Banning, 1985.

Niditch, Susan. "The Wronged Woman Righted: An Analysis of Genesis 38." *Harvard Theological Review* 72:1/2 (1979) 143–49.

Noble, Alan. *Disruptive Witness: Speaking Truth in a Distracted Age*. Downer Grove, IL: InterVarsity, 2018.

Northeastern Pennsylvania Synod. "ELCA Sanctuary Background and Recommendations." http://nepasynod.org/documents/sanctuary-background-recommendations.pdf.

Nouwen, Henry J. M. *Reaching Out: The Three Movements of the Spiritual Life*. New York: Doubleday, 1975.

Odozor, Paulinus Ikechukwu. *Morality Truly Christian, Truly African: Foundational, Methodological, and Theological Considerations*. Notre Dame, IN: University of Notre Dame Press, 2014.

Office of Vocation of the United Church of Canada. "Candidacy Pathway Policy Office of Vocation United Church of Canada." Toronto: United Church of Canada, 2019. https://united-church.ca/sites/default/files/candidacy-pathway_policy.pdf.

Origen. *Commentary of the Gospel of Matthew*. Translated by John Patrick. In *Ante-Nicene Fathers*, vol. 9. Edited by Allan Menzies. Buffalo, NY: Christian Literature,1896. Revised and edited for New Advent by Kevin Knight. https://www.newadvent.org/fathers/1016.htm.

———. *The Philocalia of Origen: A Compilation of Selected Passages from Origen's Works Made by St, Gregory of Nazianzus and St Basil of Caesarea*. Translated by George Lewis. Edinburgh: T. & T. Clark, 1911.

Osmer, Richard. *Practical Theology: An Introduction*. Grand Rapids: Eerdmans, 2008.

Owens, Roger. "Don't Talk Nonsense: Why Herbert McCabe Still Matters." *Christian Century*, January 25, 2005, 20–25.

Paas, Stefan. *Church Planting and the Secular West*. Grand Rapids: Eerdmans, 2016.

Palad, Bukas. "God of Silence." Video. Posted to YouTube June 2017. https://youtu.be/vtXJWqkosQo.

Pardue, Stephen T. *The Mind of Christ: Humility and the Intellect in Early Christian Theology*. London: T. & T. Clark, 2015.

Parks, Sharon Daloz. *Big Questions, Worthy Dreams*. San Francisco: Jossey-Bass, 2000.

Penner, Todd, and Davina Lopez. *De-Introducing the New Testament: Texts, Worlds, Methods, Stories*. Oxford: Wiley, 2015.

Peterson, Eugene. *Tell It Slant: A Conversation on the Language of Jesus in His Stories*. Grand Rapids: Eerdmans, 2012.

Pew Research Center. "The Future of World Religions: Population Growth Projections, 2010–2050." April 2, 2015. https://www.pewforum.org/2015/04/02/religious-projections-2010-2050/.

Pius XI. *Studiorum Ducem: On St. Thomas Aquinas*. Papal encyclical. Vatican, June 29, 1923. https://www.papalencyclicals.net/pius11/p11studi.htm.

Rad, Gerhard von. *Genesis: A Commentary*. Translated by John H. Marks. Philadelphia: Westminster, 1972.

Ricouer, Paul. *Critique and Conviction: Conversations with Francios Azouvi and Marc de Launay*. Translated by Kathleen Blamey. New York: Columbia University Press, 1998.

———. *Interpretation Theory: Discourse and the Surplus of Meaning*. Fort Worth: Texas Christian University Press, 1976.

———. *Political and Social Essays*. Athens: Ohio University Press, 1975.

———. "Toward a Hermeneutic of the Idea of Revelation." *Harvard Theological Review* 70:1–2 (1977) 1–37.

Rigby, Cynthia. *Holding Faith: A Practical Introduction to Christian Doctrine*. Nashville: Abingdon, 2018.

Robert, Dana Lee. *American Women in Mission: A Social History of Their Thought and Practice*. Macon, GA: Mercer University Press, 1997.

———. *Christian Mission: How Christianity Became a World Religion*. Oxford: Wiley-Blackwell, 2009.

Roberts, Kyle. "Six Tensions in Curriculum Revision." *In Trust*, Summer, 2017: https://www.intrust.org/Magazine/Issues/Summer 2017.

Rolheiser, Ronald. *The Holy Longing: The Search for a Christian Spirituality*. New York: Image, 2014.

Roxburgh, Alan J., and M. Scott Boren. *Introducing the Missional Church: What It Is, Why It Matters, How to Become One*. Grand Rapids: Baker, 2009.

Sanneh, Lamin O. *Abolitionists Abroad: American Blacks and the Making of Modern West Africa*. Cambridge, MA: Harvard University Press, 1999.

———. *Translating the Message: The Missionary Impact on Culture*. Maryknoll, NY: Orbis, 1989.

———. *Whose Religion Is Christianity?: The Gospel Beyond the West*. Grand Rapids: Eerdmans, 2003.

Sanneh, Lamin O., and Joel A. Carpenter, eds. *The Changing Face of Christianity: Africa, the West, and the World*. Oxford: Oxford University Press, 2005.

Santayana, George. *Reason in Religion*. Vol. 3 of *The Life of Reason*. New York: Scribner, 1906.

Schloen, J. David. *The House of the Father as Fact and Symbol: Patrimonialism in Ugarit and the Ancient Near East*. Studies in the Archaeology and History of the Levant 2. Winona Lake, IN: Eisenbrauns, 2001.

Schneersohn, Rabbi Shmuel. *True Existence*. Translated by Yosef Marcus. New York: Kehot, 2002.

Segovia, Fernando F., and Mary Ann Tobert, eds. *Reading from This Place*. 2 vols. Minneapolis: Fortress, 1995.

Skelton, Melissa, and the Diocese of Olympia. *The College for Congregational Development; Manuals Year A and Year B*. Seattle: Diocese of Olympia, 2021.

Smith, Mark S. *The Early History of God: Yahweh and the Other Deities in Ancient Israel*. San Francisco: Harper & Row, 1990.

Sölle, Dorothee. *The Silent Cry: Mysticism and Resistance*. Minneapolis: Fortress, 2001.

"The Southern Baptist Convention Must Enact Tough Reform on Its Sexual Abuse Crisis." *Washington Post*, June 10, 2019. https://www.washingtonpost.com/opinions.

Sparks, Paul, Tim Soerens, and Dwight Friesen, eds. *The New Parish: How Neighborhood Churches Are Transforming Mission, Discipleship and Community*. Downers Grove, IL: InterVarsity, 2014.

Stout, Jeffrey. *Ethics After Babel: The Languages of Morals and Their Discontents*. Boston: Beacon, 1988.

Stringfellow, William. *An Ethic for Christians and Other Aliens in a Strange Land*. Eugene, OR: Wipf & Stock, 2004.

———. *Conscience and Obedience*. Eugene, OR: Wipf & Stock, 2004. Originally published 1973.

Stroup, George. *Before God*. Grand Rapids: Eerdmans, 2004.

Tanner, Kathryn. *Christ the Key*. Cambridge: Cambridge University Press, 2010.

———. "Public Theology and the Character of Public Debate." *The Annual of the Society of Christian Ethics*, 1996, 79–101.

Taylor, Charles. *A Secular Age*. Cambridge: Harvard University Press, 2007.

Tertullian. *Apologeticus*. Translated by S. Thelwall. In *Ante-Nicene Fathers*, vol. 3. Edited by Philip Schaff and Henry Wace. Buffalo, NY: Christian Literature, 1885. Revised and edited for New Advent by Kevin Knight. https://www.newadvent.org/fathers/0301.htm.

Thiselton, Anthony C. *New Horizons in Hermeneutics: The Theory and Practice of Transforming Biblical Reading*. London: HarperCollins, 1992.

Thysell, Carol. *The Pleasure of Discernment: Marguerite de Navarre as Theologian*. New York: Oxford University Press, 2000.

Tienou, Tite. "Indigenous Theologizing: From the Margins to the Center." Paper presented at the North American Institute for Indigenous Theological Studies Missiological Symposium, Los Angeles, California, 2004.

Tissot, Samuel-Auguste. *Thoughts on the Sin of Onan: Chiefly Extracted from a Late Writer*. London, 1767.

Tracy, David. *The Analogical Imagination: Christian Theology and the Culture of Pluralism*. New York: Crossroad, 1981.

The Truth and Reconciliation Commission of Canada. *Honouring the Truth, Reconciling for the Future: Summary of the Final Report of the Truth and Reconciliation Commission of Canada*. Truth and Reconciliation Commission of Canada, 2015. https://web-trc.ca/.

Tshaka, Rothney S. *Confessional Theology?: A Critical Analysis of the Theology of Karl Barth and Its Significance for the Belhar Confession*. Newcastle upon Tyne: Cambridge Scholars, 2013.

Turner, Denys. *The Darkness of God: Negativity in Christian Mysticism.* New York: Cambridge University Press, 1998.

Walls, Andrew F. *The Missionary Movement in Christian History: Studies in the Transmission of Faith.* Maryknoll, NY: Orbis, 1996.

Walshe, Maurice O. C., trans. and ed. *The Complete Mystical Works of Meister Eckhart.* New York: Crossroad, 2009.

Ward, Kevin. *A History of Global Anglicanism.* Cambridge: Cambridge University Press, 2006.

Warner, Michael. "Uncritical Reading." In *Polemic: Critical or Uncritical.* Edited by Jane Gallop, 13–39. New York: Routledge, 2004.

Webber, Robert. *Ancient-Future Evangelism: Making Your Church a Faith-Forming Community.* Grand Rapids: Baker, 2003.

Weinfeld, Moshe. "Zion and Jerusalem as Religious and Political Capital: Ideology and Utopia." In *The Poet and the Historian: Essays in Literary and Historical Biblical Criticism.* Edited by Richard Elliott Friedman, 75–115. Chico, CA: Scholars, 1983.

Wells, H. G. *The War That Will End War.* London: Frank Cecil Palmer, 1914.

Wesley, Andrew. "Traditional Aboriginal Spirituality." Paper presented at the Consultation on First Nations Theological Education, Thornloe University, Sudbury, Ontario, May 21, 2009.

Westermann, Claus. *Genesis 37–50: A Commentary.* Translated by John J. Scullion. Minneapolis: Augsburg, 1986.

Wheatley, Margaret. *Perseverance.* San Francisco: Berrett-Koehler, 2010.

Whitehead, James D., and Evelyn Eaton Whitehead. *Method in Ministry: Theological Reflection and Christian Ministry.* Lanham: Sheed and Ward, 1995.

Whyte, David. "Sometimes." In *Everything is Waiting for You,* 4–5. Langley, BC: Many Rivers, 2003.

Williams, Rowan. *Being Human: Bodies, Minds, Persons.* London: SPCK, 2018.

———. *Faith in the Public Square.* London: Bloomsbury, 2012.

———. "Making Moral Decisions." In *The Cambridge Companion to Christian Ethics.* Edited by Robin Gill, 3–15. Cambridge: Cambridge University Press, 2000.

Wilson, Shawn. *Research Is Ceremony: Indigenous Research Methods.* Halifax, NS: Fernwood, 2008.

Wilson, Todd A., and Gerald Hiestand, eds. *Becoming a Pastor Theologian: New Possibilities for Church Leadership.* Downers Grove, IL: IVP Academic, 2016.

Wittgenstein, Ludwig. *Philosophical Investigations.* Translated by G. E. M. Anscombe. 3rd ed. New York: Macmillan, 1958.

Wolterstorff, Nicholas. *Justice in Love.* Eerdmans: Grand Rapids, 2011.

Woodberry, Robert. "Reclaiming the M-Word: The Legacy of Missions in Nonwestern Societies." *Review of Faith and International Affairs,* March 2006, 3–12.